Toward a
North American Community?

The Political Economy of Global Interdependence
Thomas D. Willett, Series Editor

Toward a North American Community?

Canada, the United States, and Mexico

EDITED BY

Donald Barry
with Mark O. Dickerson
and James D. Gaisford

Westview Press

BOULDER • SAN FRANCISCO • OXFORD

The Political Economy of Global Interdependence

Copyright © 1995 by Westview Press, Inc.

Published in 1995 in the United States of America by Westview Press, Inc., 5500 Central Avenue, Boulder, Colorado 80301-2877, and in the United Kingdom by Westview Press, 12 Hid's Copse Road, Cumnor Hill, Oxford OX2 9JJ

Library of Congress Cataloging-in-Publication Data
Barry, Donald D.
    Toward a North American community? : Canada, the United States,
and Mexico / edited by Donald Barry with Mark O. Dickerson and James Gaisford.
        p.   cm.
    Includes bibliographical references and index.
    ISBN 0-8133-8897-X
    1. United States—Relations—Canada.   2. Canada—Relations—United
States.   3. United States—Relations—Mexico.   4. Mexico—Relations—
United States.   5. Canada—Relations—Mexico.   6. Mexico
—Relations—Canada.   I. Dickerson, M. O., 1934–   .   II. Gaisford,
James.   III. Title.
E183.8.C2B345   1995
327.7—dc20   94-43288
                                                                              CIP

Printed and bound in the United States of America

The paper used in this publication meets the requirements
of the American National Standard for Permanence of Paper
for Printed Library Materials Z39.48-1984.

10   9   8   7   6   5   4   3   2   1

Contents

Acknowledgments

Most of the chapters in this volume are revised versions of papers presented at a conference on the North American Free Trade Agreement held at The University of Calgary in October 1993. The conference was sponsored by The University of Calgary and the Canada West Foundation, with the support of Alberta Federal and Inter-governmental Affairs, the Canadian Foundation for the Americas (FOCAL-West), the Canadian Department of Foreign Affairs and International Trade (International Higher Education Division), the Embassy of Mexico, the Social Sciences and Humanities Research Council of Canada, the United States Information Service and The University of Calgary's Department of Political Science, Faculty of Social Sciences, International Centre, Research Grants Committee and Special Projects Fund.

James Frideres, Roger Gibbins, Stephen Randall and William Warden made important contributions to the project. David Elton, president of the Canada West Foundation, put its resources and expertise at our disposal in arranging the conference, and the Foundation provided support for this volume. My coeditors, Mark Dickerson and James Gaisford, made a significant contribution to the conference and to the completion of the book. The contributors generously agreed to revise and update their papers for publication. Thomas Willett's insightful comments helped sharpen the volume's focus and organization. Alison Auch facilitated arrangements with Westview Press. Judi Powell provided administrative support for the conference and applied her impressive word processing skills to the manuscript. Cameron Brooks prepared the list of acronyms and the index. To all I offer my thanks.

Donald Barry

Introduction

Donald Barry

The North American Free Trade Agreement (NAFTA), which came into effect on January 1, 1994, is a milestone in the affairs of the continent and in international trade. It is the first formal arrangement among Canada, the United States and Mexico and also the first trade pact involving countries of such disproportionate power and levels of development. In global economic terms NAFTA furthers a trend toward regional economic arrangements and establishes a precedent for cooperation between developed and developing countries.

Relations among the three countries have evolved along bilateral rather than trilateral lines. Canada and Mexico have depended heavily on their superpower neighbor, it being their largest trading partner, leading source of foreign investment and the principal guarantor of their security. American reliance on those countries has been less substantial but still significant. Canada and Mexico are the first and third largest trading partners respectively of the United States, and they have also been important in American strategic calculations. As well, the long U.S.-Canada and U.S.-Mexico borders have given rise to a wide range of interactions and issues. By contrast, relations between Canada and Mexico have not been extensive, although due to recent mutual interests they are expanding.

Canada and Mexico share a long-standing ambivalence toward the United States, which at times has caused them to move toward that country and at other times to follow a more nationalistic course. The U.S., reflecting its overwhelming power, has traditionally favored an expansive approach in its relations with its neighbors. Canada and Mexico, on the other hand, have been distant friends. Despite their shared preoccupation with the U.S., Mexico's orientation has been southward towards Latin America, while Canada's has been northward across the Atlantic. NAFTA thus represents a significant departure in North American relations.

This volume focuses on the management of Canadian-United States-Mexican relations in an era of emerging continental cooperation. It goes beyond the economic questions that have been at the center of much of the discussion of NAFTA to examine a range of issues, including the interrelationship between economic integration, national values and security, and explores the implications for national policies and community building in North America. Is NAFTA the first step in a wider integration process, as some observers contend? Or will its effects be more limited, as others claim? The essays consider whether the agreement will become a point of departure for broader cooperation among the three countries and identify areas in which collaboration is likely.

The volume is divided into five sections. Part One discusses how and why the North American Free Trade Agreement came about, the major elements of the pact, and NAFTA's place in the global trading system.

Donald Barry observes that NAFTA grew out of the decisions of Canada and Mexico to liberalize their economies, together with the interest of the United States in forging closer economic ties. While the three countries have taken a major step toward economic integration in NAFTA, Barry suggests that Canadian and Mexican insistence on the inclusion of a dispute settlement mechanism to adjudicate trade complaints demonstrates their continuing interest in constraining U.S. behavior.

Gilbert Winham and Heather Grant, in their discussion of the economic foundations of NAFTA, point out that, while each country had its own reasons for entering into the pact, all shared the common objective of enhancing their competitiveness in order to stimulate exports within and beyond their region and to alleviate debt and deficit problems. The agreement's strengths, according to Winham and Grant, include the fact that it encompasses developed and developing countries, that it opens up the Mexican automobile market, that it contributes to the liberalization of trade in services, and that it contains advances in dispute settlement. Weaknesses concerning rules of origin, however, are likely to spawn new types of trade disputes.

Michael Hart considers NAFTA in the context of the evolving international trade regime. He starts from the premise that the world is experiencing a "techno-economic paradigm shift" that is driven by developments in communication, transportation and information sharing. This shift compels a move beyond national markets toward global markets. He argues that intellectuals and policy-makers are struggling to catch up with this new reality. As a result, global trade agreements like the General Agreement on Tariffs and Trade (GATT)

Uruguay Round are more "attuned to the realities of the 1970s" than to the 1990s. While the 1989 Canada-U.S. Free Trade Agreement (CUSFTA) and NAFTA help lay the foundation for the future prosperity of North America, Hart contends that more needs to be done intellectually and practically in order to comprehend and take advantage of the global initiative.

Part Two examines the conduct of post-war Canada-U.S., U.S.-Mexico and Canadian-Mexican relations, and speculates about NAFTA's impact on those relationships.

Denis Stairs, in his essay on Canadian-American relations, discusses three dominant strategies -- multilateralism, diversification and execu-tive pluralism -- by which Canada has sought to offset its unequal relationship with the U.S. During the past two decades, he argues, this "strategic edifice" has come under increasing stress. CUSFTA, through which Ottawa attempted to exploit interdependence with the U.S. while subjecting American power to legal constraint, represents a fundamental shift in approach. Canada's strategic options, Stairs suggests, will evolve in accordance with its ability to manage the continental relationship, Mexico's participation in NAFTA, and the admission of new members into that agreement.

Stephen Randall argues that historically the management of U.S.-Mexico relations was affected by their divergent views of the relationship. Despite this, interdependence between the two countries grew steadily, giving rise to an extensive pattern of bilateral consultation. NAFTA represents an acknowledgment of U.S.-Mexican interdependence and offers an improved mechanism for managing their interaction. Randall points out, however, that the reorientation of the two countries' bilateral approaches will do little to alter their long-held images of each other. A lengthy period of adjustment can be expected.

Gustavo del Castillo contends that the asymmetrical relationship that Canada and Mexico share with the U.S. has forced them to focus their attention on that country rather than on each other. Continental relations, however, are becoming more integrative as issues become increasingly "intermestic," that is, as the domestic policies of the three countries encroach upon each other's politics. Given the prospect of continued integration and the high costs of withdrawal from the emerging continental economic system, del Castillo asserts, trans-national mechanisms will have to be found to regulate the "dominions of intermesticity" in North America.

Part Three discusses Mexican, Canadian and United States perspectives on trilateralism and region building and considers how economic integration will affect the three countries' policies.

Gustavo Vega Canovas argues that consolidating economic ties with the U.S. was part of a larger Mexican strategy of opening up the whole Latin American region to trade in order to expand Mexico's markets and to enhance its commercial autonomy. He maintains that the patterns of cooperation built up within the Group of Three (G3), composed of Mexico, Colombia and Venezuela, make it the most effective forum for facilitating "regional economic plurilateralism."

Maxwell Cameron and Brian Tomlin hold that Canada's main aim was to protect its access to the American market and only secondarily to expand its access to Mexico. Relations with the United States remain its preoccupation. Canada will not likely take the initiative in promoting hemispheric free trade, Cameron and Tomlin conclude. Instead it will probably follow the lead of the U.S. should that country decide that NAFTA should be extended to other countries in the region.

Alan Henrikson contends that the recent debate over NAFTA in the U.S. was not about isolationism versus internationalism, as is generally assumed. Rather it involved competing notions -- continentalism, hemispherism and globalism -- of how best to engage in international cooperation. While others have focused on the agreement's effects on American power and interests, Henrikson suggests that its ultimate significance for the U.S. (as well as for Canada and Mexico) may depend upon the interaction of emerging "geoeconomic regions" in North America and elsewhere.

Neil Nevitte explores the relationship between economic integration and value change in Canada, the United States and Mexico. He shows that despite the historic wariness of Canadians and Mexicans toward the United States there is a surprising degree of value convergence among the three publics. There is little evidence that this is due to "Americanization" since U.S. values do not seem to lead those of Mexico and Canada. In accordance with the "Deutsch hypothesis," levels of cross-national trust correlate strongly and positively with support for economic integration in all three countries. In turn, support for increased economic cooperation is closely related to support for political integration. Nevitte concludes that, while Canadians and Mexicans share a concern about the cultural implications of greater economic interdependence, they are less reluctant "continentalists" than is often thought.

Joseph Jockel addresses the implications of economic integration for security cooperation among the three countries. Currents influencing transnational defense relations, he observes, are at variance with the forces of globalization that are compelling closer economic ties. The end of the Cold War, the collapse of the USSR and budgetary pressures will make the previously close Canadian-American military collaboration more problematic. Consequently, U.S.-Canada defense relations will come to resemble the much more limited U.S.-Mexico relationship. Three areas in which Jockel identifies possibilities for quasi-military trilateral collaboration are sovereignty protection and the cross-border drug trade, environmental protection, and rescue and disaster relief.

Part Four considers whether the European Union's (EU) experience in managing economic integration contains lessons for North America and assesses the impact that the intensification of European and North American economic cooperation may have on future transatlantic relations.

Gretchen MacMillan examines similarities and differences between these regional regimes. The EU's goal is to achieve political union through economic integration. NAFTA's more modest aim is to enhance competitiveness by removing barriers to trade and investment. MacMillan is skeptical about the relevance of the EU model for the NAFTA countries, but she notes that the experience of the Union suggests that "incremental centralization" is difficult to halt after the integration process has been set in motion.

Evan Potter, in his analysis of the relationship between the EU and North America in the post-Cold War environment, suggests that the absence of unifying pressure generated by East-West tension could lead to the erosion of cooperation between the two sides. Canada and Mexico could find themselves "side swiped" in the event of future trade confrontations between the EU and the U.S. Potter argues that a strengthened GATT, together with an expanding network of bilateral sectorial and specific issue agreements, may provide the most effective framework for transatlantic cooperation.

In the concluding section Charles Doran reflects upon the preceding chapters and ponders the future of North American integration. He argues that NAFTA exemplifies an emerging new paradigm consisting of "clusters of intense trade interaction that have emerged around regional dynamos of development and growth." Because North Americans do not support political union they will likely decide to "widen" NAFTA by adding new members rather than to "deepen" cooperation by means of policy harmonization. Doran suggests that the lack of progress in deepening might be offset somewhat by the fact that the United States already wields considerable "decision authority" within the region.

PART ONE

North American Free Trade in Perspective

1

The Road to NAFTA

Donald Barry

The North American Free Trade Agreement (NAFTA) has ushered in a new era in Canadian-U.S.-Mexican relations, adding a trilateral dimension to relations that were previously managed on a bilateral basis. For Canada and Mexico the agreement represents a reversal of long-standing efforts to resist the embrace of their powerful neighbor. For the U.S. it is the culmination of an equally enduring aim of achieving closer continental relations. This essay describes the factors that led the three countries to conclude NAFTA and considers whether this convergence amounts to a qualitative change in their relations.

Origins of Trilateralism

As Werner Feld and Cheron Brylski note, proposals for North American economic union "are not ideas foreign to American policy goals." Past proposals, however, "referred either to U.S.-Canada or U.S.-Latin America cooperation."[1] It was not until 1979 that trilateralism became the subject of serious debate in American political circles: in the National Governors Association, in Congress and among contenders for the Democratic and Republican party presidential nominations.[2]

Building on patterns of collaboration between northeastern and western state governors and the premiers of Canada's eastern and western provinces, and between southwestern governors and their Mexican counterparts, the National Governors Association, in early 1979, commissioned a study on the prospects for broader North American cooperation by the University of Georgia's Dean Rusk Center. In October 1980, the association, acting on the center's recommendation, established a task force to explore with corresponding Canadian and Mexican bodies the feasibility of a North American Council to "provide a forum to allow representatives of all levels of government and the private sector from the three countries to discuss issues of mutual concern."[3]

Proposals for tripartite arrangements, including a North American common market, a continental energy policy and a trilateral trade commission also surfaced in Congress. A prime mover was Senator Max Baucus (D., Mt.) who chaired hearings of the Subcommittee on International Trade on North American cooperation.[4] On his initiative an amendment was added to the U.S. Trade Agreements Act of 1979, which directed the president to undertake a study of economic interdependence among Canada, the U.S. and Mexico. A further step was taken in the spring of 1980, when North American trade caucuses were formed in the Senate and the House of Representatives.

Public attention centered on schemes for closer North American ties put forward by challengers for the 1980 Democratic and Republican presidential nominations. The leading Democratic advocates were Massachusetts Senator Edward Kennedy, who called for the creation of a continental energy market, and Governor Jerry Brown of California who championed a "North American Community." On the Republican side former Texas governor and Treasury secretary John Connally and Senators Robert Dole of Kansas and Howard Baker of Tennessee echoed Kennedy's common energy market proposal.[5]

The most prominent proponent was former California governor Ronald Reagan who made the concept of a "North American Accord" -- a vague scheme for economic cooperation, presumably including energy sharing, among Canada, the U.S. and Mexico -- the centerpiece of his foreign policy platform in declaring his candidacy for the Republican party's presidential nomination in November 1979. Reagan could not say "precisely what form" collaboration among the three countries might take, but he promised that if elected president he would "immediately seek the views and ideas of Canadian and Mexican leaders ... and work tirelessly with them to develop closer ties among our peoples." Significantly, he added, "It is time we stopped thinking of our nearest neighbors as foreigners."[6]

Underlying these expressions of continentalism was a growing sense of America's vulnerability in an increasingly uncertain world. The energy shocks of 1973 and 1979 had highlighted U.S. dependence on interruptible foreign supplies. The search for more reliable sources focused attention on Canadian and Mexican oil and gas and Canada's hydroelectric power.

A related concern was the weakness of the U.S. economy evidenced by continuing balance of payments deficits and declining productivity. This, together with the growing impact of the Organization of Petroleum Exporting Countries (OPEC) and the European Community (EC), highlighted the importance of regional trade blocs a n d contributed to pressures to strengthen continental ties as a means of restoring America's competitive edge. "Analysis of where we stand in regard to energy or trade," said Senator Baucus, "leads inevitably to a discussion of our relations with our two major neighbors."7

At the same time, North American cooperation appeared to offer a way of enhancing U.S. strength in the face of the perceived decline of American power, emerging strains between Washington and its allies, and rising East-West tension. As Ronald Reagan put it, "The key to our own future security may lie in both Mexico and Canada becoming much stronger countries than they are today."8

Another important factor was the emergence of "self-conscious regions" within North America, some of which, Alan Henrikson observes, "were transborder regions, an aspect giving rise to the idea of an inclusive continental identity overarching them all."9 Reinforcing this development was the existence of mutual problems such as pollution, resource management, migration, transportation and communications arising from shared borders that could be addressed most effectively on a continental basis.

Canadian and Mexican Responses

Canada and Mexico were cool to the American proposals. Ronald Reagan travelled to Mexico City in July 1979, to discuss his North American accord idea with President José López Portillo and dispatched senior campaign aids to Ottawa to meet with members of Canadian Prime Minister Joe Clark's staff. The responses were not encouraging.10 When López Portillo and the recently reelected prime minister, Pierre Trudeau, met in Ottawa in May 1980, they issued a joint statement reaffirming their opposition to tripartite schemes which they agreed "would not serve the best interests of their countries."

At the root of Canadian and Mexican opposition was their traditional sense of insecurity vis-à-vis their superpower neighbor. López Portillo described the American proposals as being "incompatible with Mexico's social and economic development objectives, since the great disparity among the levels of development of the three countries would mean that any benefit resulting from such a union would be distributed unevenly, thereby emphasizing existing differences, and with the additional risk of endangering Mexico's sovereign ability to decide on the application of its economic policies." Trudeau declared that Canada's interests "were unlikely to be enhanced by mechanisms for comprehensive trilateral economic cooperation."[11] Their views received support from the Canadian and Mexican business communities which, while favoring increased trade and investment cooperation, were concerned about being overwhelmed by more powerful American competitors. Significantly, support for a trilateral arrangement was higher in the U.S.[12]

On the other hand, what made Americans conscious of their vulnerability, especially the energy crisis, appeared to strengthen the hands of Canada and Mexico. Both countries saw their resource wealth as a means of achieving a more arms length relationship with the U.S. In 1980, the Trudeau government adopted its National Energy Program (NEP) to increase Canadian participation in the largely foreign (mainly American) owned oil and gas industry and stiffened the government's existing foreign investment review process to scrutinize more closely the activities of multinational corporations in Canada. These actions were combined with a strategy of "concentrated bilateralism" to diversify trade. Mexico had also embarked on an ambitious economic development program and attempted to reduce reliance on the U.S. by broadening its export markets and imports of equipment and technology.

The inauguration of Ronald Reagan as president in January 1981, intensified this clash of perspectives. Tensions grew between Washington and Ottawa over the Canadian government's restrictive energy and investment measures and among all three countries over the U.S. government's economic policies and its hard-line foreign policy. By the summer of 1981, Reagan acknowledged that "North America's great disparities in levels of economic development, resources, and economic philosophies make trade liberalization difficult." He added "Improving trade relations with Mexico and Canada separately rather than on a regional basis seems appropriate at the present time."[13]

"The Canadian-Mexican negation of American trilateralism," according to Henrikson, became "a Canadian-Mexican affirmation of their own bilateralism."[14] Each saw the other as an important economic partner and foreign policy ally. Mexico looked to Canada as a source of North American technology, while Canada saw Mexico as a secure supplier of oil for its eastern provinces. Increased cooperation between the two countries was reflected in their trade which more than doubled between 1979 and 1981. They also worked together in an attempt to advance the North-South agenda. This pattern of collaboration, however, was short lived. By 1982, a severe global recession, high interest rates, falling energy prices and the debt crisis prompted Canada and Mexico to reassess their economic strategies. Their efforts to promote the North-South dialogue also bore little fruit.

Canada Changes Course

In 1982, the Trudeau government launched a major trade policy review. The study, which was released in August 1983, signalled the end of the government's trade diversification approach by proposing the negotiation of free trade with the U.S. on a sectoral basis.[15] The Reagan administration reacted favorably and by February 1984, the two sides had identified a number of sectors for potential action. But by summer discussions had stalled because of difficulties encountered in balancing trade-offs among the various sectors.

Despite their failure, the sectoral talks focused attention on the possibility of concluding a broader free trade agreement. Impetus was provided by the election of Prime Minister Brian Mulroney's government in September 1984. It made economic renewal and refurbished relations with the U.S. a key part of its policy and moved quickly to dismantle the National Energy Program, to soften the country's foreign investment regulations, and to give Washington "the benefit of the doubt" on foreign policy. Also important was the passage of American legislation in the fall of that year which urged the administration to begin negotiating bilateral trade agreements, Israel and Canada being identified as leading candidates.

At their "Shamrock Summit" meeting in Quebec City in March 1985, Mulroney and Reagan directed the U.S. Trade Representative, William Brock, and Canadian trade minister James Kelleher to examine ways of reducing or eliminating barriers to trade. After undertaking extensive consultations the two ministers recommended that their governments explore the prospects for a free trade accord. Mulroney and Reagan expressed agreement in an exchange of letters on October 1, 1985. Two years of difficult negotiations were brought to a dramatic conclusion by Canadian and U.S. cabinet level representatives in early October 1987. The prime minister and the president signed the final text of the Canada-U.S. Free Trade Agreement (CUSFTA) on January 2, 1988, and the pact came into effect on January 1, 1989, after a bitterly contested general election in Canada which saw the government returned to power.[16]

The Mulroney government's decision to seek comprehensive free trade with the U.S., Gilbert Winham has written, "represented a fundamental change of Canadian economic policy, both domestic and toward the United States."[17] Contributing to the shift was the 1985 report of the Royal Commission on the Economic Union and Development Prospects for Canada, which had been set up by the Trudeau government during the recession in 1982, to examine Canada's economic situation. The commission argued that economic growth required a reduced role for government and more reliance on market forces. Free trade with the U.S. was seen as an important instrument for bringing about this domestic transformation. "By exposing the Canadian economy to greater international competition while simultaneously improving access to the large market to the south," Michael Hart says, "Canadian firms would have an incentive to restructure and modernize and become more efficient and productive."[18] This conclusion was supported by Canadian businesses, now more confident of their ability to compete with their American counterparts.

Support for free trade was reinforced by a sharp rise in protectionist pressures in the U.S. which threatened to limit Canadian exports to that market. A common set of trade rules and the creation of an effective mechanism to adjudicate trade disputes were considered necessary to maintain security of access to the U.S. market for Canadian products. Also important was the increasing inability of the General Agreement on Tariffs and Trade (GATT) to provide an adequate framework for international trade and the failure to agree on the major issues facing that body. Reaching a similar conclusion, the U.S. government realized that "a bilateral agreement with Canada would probably represent the only trade agreement it could achieve."[19]

CUSFTA provided for the gradual elimination of all tariffs between the two countries over a ten year period and liberalized trade in agriculture and financial services. Energy trade and cross border investment restrictions were reduced. The 1965 Canada-U.S. auto pact was confirmed as the basis of bilateral automotive trade. At the heart of the agreement was a pioneering trade dispute settlement process. Bilateral panels with binding powers were established to ensure that each country's anti-dumping and countervailing duty laws would be fairly applied. Changes to current trade remedy laws would also be subject to consultation and review. (The two governments gave themselves seven years to negotiate a uniform set of rules regarding subsidies and dumping.) "By these means," Henrikson states, "an emergent 'supranationality' was delicately balanced with national sovereignty, 'interdependence' was intricately adjusted to independence, and 'North America' was judiciously integrated with the separateness of the two countries."[20]

Mexico's Shift

Meanwhile, Mexico had launched what would ultimately become a far-reaching program of economic reform of its own. Beginning in 1983, the governments of President Miguel de la Madrid and especially his successor, Carlos Salinas de Gortari, embarked on a policy of liberalization to open up the Mexican economy. Between 1985 and 1989, Mexico sharply reduced its tariffs and began easing import restrictions. It also took a number of external initiatives, including membership in GATT in 1986, and the signing of agreements with the U.S. dealing with such matters as subsidies and countervailing duties, trade and investment consultative procedures, steel and textiles. In addition, in 1989, Salinas unveiled a national development plan aimed at attracting foreign investment, liberalizing financial markets and further reducing trade barriers.[21]

The culmination of this process was the decision taken in early 1990, to seek a free trade agreement with the U.S. On June 10, Salinas and President George Bush issued a joint statement endorsing the goal of a comprehensive accord and they directed the U.S. Trade Representative, Carla Hills, and Mexican trade minister Jaime Serra Puche to undertake exploratory talks. In late August the representatives recommended that the two sides take the necessary steps to start the negotiation. Shortly after Salinas made a formal request to begin discussions and Bush responded by notifying Congress of his intention to negotiate an agreement. Prime Minister Mulroney, after some hesitation, indicated Canada's interest in participating on September 24. The three governments formally announced their decision to negotiate a trilateral trade agreement on February 5, 1991.

Mexican, U.S. and Canadian Motives

Mexico's decision to seek free trade with the U.S., even more so than Canada's, signified, according to Sidney Weintraub and Delal Baer, "a fundamental shift in attitude from deliberate distancing to formally linking the nation's future to its relations with the United States."[22] But while Mexico's policy shift was more dramatic than that of Canada, given the former's long history of a closed economy, the reasons for the change were similar.

The steep decline in oil prices and the debt crisis of the early 1980s, which brought Mexico's economy close to collapse, pointed to the failure of the country's economic development model based on the concept of growth through import substitution and convinced the government of the need to adopt a more market driven approach. The Mexican business community, reversing its earlier view, agreed.

A free trade agreement with the U.S., which assured access to the American market, would solidify Mexico's new economic thrust, making it difficult for future governments to roll back the reforms undertaken. It would also provide insurance against American protectionism thereby increasing investor confidence in Mexico. The likelihood that the Canada-U.S. free trade accord would adversely affect Mexican exports to the Canadian and American markets, and the protection that Canada had received from many current and future U.S. non-tariff barriers as a result of the agreement, reinforced Mexico's determination to act.[23]

For Washington the Mexican initiative presented what a senior State Department official called, "a rare strategic opportunity to secure, strengthen, and develop our continental base, economically and politically, in a way that will promote America's foreign policy agenda, our economic strength and leadership, and U.S. global influence."[24] In addition to increasing American trade with Mexico an agreement would support that country's economic reforms thereby contributing to Mexican economic and political stability. It would also give impetus to U.S. efforts to deal with such pressing bilateral problems as the environment, the drug trade and illegal immigration. Moreover, it was anticipated that economic rationalization on a continental scale would strengthen America's competitive position vis-à-vis Europe and Asia. Finally, consistent with a new hemispheric thrust in American policy expressed in President Bush's June 1990 Enterprise for the Americas Initiative (EAI), a free trade pact would "send a strong, encouraging signal throughout Latin America to a new generation of leaders pledged to democracy, human rights, and market economics."[25]

In contrast, the Canadian government was a less than eager participant. Canada's limited economic links with Mexico provided little incentive to join the talks; nor was the government anxious to reignite the divisive domestic debate that had accompanied CUSFTA. But it concluded that it could not remain aloof. Ottawa's main concerns were to protect the gains it had achieved in CUSFTA and to prevent the creation of a "hub and spoke" arrangement that would give the U.S. special access to Canada and Mexico while restricting their advantage to the American market. Once the negotiation began its main aim would be to secure improvements to CUSFTA.

NAFTA and Its Aftermath

Formal negotiations for a North American free trade pact began on June 12, 1991, and concluded in Washington on August 12, 1992, just prior to the Republican National Convention that would confirm President Bush as his party's standard bearer in the fall presidential election. The agreement that was reached essentially strengthened and extended the provisions of CUSFTA to all three countries. It provided for the phasing out of tariffs and investment restrictions, and set out rules covering such matters as agriculture, energy, goods and services, intellectual property, government procurement, and dispute settlement.[26]

Bush made the agreement a key element of his reelection strategy. But the pact soon came under fire from a broadly based coalition of environmentalists, labor unions, human rights groups and America First proponents. Democratic presidential nominee Bill Clinton, who would go on to win the election, expressed support for NAFTA while calling for parallel agreements to meet domestic concerns.[27] Encouraged by Clinton's endorsement, Mulroney, Salinas and the outgoing Bush formally signed the agreement on December 17, 1992.

In an effort to shore up support for NAFTA, President Clinton announced that his administration would seek supplementary agreements on the environment, labor, and import surges. Canada and Mexico reluctantly agreed to enter into discussions which began in March 1993, and concluded five months later. Three deals were reached: an agreement on the environment which created a North American Commission on the Environment to oversee the enforcement of national environmental regulations, a labor agreement which established a North American Commission on Labor to promote the enforcement of labor standards, and an agreement on import surges which set up a tripartite working group to ensure the effective application of import surge provisions.[28] NAFTA still faced an uphill battle in Congress, but the president ultimately prevailed, winning a dramatic come from behind victory in a crucial vote in the House of Representatives on November 17, 1993. The Senate voted in favor of the agreement a few days later.

By this time NAFTA was facing criticism from Prime Minister Jean Chretien's newly elected Canadian government. Although Parliament had approved the pact the previous spring, Chretien threatened to withhold ratification without a clearer definition of subsidies and dumping, changes to protect Canada's energy supplies, and agreement that water resources were not included. However, Ottawa gave its final approval in early December after settling for a non-binding agreement to reach an accord on subsidies and dumping within two years, and a joint statement confirming that water exports were excluded from NAFTA. It also issued a unilateral declaration setting out its position on energy.[29] Mexico, which had delayed its assent pending U.S. and Canadian approval, ratified the agreement shortly thereafter, paving the way for it to come into force as scheduled on January 1, 1994.

Change or Continuity?

The conclusion of an integrative economic arrangement in North America was a marked departure from the long-established efforts of Canada and Mexico to counter the push and pull of the U.S. It also fulfilled the American goal of establishing closer economic linkages with its neighbors. This convergence followed parallel decisions taken by Canada and Mexico to adopt more market oriented domestic economic strategies and to pursue free trade with the U.S. as a means of effecting and consolidating those changes.

At the same time both countries remained concerned about their vulnerability to American actions. A critical Canadian objective during the Canada-U.S. free trade deliberations was the establishment of a legal mechanism to protect its economic interests from American protectionism. Allan Gotlieb, a former Canadian ambassador to the U.S., describes the dispute settlement process as "the most important part of the Agreement."[30] For the same reason, such a mechanism was high on the list of Canadian and Mexican priorities in the negotiation of NAFTA,[31] which contains a dispute settlement provision similar to that found in CUSFTA.

Thus the "new continentalism"[32] contains elements of both change and continuity. On the one hand, the adoption of more liberal economic approaches by Canada and Mexico has made their economies more like that of the U.S. and facilitated closer relations. On the other hand, the inclusion of the dispute settlement procedure in NAFTA demonstrates their continuing efforts to constrain the exercise of American power.

Notes

1. Werner J. Feld and Cheron Brylski, "A North American Accord: Feasible or Futile?," *Western Political Quarterly*, Vol. 36, No. 2 (June 1983), p. 289.

2. Ironically, the first proposal for formal trilateral cooperation appeared in Canada in 1977 when Duncan Edmonds, then a senior advisor to Progressive Conservative Party leader Joe Clark, drew up a plan for a "Treaty of North America" for the economic and political union of Canada, the U.S. and Mexico, an end he considered inevitable. Edmonds' plan, which was designed to provide a means of managing this process, envisaged the creation of a Council of North America, modelled on the Council of Europe, to oversee the selective integration of the three countries. The idea was politically very sensitive and was not taken up, but Edmonds continued to promote it in Canadian political circles and also in some American quarters. See Lawrence Martin, *Pledge of Allegiance: The Americanization of Canada in the Mulroney Years* (Toronto: McClelland and Stewart, 1993), pp. 12-22. The text of the proposal was published in the *Ottawa Journal*, January 5, 1980.

3. *Canadian Press Report*, October 16, 1980. The report on which the Center's recommendation was based is entitled *Comparative Facts on Canada, Mexico and the United States: A Foundation for Selective Integration and Trilateral Cooperation* (The Dean Rusk Center for International and Comparative Law, University of Georgia, 1979).

4. *North American Economic Interdependence* and *North American Interdependence II*, Hearings Before the Subcommittee on International Trade of the Committee on Finance, United States Senate, Ninety-Sixth Congress, First Session, June 6, 1979, October 1, 1979.

5. *Globe and Mail*, July 20, 1979; July 24, 1979; July 27, 1979, August 17, 1979, *Toronto Star*, October 17, 1979.

6. Quoted in Alan K. Henrikson, "American Rediscovery of North America," Paper presented to the Western Social Science Association, Denver, Colorado, April 21-24, 1982, p. 7.

7. *North American Interdependence*, June 6, 1979, p. 3.

8. Quoted in Henrikson, "American Rediscovery of North America," p. 6.

9. Alan K. Henrikson, "A North American Community: From the Yukon to the Yucatan," in Hans Binnendijk and Mary Locke, eds., *The Diplomatic Record, 1991-1992* (Boulder: Westview Press, 1993), p. 78.

10. William A. Orme, Jr., *Continental Shift: Free Trade and the New North America* (Washington: Washington Post Company, 1993), p. 24; *New York Times*, November 15, 1979.

11. Quoted in James Basche, "North American Economic Relations: A Survey of Canadian, Mexican and U.S. Business Leaders," The Conference Board, *Information Bulletin*, No. 88, 1981.

12. Ibid.

13. President Ronald Reagan to Hon. Dan Rostenkowski, August 4, 1981.

14. Henrikson, "American Rediscovery of North America," p. 25.

15. Canada, Department of External Affairs, *Trade Policy for the 1980's: A Discussion Paper* (Ottawa: Minister of Supply and Services Canada, 1983).

16. The leading accounts of the negotiation of the agreement are G. Bruce Doern and Brian W. Tomlin, *Faith and Fear: The Free Trade Story* (Toronto: Stoddart, 1991) and Michael Hart, Bill Dymond and Colin Robertson, *Decision at Midnight: Inside the Canada-U.S. Free Trade Negotiations* (Vancouver: University of British Columbia Press, 1994).

17. Gilbert R. Winham, *Trading With Canada: The Canada-U.S. Free Trade Agreement* (New York: Priority Press Publications, 1988), p. 21.

18. Michael Hart, "Negotiating Free Trade, 1985-88," in Don Munton and John Kirton, eds., *Canadian Foreign Policy: Selected Cases* (Scarborough: Prentice Hall, 1992), pp. 326-327.

19. Winham, *Trading With Canada*, p. 21.

20. Henrikson, "A North American Community," p. 76.

21. Nora Lustig, "NAFTA: A Mexican Perspective," *SAIS Review*, Vol. 12, No. 1 (Winter-Spring 1992), pp. 58-59.

22. Sidney Weintraub and M. Delal Baer, "The Interplay Between Economic and Political Opening: The Sequence in Mexico," *The Washington Quarterly* (Spring 1992), p. 198.

23. Sidney Weintraub, "Free Trade in North America: Has Its Time Come?" *The World Economy*, Vol. 14, No. 1 (March 1991), p. 58.

24. Robert O. Zoellick (Counselor, Department of State), "The North American FTA: The New World Order Takes Shape in the Western Hemisphere," *US Department of State Dispatch*, Vol. 3, No. 15 (April 13, 1992), p. 290.

25. "North American Free Trade Agreement," ibid., Vol. 3, No. 7 (February 17, 1992), p. 112.

26. See, in this volume, Chapter 2 by Gilbert R. Winham and Heather A. Grant.

27. The U.S. debate over NAFTA is discussed in Orme, *Continental Shift*.

28. United States Embassy, Ottawa, "Procedures Involved in Implementing NAFTA Agreement," *Backgrounder*, 9-17-93.

29. Canada, Office of the Prime Minister, "Prime Minister Announces NAFTA Improvements: Canada to Proceed With Agreement," *Press Release*, December 2, 1993.

30. Allan Gotlieb, "The United States in Canadian Foreign Policy," O.D. Skelton Memorial Lecture, December 10, 1991, External Affairs and International Trade Canada, p. 17.

31. For a discussion of Mexico's objectives in the negotiation see Gerardo M. Bueno, "Mexico's Options in Trade Negotiations," *The World Economy*, Vol. 14, No. 1 (March 1991), p. 75.

32. M. Delal Baer, "North American Free Trade," *Foreign Affairs*, Vol. 70, No. 4 (Fall 1991), p. 132.

2

NAFTA: An Overview

Gilbert R. Winham and
Heather A. Grant

The North American Free Trade Agreement (NAFTA) has created the world's largest free trade region, encompassing 360 million people producing approximately $7 trillion in goods and services.[1] NAFTA is a comprehensive agreement that provides for the gradual reduction in tariffs among the parties, and establishes rules and principles to govern such areas as intellectual property, government procurement, services, energy and dispute settlement, which will ensure a more stable climate for trade and investment among the parties.

Each country had its own particular reasons for becoming involved in the negotiations. However, according to Gary Hufbauer and Jeffrey Schott, NAFTA's unifying appeal was likely the prospect that "substantial synergy" among the parties' economies could generate significant increases in income and employment and improve the efficiency and productivity of North American firms so that they could become more internationally competitive.[2] NAFTA's most important objective is export-generated growth outside North America that will allow all three parties to decrease their respective debts and current account deficits in a way they cannot achieve through trade among themselves.[3]

The purpose of this paper is to canvass briefly each party's reasons for entering into the negotiations, and to provide an overview of the structure and substance of the agreement. Finally, some of the more important implications of the agreement will be summarized.

Pre-NAFTA Considerations

Mexico

The NAFTA negotiation commenced with a declaration in June 1990, by Mexican President Carlos Salinas de Gortari and U.S. President George Bush that committed their two countries to negotiate a comprehensive bilateral trade agreement.[4] For Mexico the declaration was the culmination of a series of far-reaching reforms undertaken by the government to address fundamental problems in the Mexican economy.

Prior to 1985, Mexico pursued an economic plan focussed on import substitution.[5] However, the country's debt crisis in 1982, followed by a weak international oil market and limited external funding, caused the government to re-evaluate its policies and to turn towards greater trade and investment liberalization in order to improve its economy. Actions taken included joining the General Agreement on Tariffs and Trade (GATT) in 1986, reducing its maximum tariff from 100 per cent to 20 per cent between 1985 and 1990, and liberalizing foreign investment and intellectual property rights.[6] Other areas of reform included the virtual elimination of all licensing requirements, reduction of government subsidy practices, and privatization of key industries such as banking, telecommunications and transport.[7]

During this period, Mexico's exports also began to shift from predominantly primary and simple secondary goods, such as textiles, liquor and tobacco, to more complex manufactured products, including chemical compounds, machinery and equipment.[8] With the shift in focus, Mexico became increasingly reliant on the export of manufactured goods to the U.S., and therefore more dependent on its northern neighbor for further economic development. Correspondingly, Mexico became increasingly vulnerable to possible American trade restrictions.

Given these trends, one of Mexico's primary objectives in participating in a free trade agreement with the U.S. was to ensure more open and secure access to the American market which, prior to the negotiations, accounted for three-fourths of Mexico's total exports.[9] Another major consideration was the prospect of increased foreign investment and capital in-flows from the U.S. which would be particularly welcome in view of the diversion of capital that had taken place from countries such as Mexico to former Communist regimes. Mexico was also concerned about the possible diversion of trade with the European Community (EC) should the Uruguay Round fail, as well as Canada's preferred access to the American market resulting from the

Canada-U.S. Free Trade Agreement (CUSFTA).[10] A free trade pact with the U.S. would mean that Mexico's domestic reforms would likely become more solidly entrenched, and continue to evolve towards greater symmetry with the U.S. system. Although not as yet a major trading partner, Canada's involvement in the negotiations would broaden Mexico's potential export horizons and sources of investment.

United States

The interests of the U.S. in pursuing a NAFTA were both economic and political. In addition to the broad objectives of promoting efficient use of labor and natural resources within the free trade region, as well as improved international competitiveness, NAFTA was seen as an opportunity for the U.S. to enhance its export markets. It was generally held that economic growth in Mexico flowing from a free trade agreement would increase Mexican demand for American goods and services.[11] Arguably, the primary U.S. objective in negotiating NAFTA was greater political and economic stability within Mexico's borders. As indicated above, Mexico had made considerable strides towards economic and political reform over the previous eight years, yet these reforms remained fragile.[12] A NAFTA would be perceived as a reinforcement of support for the reforms. Also important was the perception that a free trade arrangement with Mexico might help stem the flow of illegal immigrants across the U.S. border from Mexico in search of better jobs and higher wages.

Canada

The announcement by Presidents Salinas and Bush to commence a bilateral trade negotiation created a difficult situation for Canada. The Conservative government of Prime Minister Brian Mulroney had narrowly survived a divisive national election in 1988 over CUSFTA, and was wary of entering what appeared to be a controversial negotiation for Canada.[13] Furthermore, in sharp contrast to the Canada-U.S. relationship, the value of trade between Canada and Mexico was not sufficient for the government to defend a negotiation with Mexico on economic grounds.

Canada's interests in joining the Mexican-U.S. initiative were initially defensive. The Canadian government wanted to ensure that the gains it had made under CUSFTA were not diluted as a result of a bilateral deal between the U.S. and Mexico. Conversely, the govern-

ment wanted to ensure that it received the same access provisions to the
Mexican market as the U.S. As succinctly stated by Hufbauer and
Schott, "[Canadian negotiators] would [have been] happy with the
status quo ante, but they realize[d] that reforms by the U.S. and Mexico
[would] affect the Canadian position in the world market whether
Canada participate[d] or not."[14] Furthermore, Canada had historically played a significant role in developing world trade policy. In
order to maintain its status as an important contributor to trade policy
reform in spite of its relatively small economic position in the world,
Canada was essentially obliged to participate in the NAFTA
negotiations.

Another Canadian concern was that a separate Mexico-U.S. trade
agreement could set a precedent for a "hub and spoke" model of
bilateral agreements between the U.S. and other individual hemispheric nations. This could potentially neutralize the gain that
Canada had realized from trade preferences under CUSFTA, without
providing any compensating benefit in the way of more liberalized
access to the domestic markets of prospective new trade partners of the
U.S. The only way to avoid the hub and spoke model was to ensure
that Canada and Mexico engaged the U.S. in a regional trade
agreement in lieu of separate bilateral agreements.

Finally, Canada recognized the potential economic benefits that
could accrue from a NAFTA, which included a large export market,
enhanced investment opportunities, and corresponding prospects for
improved efficiency and productivity among Canadian firms. In
concrete terms, Canada sought to use NAFTA to make improvements to
CUSFTA, to gain access to the Mexican market, and to ensure that, by
maintaining a liberal trade policy, Canada would continue to be an
attractive location for both Canadian and foreign capital.[15] As
Canada engaged in the NAFTA negotiation, the positive benefits of an
agreement took on greater importance than the defensive concerns that
initially motivated the country.

The Structure and Substance of the Agreement

NAFTA is divided into eight principal areas: objectives and scope
of the agreement, trade in goods, technical barriers to trade,
government procurement, investment and services, intellectual property
and institutional provisions, such as dispute settlement, and finally
general provisions governing entry into force and accession. Although
labor and environment were dealt with more comprehensively in the
original NAFTA text than in any previous free trade accord,

supplemental agreements on these issues were reached on August 13, 1993. In many respects, NAFTA builds upon the substance of CUSFTA, but goes considerably beyond its scope in some areas such as services, and expands into new ones such as intellectual property.

NAFTA primarily establishes mutual obligations among the parties. However, in some instances the agreement only creates bilateral or unilateral obligations in order to take into account specific aspects of a party's economic, political or legal systems. For example, between Canada and the U.S., the provisions of CUSFTA continue in effect except where NAFTA specifically goes beyond it. As such, Canadian and U.S. obligations under CUSFTA were either incorporated by reference, extended trilaterally or made generic under the agreement. Similar to CUSFTA, NAFTA does not apply to cultural industries, and government health and social programs remain protected. Furthermore, NAFTA, like CUSFTA, is subject to the parties' obligations under GATT. As noted above, NAFTA provides for the accession of other countries. In order to accede, a country must fulfil certain criteria and agree to the terms of the pact, subject to final approval by each of the three original NAFTA members.

The following sections will highlight some of the general areas of NAFTA and the side agreements. The implications of some of these provisions will be given greater consideration in the third part of the paper.

Tariffs and Non-Tariff Barriers

The reduction of tariffs and non-tariff barriers remains a cornerstone of regional free trade agreements. The elimination of these barriers to trade on substantially all goods traded between the parties is required by GATT Article XXIV in order for the parties to comply with the exception to the principles of most-favored nation (MFN) and national treatment under the GATT. To this end, NAFTA does provide for the virtual elimination of all tariffs between the parties. However, this issue was overshadowed during the negotiations by more current issues, such as the formulation of rules governing intellectual property and dispute settlement. The main reason for this is that, during its years of reform, Mexico had already reduced its tariffs significantly and eliminated many of its import licensing requirements which had previously posed serious obstacles to access for foreign producers, thereby making this issue less contentious than others.

Under the agreement, Canada, the U.S. and Mexico will phase out virtually all of the tariffs applying to each other's goods over the next

10 years. The tariffs will either be eliminated immediately, or phased out over periods of five, ten or fifteen years, in order to provide temporary protection to sensitive industries and allow them to restructure and adapt to the new trading conditions. For Canada, clothing and footwear are among the more sensitive industries covered by a lengthy phase-out period, while for Mexico the sensitive products include certain vegetables, powdered milk and pharmaceutical products.

The tariff schedule provides Mexico with faster access to the Canadian and U.S. market in recognition of the "disparity in the level of development of Mexico, the U.S. and Canada."[16] Where import surges resulting from the agreement injure a party's domestic industry, that party may invoke safeguard measures to protect the industry.

Auto Industry

One of Canada's primary objectives in entering the negotiations was to ensure that the auto pact between Canada and the U.S. was preserved and not diluted by any bilateral arrangement between the U.S. and Mexico.[17] Canada succeeded in this objective. The agreement further provides that the duty remission schedule in CUSFTA is maintained. Mexico's automotive industry which had previously been insulated from competition by the Mexican "Automotive Decree," will open up to competition from Canadian and U.S. exports of auto parts and vehicles over a phase-in period as a result of NAFTA. A significant change from CUSFTA is that the rules of origin have increased the percentage of domestic content from 50 per cent to 62.5 per cent on cars, light trucks and major parts, and to 60 per cent on all other parts. Tariffs on all automotive goods will finally be eliminated by the year 2003. NAFTA also incorporates new rules and procedures to avoid customs disputes of the sort that had previously occurred between Canada and the U.S. over Honda automobiles. In this case U.S. and Canadian customs authorities could not agree on the application of a "roll-up/roll-down" formula that counted auto components originating in a CUSFTA party as wholly foreign (and therefore not subject to duty-free treatment) if the foreign content of the component comprised over 50 per cent of its total value. Specifically, NAFTA includes a tracing requirement designed to facilitate the application of rules of origin to goods containing foreign and territorial (i.e., NAFTA) materials.[18]

Agriculture[19]

NAFTA actually establishes two bilateral arrangements among the parties with respect to agricultural products. While the CUSFTA provisions governing agriculture remain in effect between Canada and the U.S., Mexico reached separate deals with both countries. The agreement focuses on phasing out tariffs and other restrictive measures such as import quotas and import licenses on agricultural products over specified periods of time. Canada and Mexico did, however, negotiate the exclusion of certain agricultural products such as eggs, poultry and dairy products, thus allowing Canada to continue to impose import quotas on these products. Furthermore, NAFTA permits each party to impose health and safety standards on agricultural imports, but these standards must have a scientific basis in order to comply.

Textiles and Apparel [20]

NAFTA's rules of origin are much tighter than those under CUSFTA, and are designed to limit the use of non-NAFTA yarns and fabrics in the production of textiles and clothing. To qualify for preferential duties under NAFTA, yarns and fabric must originate in North America. Likewise, apparel must be made with yarns and fabrics originating in North America in order to qualify for preferential tariffs. However, some exceptions were incorporated into the agreement, permitting certain specified quotas on products not meeting the strict rules of origin to qualify. Similar quotas which were incorporated into CUSFTA proved to be beneficial to Canada's textile and clothing manufacturers because, in comparison with American producers, the Canadian industry has tended to use a significantly higher proportion of yarns and fibers imported from outside North America. Under NAFTA, these quotas have been expanded and increased to compensate, in part, for the stricter rules of origin. Many quotas on various Canadian exports to the U.S. will increase between 1 per cent and 2 per cent annually, beginning in 1995, subject to review in the year 2000.

Energy [21]

The NAFTA energy chapter largely parallels the provisions of the Canada-U.S. Free Trade Agreement. Trilaterally, the chapter provides for greater trade and investment opportunities between the parties in the energy sector. However, even though the provisions focus on the elimination or reduction of trade and investment restrictions, a significant portion of Mexico's sector is excluded from the application of these provisions. The most important areas of exclusion are Mexico's oil and gas industries. Mexico prohibits not only investment but also the provision of services in these areas, which are considered resources protected from foreign ownership and exploitation under the Mexican constitution. It should be noted, however, that because certain sectors are excluded from the application of these provisions, Mexico does not receive the benefit of NAFTA in the areas of exclusion. For example, Mexico does not benefit from unrestricted access to the other parties' markets subject only to limited exceptions on the basis of national security.

Services[22]

Pursuant to Chapter 12 of the agreement, each party is obliged to extend national treatment to many commercial services. The scope of these services is broader under NAFTA than previously under CUSFTA. Both land transportation and speciality air services, such as aerial surveying and forest fire management are two new areas into which NAFTA has expanded. Although basic telecommunications, such as local and long distance services are not covered by NAFTA (similar to CUSFTA), enhanced services are within the agreement's scope. NAFTA also provides for greater transparency and simplicity in the procedures governing the temporary entry of business and professional persons from the other two parties, and as such it builds upon the corresponding CUSFTA chapter.

Financial Services[23]

The NAFTA chapter governing financial services between the parties builds in substance on CUSFTA. However, the framework has been changed to make the agreement more appropriate for the accession of future parties. The financial services chapter succeeds in providing Canadian and U.S. financial institutions with access to Mexico's financial markets, although full access will only be achieved after a lengthy transition period ending in the year 2000. NAFTA establishes a set of principles applicable to all parties. These include national treatment, greater transparency in the regulation of their respective financial sectors, and MFN treatment where a non-NAFTA party is granted a concession beyond the privileges enjoyed by NAFTA partners. A state or provincial government may, however, take reservations to the agreement, provided this is done within a certain period of time. Otherwise sub-national governments are also bound by the agreement. Unlike CUSFTA, NAFTA provides for dispute settlement regarding issues pertaining to the financial services sector.

Government Procurement[24]

Chapter 13 provides NAFTA parties with access to each other's government markets. The agreement increases the scope and coverage of opportunities for NAFTA suppliers to vie for government procurement contracts in goods, services and construction. The procedures governing the tendering of bids, challenging bids and dispute settlement have also been improved under NAFTA compared to the provisions in CUSFTA.

Investment[25]

The investment chapter obliges parties to extend the better of national treatment or MFN treatment to investors from NAFTA countries. It specifically prohibits the parties from imposing trade-distorting performance requirements on the export of goods and services, domestic content, domestic sourcing, trading balancing, the transfer of technology and obligations to supply exclusively a certain regional or world market. These obligations are subject to specific exceptions or reservations each party has taken, or will take, as set out in the agreement. For example, Canada's cultural industries are exempt from the agreement entirely while Mexico has reserved to the right to impose performance requirements on its *maquiladora* industry. The specific reservations to the general principles governing investments between the parties are set out in lengthy annexes to the agreement. The scope of the investment chapter is broader under NAFTA than CUSFTA and includes investments incorporated in a NAFTA country regardless of country of origin. The chapter also provides for dispute resolution in the form of international arbitration on a state-to-state basis and the investor-state level.

Intellectual Property[26]

NAFTA goes a long way towards establishing standards in the trade and transfer of intellectual property between the parties, and to provide for their protection and enforcement. The substance of the chapter is largely based on the Agreement on Trade-Related Aspects of Intellectual Property Rights (TRIPs) in the Uruguay Round draft code. This chapter sets both standards designed to protect such property and remedial provisions to deal with infringements on these rights. NAFTA further obliges parties to give effect to the substance of numerous international conventions designed to protect intellectual property rights.

Dispute Settlement[27]

In addition to sector-specific dispute settlement provisions in NAFTA, two other chapters are set aside to provide mechanisms for resolving disputes between the parties. Chapter 20 adopts the basic institutional arrangements and dispute settlement procedures established in CUSFTA to resolve disputes over the interpretation and implementation of NAFTA. Incremental improvements were made to the procedures for selecting panelists and obtaining expert advice on scientific matters where appropriate. Greater emphasis has been placed in NAFTA on resolving disputes prior to invoking the formal dispute settlement mechanism.

Chapter 19 provides a dispute settlement mechanism for countervailing and anti-dumping disputes. The mechanism provides for the creation of ad hoc bi-national panels to replace domestic courts in reviewing final anti-dumping and countervailing duty findings by domestic agencies. NAFTA adds to the mechanism originally conceived in CUSFTA by incorporating new safeguard provisions to ensure that a party's domestic laws do not impede the panel process or the implementation of panel decisions. Where the benefit of the mechanism is denied, a party may take recourse against its offending counterpart.

The NAFTA Side Agreements on Labor and the Environment[28]

The side agreements are designed to confront a situation where a party demonstrates a persistent pattern of failure to effectively enforce its laws pertaining to workplace health and safety, minimum wages and child labor, or environmental protection. Each agreement sets up machinery for cooperation and dispute settlement, including a Commission consisting of a Ministerial Council, an independent Secretariat, and a Public Advisory Committee. The most important function of the Commission is to undertake consultations in the event that a party is charged with not enforcing its relevant legislation. An independent panel can be established to investigate a situation of non-enforcement, and if the situation is not rectified the panel may ultimately recommend sanctions against the party. Sanctions are to be fines against governments or withdrawal of equivalent NAFTA trade benefits. Although the side agreements provide for the possibility of punitive actions, the procedure is lengthy and it provides much in the way of opportunities for consultation and cooperative problem-solving between the parties. In sum, the side agreements succeed in ratcheting up the concern for environment and labor issues, while avoiding an adversarial approach which could undermine the cooperation needed to carry out a working trade agreement.

Evaluation of the Agreement

Following on two GATT multilateral rounds and CUSFTA, NAFTA is the fourth major trade negotiation Canada has participated in during the past two decades. There is a reason for this extraordinary effort in international policy making. It is that the world economy has under-gone rapid change over the same period, which in turn has made obsolete many of the rules and policies by which nations previously governed their international economic exchanges.

The obsolescence of national trade policies is driven by several factors. There is high mobility of capital, technology and information in the international economy today, which creates conditions for an international marketplace and makes it effectively impossible to defend national markets with traditional tools like protective tariffs. In turn, producers recognize that national markets are inadequate for efficient production, which encourages large and even smaller firms increasingly to orient their production and sales toward foreign markets. The result is that pressures are created -- especially in trade-dependent countries like Canada -- to forego economic policies that segment and divide markets in favor of policies that respond to an interdependence already established in the international economy.

NAFTA represents a deepening of the obligations Canada has already undertaken toward its principal trade partners in GATT and CUSFTA. GATT contains the fundamental rules necessary to create a liberal trading system: for example, non-discrimination (Article I), national treatment (Article III), and renunciation of quantitative and certain non-border measures (Article XI).[29] CUSFTA was concluded within the legal framework of GATT, but it effectively expanded GATT disciplines between Canada and the U.S. by applying them to new areas such as services and investment. NAFTA in turn is GATT-consistent, but it is a yet more sophisticated attempt to create rules that support an international business environment.[30] For example, NAFTA includes rules on relations between private investors and states, whereas CUSFTA dealt only with state-to-state obligations; NAFTA establishes, within limits, principles of right-to-establish and national treatment in financial services, while CUSFTA simply made marginal changes to restrictive legislation in Canada and the United States; and NAFTA includes a chapter on intellectual property that incorporates many of the disciplines negotiated in the Uruguay Round draft text. The upshot is that NAFTA should be seen not only as incorporating a third nation into a bilateral U.S-Canada trade regime, but also as a substantial improvement of that regime itself.

NAFTA has a series of strong points, beyond those mentioned above. At a most basic level, the agreement is a commitment to move to tariff-free trade between a developing and two developed countries. Developed and developing countries have generally been unwilling to trade with each other without numerous protective restrictions, and simply concluding a deal is a breakthrough equivalent to the expansion of the European Community to include southern Mediterranean countries. Moreover, the deal makes remarkable progress in troublesome areas like textiles, where Canada and the U.S. accepted significant liberalization in a heavily-protected sector, and in agriculture, where the bilateral accord between Mexico and the U.S. established tariff-rate quotas that can be gradually phased out in lieu of all non-tariff restrictions.[31]

A second strong point is that NAFTA dismantles Mexico's Auto Decree and opens its domestic market to Canadian and U.S. exports. This is a substantial benefit to the North American auto makers, which will now have the potential to trade into Mexico in lieu of being forced to locate investment there in order to access the Mexican market. Other aspects of the NAFTA automotive chapter are less desirable from the perspective of liberalized trade, such as a restrictive rule of origin that in time will extend duty free treatment only to vehicles that contain 62.5 per cent North American content. The equivalent figure for CUSFTA is 50 per cent, as noted earlier.

A third strong point is the advance made by NAFTA in liberalizing trade in services. The agreement calls for both national and MFN treatment in services, and it prevents parties from requiring service providers from other parties to establish local offices as a condition of providing the service.[32] The agreement liberalizes exchanges of professional services, especially engineering services, and it makes major progress in opening up services and cross-border investment in land transportation. The latter development is significant because of the important role of rail and truck transportation in North America.[33] Finally, NAFTA includes a chapter on telecommunications which substantially liberalizes markets, particularly Mexico's, in telecommunications equipment. The chapter further provides private firms access to public telecom networks in other parties on a reasonable and cost-oriented basis. However, the provision of basic telephone and telecommunication services will continue to be controlled by national governments.

A fourth strong point of NAFTA concerns the provisions for dispute settlement, which, as noted above, were modeled after those in CUSFTA. NAFTA provides for a GATT-like general dispute-settlement procedure that is an incremental improvement over its predecessor in that it will promote dispute settlement at the level of working groups and technical committees before disputes take on political and therefore more serious proportions. An innovative procedure has also been established for settling disputes between private investors and state parties. On disputes over antidumping and countervailing duties, Chapter 19 of CUSFTA has been established on a permanent basis and extended to Mexico, contingent on the latter undertaking legislative reforms necessary to provide judicial review and due process for foreign parties. These reforms will create a more transparent and rules-based unfair trade remedy regime in Mexico, and will permit the U.S. and Canada to extend the benefits of Chapter 19 to Mexican governments and private parties.

NAFTA also contains some weak points, when assessed from the perspective of trade liberalization. The principal weakness is the provision for rules of origin. Rules of origin are a necessary part of a regional free trade agreement, and it is the application of these rules by customs officials that insures that only goods which have been mainly produced within the free trade area are given preferential treatment. Conversely, rules of origin offer an opportunity for protectionism by restricting the amount of foreign content that is acceptable in goods originating in the free trade area.

The basic rule in NAFTA is that a good qualifying for preferential treatment should be wholly obtained within the NAFTA area, or if it incorporates intermediate products from outside the area, the final product must undergo a change in tariff classification.[34] In the event that an intermediate product is not reclassified, or if in certain circumstances it is shipped in an unassembled state, an analysis must be made of the North American content of the final product. The latter procedure, which is complicated, applies particularly to the automotive and textile/apparel sectors.

As noted earlier, under NAFTA the content requirement for automobiles, engines and transmissions will rise from 50 per cent under CUSFTA to 62.5 per cent and to 60 per cent for other vehicles and parts. Increased content requirements will mean that non-North American automakers (e.g., Honda) will be more constrained in their ability to use offshore parts in vehicles assembled in North America, thereby reducing the attractiveness of investment in the NAFTA area.

In textiles/apparel, content rules will require that fibers produced in a NAFTA country must be used in textiles and apparel for the latter to qualify for preferential treatment. This provision is variously called "yarn forward," or "double transformation" in the case of textiles or "triple transformation" for apparel. This rule threatened Canada's growing apparel exports to the United States established under CUSFTA rules that allowed a larger proportion of foreign fibers than would be permitted under NAFTA. In response to Canada's concerns, the U.S. negotiated tariff-preference levels (TPLs) that effectively establish quotas for designated Canadian textile and apparel products which do not meet NAFTA rules of origin. However, this does not change the fact that NAFTA has reduced overseas competition to largely U.S-based textile producers.

Despite its drawbacks, NAFTA has won widespread praise from American economists.[35] These conclusions are consistent with the Canadian experience, where exports to the U.S. in sectors liberalized by CUSFTA (i.e., not previously liberalized) increased 33 per cent in value between 1988 and 1992, compared to a 2 per cent growth in exports to the rest of the world.[36] In terms of aggregate trade flows, the data indicate that CUSFTA has proved its value to the Canadian economy at a time when other economic indicators have been depressed. However, this has not translated into public support for CUSFTA, due largely to the loss of employment that also occurred during the 1988-1992 period, and which is associated in the public consciousness with free trade.

The impact of free trade on jobs is the most important political issue at stake in the creation of trade agreements, and the recent politics of NAFTA in the U.S. bear this out. The American debate over NAFTA was reminiscent of the earlier debate in Canada over CUSFTA, and in both countries the exchange was driven more by hyperbole than economics. What the Canadian experience appears to confirm is that job losses are likely to be taken in the sectors already experiencing difficulty from global competition, while offsetting gains are taken in the higher-value-added sectors.[37] The result is an improvement for the overall economy, but the appearance of winners and losers across a broad spectrum of society has created a politics of class in addition to the politics of special interest that has always accompanied trade policy making. The potential of NAFTA to stimulate a class-based politics in the U.S. offers opponents like Ross Perot a golden opportunity to oppose the deal, and conversely it constitutes the greatest threat to the future workability of the agreement.

Notes

1. The Honorable Michael Wilson, Minister of Industry Science and Technology and Minister for International Trade, *News Release*, February 25, 1993, "Government Introduces Bill to Implement North American Free Trade Agreement."

2. Gary Clyde Hufbauer and Jeffrey J. Schott, *North American Free Trade: Issues and Recommendations* (Washington, D.C.: Institute for International Economics, 1992), p. 4.

3. *Ibid.*, p. 4. Professor Peter Morici defines three general reasons for the appeal of regional free trade agreements at a time when the future of the General Agreement on Tariffs and Trade (GATT) was uncertain and political instability throughout the world was increasing, such as in the former Communist states: (1) security risks are greater when one's neighbors have fragile economies and are politically unstable; (2) regional trade blocs generally reduce, or eliminate political friction between neighbors; and (3) developing nations can be persuaded to undertake certain reforms consistent with the wishes, or in the image, of their "trading partners," provided that goals of structural reform are clearly defined in conjunction with an orderly plan for integration which includes "attractive market access awards." "Hemispheric Free Trade: Defining the Challenge," Paper presented at the Conference on Designing the Architecture for a Western Hemisphere Free Trade Area, North-South Center, University of Miami, January 28, 1993, p. 2.

4. Larry Rohter, "U.S. and Mexico Cautiously Back Free-Trade Idea," *New York Times*, June 12, 1990.

5. For further discussion on Mexico's economic development see, Gustavo Vega Canovas, "NAFTA and the Supplemental Agreements on Environmental and Labour Standards: A Mexican Perspective," Paper presented at the Conference on "NAFTA Implementation: Side Agreements and Broader Implications," International Development Research Centre and Centre for Trade Policy and Law at Carleton University/University of Ottawa, Ottawa, June 23, 1993.

6. Ibid, p. 4.

7. Hufbauer and Schott, *North American Free Trade*, p. 12.

8. In the 1970s, Mexico's primary and simple secondary goods accounted for 60 per cent of Mexico's total exports to the U.S. while more sophisticated manufactured goods accounted for only 20 per cent. In 1990, these categories of

exports practically reversed so that manufactured goods accounted for 60 per cent of exports and primary and simple secondary goods accounted for 15 per cent. Vega, "NAFTA and the Supplemental Agreements," p. 4.

9. Hufbauer and Schott, *North American Free Trade*, p. 12.

10. Vega, "NAFTA and the Supplemental Agreements," p. 5.

11. Hufbauer and Schott, *North American Free Trade*, p. 11.

12. As stated by Professor Peter Morici: "[a]n American failure to respond forwardly to Mexico at this critical juncture [post Mexico's significant political and economic reforms] could substantially alter the pace and path of economic reform, derail growth and bolster the position of critics of closer bilateral ties within the dominant Institutional Revolutionary Party (PRI)," in "Facing Up to Mexico," unpublished article, p. 1.

13. Michael Hart, *A North American Free Trade Agreement: The Strategic Implications for Canada*, Halifax: Institute for Research on Public Policy, 1990, p. 8.

14. Hufbauer and Schott, *North American Free Trade*, p. 21.

15. *NAFTA: What's It All About*, Ottawa: External Affairs and International Trade Canada, n.d., pp. 7-8.

16. Vega, "NAFTA and the Supplemental Agreements," p. 10.

17. See Jon R. Johnson, "NAFTA and the Trade in Automotive Goods" in Steven Globerman, ed. *Assessing NAFTA* (Vancouver: The Fraser Institute, 1993), p. 87.

18. See Peter Morici, "NAFTA Rules of Origin and Automotive Content Requirements," Ibid, p. 226.

19. See Thomas Grennes, "Toward a More Open Agriculture in North America," Ibid., p. 148.

20. See Eric Barry and Elizabeth Siwicki, "NAFTA: The Textile and Apparel Sector," Ibid., p. 130.

21. See G.C. Watkins, "NAFTA and Energy: A Bridge Not Far Enough?" ibid, p. 206.

22. See "Part Five: Investment, Services and Related Matters" in *NAFTA: What's It All About?*, p. 59.

23. See John F. Chant, "The Financial Sector in NAFTA: Two Plus One Equals Restructuring" in Globerman, *Assessing NAFTA*, p. 172.

24. See Alan M. Rugman and Michael Gestrin, "The Investment Provisions of NAFTA," ibid., p. 271.

25. See ibid., p. 271.

26. See Part Six: Intellectual Property in *NAFTA: What's It All About?*, p. 79.

27. See Gilbert R. Winham, "Dispute Settlement in NAFTA and the FTA," in Globerman, *Assessing NAFTA*, p. 251.

28. See "Side Agreements on Environment and Labor," in Gary Clyde Hufbauer and Jeffrey J. Schott, *NAFTA: An Assessment* (Revised Ed.) Washington: Institute for International Economics, 1992, p. 159.

29. These basic rules continue to be some of the most onerous obligations trading nations have undertaken toward each other, as is evident from the frequency that the Articles mentioned (especially Articles III and XI) are tested in GATT dispute settlement panels.

30. The increasing sophistication can be observed in the growing length and complexity of the documents in question. The GATT is a short document and can easily be included as an appendix to a normal book. CUSFTA would be a book itself, while the NAFTA is the size of an urban phone directory.

31. See Hufbauer and Schott, *NAFTA: An Assessment,* Section III.4 (Agriculture).

32. NAFTA, Article 1205.

33. For example, Hufbauer and Schott estimate that rail and truck transportation accounts for about 85 to 90 per cent of U.S.-Mexico trade. See *NAFTA: An Assessment,* Section 6:1.

34. NAFTA, Article 401.

35. Sylvia Nasar, "A Primer: Why Economists Favor Free-Trade Agreement," *New York Times,* September 17, 1993.

36. Daniel Schwanen, "A Growing Success: Canada's Performance Under Free Trade," C. D. Howe Institute, *Commentary* No. 52, September, 1993.

37. Ibid. The *New York Times* quotas trade economist Jagdish Bhagwati as stating: "I wouldn't say we're creating more jobs than we're destroying; that's hype. In the long run, trade only reallocates jobs." Nasar, "A Primer."

3

Searching for New Paradigms: Trade Policy Lessons from Recent and More Ancient History

Michael Hart

I would like to explore some conclusions I have drawn from three strands of intellectual and professional experience as an academic (trained as a medieval historian), as a trade policy practitioner, and as a student of Canadian economic history. I am at present engaged in thinking and writing about the implications of the current acceleration in the internationalization or globalization of the economy for Canadian trade and economic policy. I am doing this by first looking at the historical development of Canadian trade policy and then considering the implications for Canadian trade policy of today's global challenges and tomorrow's emerging opportunities.

In this paper I shall attempt to combine what I have learned into a credible explanation of the economic troubles we are currently experiencing and draw some conclusions about possible developments in North American trade policy in the medium term. The result is more in the nature of a philosophical essay than an academic research paper.

For the last three years we have been going through a period of alternating recession and slow growth, accompanied by persistent high unemployment and major structural adjustments. The media keeps reporting this as a recession, i.e., as a slowdown in the business cycle. We are not going through a recession. We are experiencing something much more fundamental. We are undergoing the fallout from what Richard Lipsey has called a techno-economic paradigm shift, i.e., a transformation in the technological basis of our economic life.[1] Changes in the technology and organization of production flowing from developments in communications, transportation and information-processing are fundamentally altering the way the economy works.

They are doing so at two levels. The new, information economy is spawning new products and industries at an unprecedented rate and creating pressures for new approaches to industrial organization, management and production techniques. Second, advances in information-processing technologies have led to a quantum leap in the internationalization of the economy. As Gilbert Winham has suggested, business used to think largely in local and national terms. Today, in order to survive, it must think in global terms. These two developments taken together underpin what has been called the globalization of the economy.

There is, of course, much more to it than just the economy. As Neil Nevitte explained in his chapter, we are also seeing a convergence in political and other values. Much of the anger we hear from national-ists, in Canada and elsewhere, for example, reflects a reaction to the erosion of local values and modes of expression and their replacement by more universal ones. Nationalists believe that local values are by definition of a higher order than those espoused on a much broader basis.

These changes have profound implications not only for business and the economy, but for many of the institutions of society. Changes in the skill requirements of industry, for example, have tremendous consequences for education and training. Changes in how to organize the design and delivery of complex tasks similarly suggest we need to recon-sider how we approach industry and government. Ultimately, what we are looking for is a new paradigm for the role of national governments in this new set of circumstances.

The dominant political/economic paradigm at mid-century revolved around the nation-state, national markets, national firms, national production and national governments. International trade and invest-ment were an add-on to national production and investment. In trade policy, the accepted paradigm among practitioners and their think tank colleagues was multilateralism, interdependence and non-discrimination. Trade was something that took place between nation states -- not within and between private entities -- and was best regulated on the basis of a series of rules and procedures that involved as many states as possible. All serious trade policy took place within the assumptions and constructs of this framework and the result was a period of remarkable stability and growth. That paradigm has now broken down, while a new one that can command broad support remains to be developed. It has broken down under the onslaught of the power of information-processing technology, the transformation in the nature of economic activity, the rise of a global market, global production and global firms, the breakdown of the relationship between the state and the individual and the other forces transforming the global economy.[2]

The literature on various aspects of this phenomenon is growing and it is tremendously exciting. In Canada, Nuala Beck and Dian Cohen and Guy Stanley have written interesting popular books explaining the nature of the new economy and Canada's place in it.[3] Both books offer stimulating insights into the changes taking place and make provocative suggestions about directions for further change.

An even larger literature can be found in the United States. Books by Peter Drucker, Kenichi Ohmae, Michael Porter, Robert Reich, Lester Thurow and others suggest that there is no shortage of controversy in explaining what is happening and in drawing policy conclusions.[4] Some of the current writings are full of insight and exciting suggestions; other pieces do little more than repeat discredited ideas from the past. That is not surprising. We have not yet reached a broad consensus on a new economic paradigm. There is still too much research and thinking required. There is, therefore, room for speculation and controversy before we settle down and accept a new dominant paradigm. More than anything else, however, we need more research and analysis to provide the necessary intellectual underpinnings for the new framework.

Research, analysis and policy development relating to socio-economic phenomena take place at three levels. Those who can be described as the plumbers in the basement perform the essential task of gathering statistics and analyzing patterns of trade and production, innovation and technological developments, industrial adaptation, employment, aggregate growth and more; they track the ever-changing nature of a dynamic economy and distill meaning from these changes.

At a second level, theories and explanations are developed to help us understand new interrelationships between, for example, innovation, the organization of production, trade and economic growth. The important research project being undertaken by Lipsey under the auspices of the Canadian Institute for Advanced Research at Simon Fraser University is a good example of this kind of work.[5] In effect, Lipsey is synthesizing the insights and data being produced by the plumbers into a coherent and satisfactory theory to explain economic growth in tune with today's circumstances.

Finally, at a third level, policy analysts and planners take the insights of the analysts, theorists and explainers and apply them to the development of appropriate policy responses by business and government to the changing nature of the economy. Much of what I am trying to do in the federal government falls into this category.

One of the problems during a period of rapid change is the long time lag between changes in the world of domestic and international business, the recognition of these changes by the plumbers, the assimilation of this information by the theorists and synthesizers, and the development of policy responses by governments, business and other institutions of society. It is not unusual for ten years to go by before the plumbers are able to gather and sift through sufficient data to map the contours of major changes in the patterns and methods of trade and production. Another few years are likely to go by before satisfactory theories and explanations begin to emerge, and even more years can pass before governments, schools and other institutions have adapted policies and practices to reflect the new realities. What this means is that during periods of rapid and fundamental transformation, there can be as much as a twenty-five year gap between changes in the structure and organization of production and the policy response to it. The result is tremendous stress on existing institutions as their inadequacy becomes increasingly apparent but the willingness to make fundamental change has not yet developed.

We are going through such a period of fundamental change today and the gap between government policies, practices and institutions and the nature of what has been called the new economy has become a chasm. Let me provide one illustration from the area of trade policy. The Uruguay Round of General Agreement on Tariffs and Trade (GATT) negotiations is now in its final stages. The intellectual spadework for this round was undertaken in the late 1970s and early 1980s, reflecting the stresses and strains in the trading system earlier in the 1970s. In effect, the successful conclusion of the Uruguay Round will provide us with a revitalized and enlarged GATT attuned to the realities of the 1970s, i.e., twenty years ago.

It is important that the round conclude successfully, if only for the psychological benefit of a positive result. But we should not assume that by concluding the round, we can coast for a while. In fact, the most important result flowing from the end of the round will be the creative energies it will release to begin looking at today's realities and problems.

For these reasons, I think that much of the debate on Canada and the international economy has an unreal quality. There are too many people pursuing issues and problems that no longer exist; they are making assumptions that have no basis in current reality; they are fighting battles based on the insights and theories of the 1960s and 1970s.

The argument can be made that the changes taking place in the global economy and in global values, popular culture and political structures are of a scale, scope and significance to rival earlier periods of substantial transformation such as the end of Rome's hegemony in the fourth and fifth centuries or the Renaissance in Europe in the fourteenth and fifteenth centuries. While there are some attractions to such a view, I believe such parallels can easily be stretched too far. The forces of change and transformation in the fourth and fifth centuries and the fourteenth and fifteenth centuries were of such duration that they can shed little light on the rapid changes facing us today, changes that are literally reshaping the world within the lifetime of a single generation. Nevertheless, a short comparison of the impact of the invention of the printing press and the computer chip is instructive, if only to whet the appetite for some of the more modest parallels that can be found in the world of industry, trade and technology over the past two hundred years.

The invention of printing in the fifteenth century in Europe transformed a world that was largely locally focused and orally organized to one where information could travel vast distances and become standardized and widely available. The changes in society that flowed from this development were of tremendous significance. It is impossible to imagine the world of commerce, urban living, bureaucratic government, nation states and industrial production without the underpinning of standardized, widely available information and record keeping, both made possible by the invention of the printing press.[6]

Similarly, the invention and widespread application of the computer chip since the 1970s have stimulated and made possible the transformation of information processing that is now revolutionizing the world of technology, industry, government and education. Given the fundamental nature of the transformation that took place in Europe in the fourteenth and fifteenth centuries and the developments that built on it, we should not be surprised to find that the changes stimulated by the computer chip are having similar repercussions.

At a more prosaic level, I think something can be learned by looking at two periods of change in our own, much shorter history. In Canada's century and a quarter of history, we can identify at least two periods where there was a similar basic shift in the technology and organization of production. The first is the period from the mid-1870s to the mid-1890s and the second is the Great Depression of the 1930s.

During both periods, we -- and the rest of the world -- were adjusting to fundamental changes in the technology and organization of production that had taken place in the two decades that preceded the period. During the 1870s and 1880s and again during the 1930s, society adjusted to these developments and adopted the necessary changes in government, industry, the universities and elsewhere to usher in a new period of growth and prosperity. That is why I am optimistic about our ability to adapt. It may be painful, but we will succeed.

Among the changes that took place were the way governments approached the international regulation of trade. The initial response was to look inward and protect domestic producers and labor. The folly of that response soon became apparent and wiser counsel succeeded in building outward-looking liberal solutions. It is a pattern that is not likely to change, but the details of it will differ. What we have to learn from the past is how to avoid adopting policies during our current transitional stage which will make it more difficult to reap the future benefits of globalization.

Let us take a more detailed look at what happened in each of these periods and see if we can draw some conclusions about what is happening and likely to happen in our own.

Confederation came at the end of a period of strong, export-led growth, largely to the United States as Canadian farmers, loggers and other producers successfully exploited the growth in the U.S. economy, the Reciprocity Treaty of 1854 and the rise in U.S. prices during the Civil War. The first railroad age further helped to boost Canadian growth. The boom only continued another five or six years beyond Confederation. Bad times hit in the mid-1870s and lasted for the next twenty years. Canada's exports to the United States stagnated while those to the UK grew only incrementally. Domestic production was also sluggish. More people left Canada than came and a lot of people concluded that Confederation was a bust.

By the 1870s, the international economy had reached the zenith of the impact of the first industrial revolution and the British-led expansion of trade. Trade within continental Europe, between Europe and Great Britain, and across the Atlantic had grown steadily and trade policy had encouraged that growth. Britain's pursuit of unilateral free trade and the negotiation of a series of interlocking most favored nation trade agreements based on the Cobden-Chevalier Treaty between England and France in 1860 had encouraged that trade.

The period from 1870 to 1890, however, was one of dislocation and slow growth; not surprisingly, protectionist sentiments steadily mounted. A number of factors were at play, including the nationalist passions released by the nation-building policies of Bismarck, Cavour and others in Germany, Italy, and elsewhere in Europe. These sentiments found expression in renewed imperial fervor in Britain. They fostered the gradual retreat from the liberalism embodied in the système de traités adopted in Europe in the 1860s. The treaties were not abandoned, but they were renegotiated and reinterpreted to provide new competitive advantages for domestic industries at the expense of foreign competitors. We can also find these protectionist sentiments in the jingoistic policies pursued by Republican administrations in the United States, steadily raising the tariff and rebuffing Canadian efforts to renew the Reciprocity Agreement of 1854.

The response in Canada was the National Policy introduced by the Macdonald government in 1878. It was built on the conviction that if others were not going to open their markets to Canadian goods, Canada would pursue what today we would call an import substitution strategy. Canada would try to go it alone and develop a more self-reliant national economy stretching from the Atlantic to the Pacific.

Underpinning these changes, however, were changes in the technology and organization of production. This is the period when steel making came into its own, fueling a revolution in production and transportation leading to the second railway boom, the development of steel hulls and steamships, the introduction of refrigerated ships and railcars, a quantum leap forward in the mechanization of production and many other innovations which fundamentally altered the nature of the economy. International trade stagnated during this period, in Canada and elsewhere. Interestingly, this was also a period of pessimism about the future. The transformation in the economy was not easy. It took time and it took adaptation. There was much pain as individuals and institutions had to adapt to new demands.

By the early years of the new century, however, a renewed upward trend was clearly discernible. Trade and production were again growing rapidly. Barriers were coming down. The adjustments made during the period of trouble were beginning to pay dividends, launching a new period of economic growth and internationalization.

On the trade front, there was a revival in the système de traités in Europe. The United States Congress adopted the Underwood Tariff, the lowest tariff in more than fifty years. At the outbreak of the first world war, trade barriers in both Europe and North America were at their lowest level in more than half a century.

In Canada, the economic boom was once again fueled by exports, including wheat from the newly opened prairies, lumber, newsprint and various agricultural commodities, as well as new investments in mining and manufacturing. Immigration patterns reversed and the population grew rapidly. The western territories were the main beneficiaries. Between 1871 and 1911, their population mushroomed from 75,000 to 1.3 million. Canada lowered its barriers to Empire goods and negotiated a new reciprocity treaty with the United States, only to have it rebuffed at the polls.

The first world war brought this boom to an end. The post-war period was one of economic stagnation, with only a few short periods of economic growth on a global basis. Canada in the 1920s was one of the few bright spots. But during this period a new set of momentous changes took place in the technology and organization of production, changes later described as Fordism and Taylorism.

During this period, the combined insights of Henry Ford and Fredrick Taylor led to a revolutionary way of organizing the inexpensive production of thousands of identical and relatively reliable automobiles. The new methods involved learning how to organize a stable work force and complex machinery in order to produce thousands of copies of identical parts which could be assembled into a wide range of consumer products. It required learning how to take advantage of economies of scale, how to generate sufficient demand to make the investment required to make economies of scale profitable, and how to distribute the resulting products to a wide range of consumers. In terms of industrial organization, the answer lay in large corporations organized to develop and manufacture new products more efficiently than the competition, source the necessary raw materials, establish distribution networks and develop and satisfy the necessary high, sustained demand.

This new type of industrial firm required a vast army of people with technical, administrative and managerial skills as well as immense numbers of unskilled assembly workers. The key to reaping rewards was to manufacture on a very large scale and maintain demand for the same product for a considerable period of time.

In conjunction with these developments in industrial technology, processes and organization, governments developed a typical set of policies and programs. These reflected the widespread acceptance of what Jan Tumlir called the planning ideology or the politicization of the economy, i.e., the involvement of political authorities in the structure and operation of the economy. The combined demands of the first world war and the depression fostered an acceptance that governments had a role to play that would have been unthinkable in the nineteenth century. The state was more and more viewed as the source of wisdom and legitimacy while the collectivist urge increasingly saw the individual's well-being as subordinate to and dependent on that of the state. The consequences of the all-pervasive grip of this statism can be seen in the secularization of society and the decline in the influence of organized religion.

This change in political ideology, when combined with the move toward democracy and universal suffrage, had profound implications for domestic economic policies and for attitudes toward the establishment of a planned international economic order.[7] It led to the modern mixed economy which accepts a significant role for government in guiding economic development at both the macro and micro levels. And it led to the interlocking arrangements which have underpinned the interdependence of national economies since the second world war.

Initially, however, the transformation of the craft economies of the early twentieth century to the industrial economies of the middle of the century created much fear and disruption. The economic instabilities of the 1920s, which led to the beggar-thy-neighbor policies of the 1930s, can in large measure be attributed to the dislocations flowing from Fordism and Taylorism. In short, the initial response to the new economy of the 1920s and 1930s was to hunker down and try to export the problems of adjustment. It took a depression and a war to convince political leaders that there had to be a better way.

That better way was the GATT. After a slow start, it succeeded in providing a regime consonant with the new business practices and governmental policies developed over the previous twenty years. The GATT allowed national firms in industrialized countries to take greater advantage of their economies of scale by finding foreign markets for their products, either directly or on the basis of foreign direct investment. The combined effect of advances in transportation, communications and the reduction in trade barriers made it possible for companies to compete for much wider markets, face much stronger competition in the home market and become increasingly specialized. The result was unprecedented expansion in global production, trade, investment and prosperity. Increased international trade and competition in turn accelerated globalization or harmonization of consumer tastes and demand, setting the stage for a new paradigm shift and a further internationalization of the economy.

The familiar characteristics of the world of Fordism and GATT appear now to be fast disappearing. Global competition, scientific and technological breakthroughs as well as consumer sophistication are shortening the product cycle and placing a premium on quality, manufacturing fluidity and innovation. These factors in turn have

called for new types of industrial processes and organizations best able
to respond to the new demands. Automotive production has most clearly
demonstrated the changes. Fordism has given way to Toyotism, the
lean production method pioneered by Toyota, capable of producing a
much wider array of high-quality vehicles which combine the benefits
of craft production and assembly line techniques. A revolution in process
technology has produced more and better products and allowed firms to
compete more effectively on the basis of not only price, but also design,
quality and after-market service.[8]

As the production of manufactured goods becomes ever more disaggre-
gated, varied and sophisticated, the cost of developing and
manufacturing new products has increased exponentially. More and
more, the costs are concentrated in developing the product -- both the
product and the most cost-effective process by which to manufacture it
-- rather than in production, devaluing the labor content in many
products and increasing the risk in producing it. Typically, labor and
raw material costs now constitute less than a quarter of the final cost of
a product.

These changes in manufacturing technology have led to massive
adjustments within industrial countries. As unskilled or semi-skilled
assembly-line workers -- the core of industrial labor -- are being
replaced by highly skilled knowledge workers, capable of understanding and adapting computer-controlled machinery, traditional
assembly-line workers are swelling the ranks of the unemployed or
accepting lower paying service jobs. Some firms are experimenting with
"leasing" rather than "hiring" their workers through temporary help
agencies, further reducing their labor costs and shifting the burden of
managing fringe benefits to such agencies. The resultant social pressures
are leading to a polarization in attitudes to business and calls for
governments to intervene and slow the adjustment process.

We are also seeing a rapid acceleration in the globalization of
production. So-called footloose industries which are not tied to
particular locations, such as mines or sawmills, are looking for the most
congenial place to invest, depending on the availability of the particular factors of production most important to that industry. Low-skill,
standard-technology, labor-intensive manufacturing firms, for example, are locating manufacturing facilities where they can find the best
combination of low-skilled labor and related factors -- productivity,
skill levels, labor laws, fringe benefits, access to inputs and distribution
networks. Old fashioned trade barriers no longer have much impact on
such decisions. Increasingly, neither firms nor products have a clear
national identity, and trade policies and practices -- including market

development programs -- geared toward promoting the interests of national firms and their products appear increasingly out of touch with reality.

Prevailing theories about economic growth and international exchange have also become much more sophisticated and varied and have robbed governments of the moral and intellectual certitude that underpinned the trade regime of the 1950s and 1960s. New ideas about dynamic comparative advantage, the international division of labor, the complementarity of international trade and investment, the role of technology, the importance of trade in services, the management and organization of production as well as the role of government policies have challenged the conventional theoretical foundations of trade policy and made governments less certain about the direction of future domestic and international policies and arrangements.[9]

As we adjust to the demands of this new techno-economic paradigm, we would do well to remember the lessons of recent and more ancient history. They are three-fold. First, the more basic the techno-economic changes, the more fundamental are changes in social and political institutions likely to be. Second, changes will take place; efforts to resist change will only complicate adjustment to the new realities. Third, the biggest obstacles to adjustment are the sacred cows of most recent origin, i.e., the values and institutions developed during the last paradigm shift.

Against this background, it is easier to appreciate why some analysts are prepared to question some deeply held intellectual, social and political values. For example, some now suggest that comparative advantage in the global economy derives as much or more from controllable factors as from natural endowments -- e.g., macro-economic stability, a highly trained and motivated labor force, a healthy population, technological innovation as well as natural resources, weather, and other less controllable factors. Are they right -- can comparative advantage be shaped by public policy and other controllable factors? If it can be shaped, can it be shaped on a national basis or is it a firm-specific attribute? Does the possibility of acquired comparative advantage and competitiveness create new challenges to public policy making? What will be the most appropriate role for local and national governments in the emerging global economy? What constitutes the national interest when a large proportion of business is pursued by global corporations? These are the questions that will shape both the national and international agenda in the years to come.

While the nation-state has become less central to organizing economic life, it continues to be critical in organizing political life. It continues to be the most acceptable basis upon which to decide who makes the laws, what the laws say and who will administer them. As noted by *The Economist*:

> The basic unit is going to remain the nation-state. Nothing else can govern whole societies without toppling, one way, into the infranationalist error of tribalism or, the other way, into the supranationalist sterility of rule by bureaucrats.[10]

Thus the policy conundrum faced by every national government: how does it ensure that it retains the capacity to govern while also providing its citizens with the benefits of a more globally integrated economy? How do governments pursue national economic interests in a world where the principal organizer of economic activity, the firm, is more likely to have global rather than national interests?

The issues that are now competing for attention on the international trade policy agenda involve not just an extension of the old trade policy to a broader range of issues, but a fundamental reconsideration of the assumptions and values that will underpin the trade regime of the future. They include efforts to develop international standards and consensus on such diverse issues as market place policies (competition policy, consumer protection, corporate structure), social policies (particularly labor market, education and income support policies), and environmental policy. Each of these policy fields raises very difficult issues, not least of which is the extent to which governments are prepared to raise the level of international agreement and accept new inroads into domestic economic decision-making. In short, the new agenda presents a direct challenge to established concepts of national sovereignty, national interest and intergovernmental cooperation. Developing international consensus will be extremely difficult because governments in Europe, North America and East Asia have traditionally seen the balance between the roles of governments, corporations and labor differently.

The search for a new paradigm may thus be complicated by the fact that there are competing visions of how the world does and should function, affecting virtually every aspect of the relationship between government and society. These competing visions strongly color people's attitudes toward the stresses and strains flowing from the changes in the technology and organization of production. One vision is grounded in concepts of individual responsibility and is philosophically committed to the ideal of equality of opportunity; the other is grounded in ideas of collective responsibility and is committed to the ideal of equality of results. Understanding these two competing visions helps to provide an analytical framework within which we can examine a host of issues.

When it comes to the role of government, for example, the equality of opportunity perspective sees a relatively small role for government involving largely negative prescriptions. Government's principal function is to guarantee and protect the right of individuals to pursue their interests. The equality of results perspective envisions a much larger and more activist role for government, dedicated to the promotion of equal results and the removal of obstacles to their achievement. Equal opportunity government is small and unobtrusive; equal results government is large and expensive. For the former, government can be a source of interference and an obstacle to the achievement of individual goals; for the latter, government is the source of solutions and the basis for achieving societal goals.

Equality of opportunity government is rooted in local, community values such as the family, and in individual responsibility; equality of results government is collectivist and rooted in statist values. On the economic front, equality of opportunity government is based on market principles; it believes that the market is the most efficient allocator of resources; government's role is limited to ensuring that markets are not abused and that individuals unable to compete within the market are protected.

Equality of results government, on the other hand, is dedicated to the proposition that the market allocates resources unfairly; instead, governments are best able to balance competing political, social and economic values and objectives which will ensure that all members of society gain their fair share of society's economic fruits.

Of course, no government or society is organized on a basis wholly consistent with one vision or another. These visions compete with one another for attention and power in democratic societies and each has left its imprint on the way governments function. All of the Organization for Economic Cooperation and Development (OECD) governments exhibit a mixture of laws, institutions, policies and programs that reflect the changing priority attached to one vision or another.

These competing perspectives have also informed how governments approach issues in the international economy and have become increasingly important as economic transactions have globalized and international economic rule-making has proliferated. In the next few years, as the process of international rule-making intensifies, we will again see how these differing perspectives, when applied to individual issues, will be sources of conflict between governments.

Much of the debate about the North American Free Trade Agreement (NAFTA), for example, like the Canada-U.S. free trade debate in Canada a few years earlier, illustrates the extent to which these competing visions can clash. Most international rule-making in the field of international economic transactions over the past fifty years has been based upon the equality of opportunity vision. The GATT and most other agreements are grounded in the concept of non-discrimination which, when worked out in detail, involves largely negative prescriptions about what governments can do to promote and protect domestic producers at the expense of foreign producers. The GATT concept of free trade is less about trade that is wholly free of government interference and more about a fixed-rule regime that guarantees equality of opportunity to all producers, no matter what their country of origin.

NAFTA stands firmly in this tradition. Opponents of NAFTA thus correctly see the agreement, and other agreements like it, as limiting the capacity of governments to pursue equality of results within the context of the nation-state. It limits what governments can do, for example, to promote sunrise industries or protect sunset industries. It limits the capacity of governments to promote full employment through direct government programs. It limits what governments can do to protect the environment. It limits the capacity of governments to pursue such objectives to the extent that governments wish to use measures that discriminate against foreign producers. It limits the capacity of governments to pursue specific, numerical results in their regulation of economic activity. Instead, it promotes a market-based view of how to solve economic problems.

It is no wonder, therefore, that much of the NAFTA debate seems like a dialogue of the deaf. Proponents and opponents speak very different languages that proceed from very different visions and values. No wonder innocent bystanders have become confused and skeptical by the cacophony of competing claims. To get through this period of change and transformation, therefore, there has to be more open debate which clearly acknowledges that there are competing visions.

Conclusions

What does this all mean for the development of a North American community and for the North American academic community?

The agreements negotiated on a bilateral and regional basis over the past decade have been singularly important in laying the groundwork for the region's participation in the emerging global economy. They are more modern, more in tune with current reality than what existed before and, therefore, they are more likely to provide business with the necessary confidence to invest in our future. Without a confident, forward-looking, outward-oriented business sector operating within a fiscal and regulatory framework that promotes risk and innovation, Canadians, Americans and Mexicans will not share in future global prosperity.

The new agreements are stimulating adjustment and adaptation to the reality of a North American economy. They provide Canada and Mexico with a more modern basis for managing trade and investment relations with their more powerful neighbor; they provide the United States with a principled set of rules within which to arbitrate competing interests at home and abroad; and they lay a sound foundation for expanding trade and investment beyond North America.

But they should be viewed as no more than a start. We need to go much further and we need to do much better. We need to begin to build a trade and economic regime for the global economy of the twenty-first century, at home and internationally. North America needs to look to Latin America and anticipate the negotiation of a Western Hemisphere trading system. It needs to look across the Pacific and build the basis for a much more vibrant trans-Pacific economy. And it needs to look across the Atlantic and see how it can draw the Europeans out of their Euro-centrism and help them become dynamic and constructive players in a much more modern global trade regime.

That regime can be built on the basis of the revitalized GATT flowing from the enthusiasm that should result from the successful implementation of the Uruguay Round and the establishment of a World Trade Organization. It can also be built more slowly on the basis of the ongoing regional experiments with deeper integration agreements. The route or process matters much less than the goal and objectives. We should stop being so hung up on process and concentrate for a while on substance. Once we know *what* we want, we can begin to revisit *how* we are going to get there. And when we revisit how, we should take a fresh look not only at the institutional setting, but also at bargaining techniques and consensus-building strategies. It is not only the substance of the GATT that is woefully out of date with reality, but also the institutional setting and the bargaining strategies and techniques.

That is where the academic community should come in. Policy makers have run out of intellectual capital. They are trying to deal with the problems and challenges of the twenty-first century on the basis of the insights and assumptions of the 1960s and 1970s within an institutional setting devised in the 1940s. That institution and its rules were devised in response to the problems of the 1930s and on the basis of the intellectual capital developed even earlier. Policy makers and academics alike need to do some fundamental research and thinking. But it needs to start in the academy and the think tanks. In short, we need a new paradigm to guide the elaboration of new international arrangements that will allow all of us -- Canadians, Americans and Mexicans -- to reap the benefits of the new economy and globalization and minimize the stresses and strains of the transition that will get us there.

Notes

The views in this article are those of Mr. Hart and do not necessarily reflect those of the Government of Canada.

1. See Richard G. Lipsey, "Notes on the Changing Technoeconomic Paradigm and Some Implications for Economic Policy," Mimeo, Canadian Institute for Advanced Research, Program in Economic Growth and Policy, Simon Fraser University, 1993. See also Richard G. Harris, "Trade, Money, and Wealth in the Canadian Economy," Benefactors Lecture, 1993, C. D. Howe Institute, Toronto, September 14, 1993.

2. I discuss these ideas at greater length in *What's Next: Canada, the Global Economy and the New Trade Policy* (Ottawa: Centre for Trade Policy and Law, 1994), and "The End of Trade Policy?" in Fen Osler Hampson and Christopher J. Maule, eds., *Global Jeopardy: Canada Among Nations 1993-94* (Ottawa: Carleton University Press, 1993).

3. Nualla Beck, *Shifting Gears: Thriving in the New Economy* (Toronto: Harper Collins, 1992), and Dian Cohen and Guy Stanley, *No Small Change: Success in Canada's New Economy* (Toronto: Macmillan of Canada, 1993).

4. Peter F. Drucker, *Post-Capitalist Society* (New York: Harper Business, 1993); Kenichi Ohmae, *The Borderless World: Power and Strategy in the Interlinked World Economy* (New York: Harper Business, 1990); Michael Porter, *The Competitive Advantage of Nations* (New York: The Free Press, 1990; Robert Reich, *The Work of Nations* (New York: Alfred A. Knopf, 1991); and Lester Thurow, *Head to Head: The Coming Battle Among Japan, Europe, and America* (New York: William Morrow, 1992).

5. See *Economic Growth: Science and Technology and Institutional Change in a Global Economy* (Toronto: Canadian Institute for Advanced Research, study No. 4, June, 1991).

6. The 1985 British television series, *The Day the Universe Changed*, hosted by James Burke and shown in North America in the fall of 1993 on The Learning Channel, very successfully dramatized the tremendous changes that flowed from the invention of the printing press and similar technological marvels.

7. Jan Tumlir, "Evolution of the concept of international economic order 1914-1980," in Frances Cairncross, ed., *Changing Perceptions of Economic Policy* (London: Methuen, 1981).

8. See James P. Womack, Daniel T. Jones and Daniel Roos, *The Machine that Changed the World* (New York: Macmillan, 1990). While the focus of the book is the revolution in the automotive industry, its analysis and findings are applicable across the full range of manufacturing.

9. For a discussion of changing theories to explain international trade and their application to trade policy, see Paul Krugman, "Does the New Trade Theory Require a New Trade Policy?" *The World Economy*, Vol. 15, No. 4 (July, 1992), pp. 423-441.

10. "The State of the Nation-State," December 22, 1990.

PART TWO

Managing Post-War Relations in North America

4

Change in the Management of Canada-United States Relations in the Post-War Era

Denis Stairs

Introduction

This is an untidy subject, complicated by an untidy reality. Almost anything that is said about it will be partly true. Almost nothing that is said about it will be wholly true. Even the title is a misnomer, for it can be argued that Canada-U.S. relations are not "managed" at all. Such an argument might even be put most vigorously by the managers themselves. As the despairing staff of Canada's embassy in Washington -- confronting yet another unexpected crisis, fighting yet another unexpected fire -- have often been heard to ask, "Why are *we* always the last to know?"

But if the relationship has not always been "managed," it has certainly been given strategic attention, particularly by Canadians, and it may be useful to begin by reviewing some of the principles and practices that have resulted. For reasons to be explored below, these may be less evident now -- or at least less helpful now -- than they were during the first two decades of the post-war period. But they persist nonetheless. The distribution of power between the two countries is, after all, disparate still, and this disparity lies at the root of the diplomatic *praxis* that Canadians, in particular, have been inclined to pursue.

Strategy 1: Multilateralism

On the Canadian side of the border, the guiding principle for the conduct of Canada-U.S. relations has traditionally been very simple: *Wherever possible, multilateralise.* The preferred course of action has thus been to facilitate, and to temper, the management of the bilateral relationship by submerging at least some of the issues that bear upon it within a multilateral context.

It should be conceded at once that this has not been the only purpose of multilateralist initiatives in Canadian foreign policy. Other Canadian objectives have included support for the institutionalization of international politics generally, and the enhancement of Ottawa's capacity for advancing specific Canadian interests abroad, not in North America alone, but in other parts of the world as well.[1] Nonetheless, it is an abiding characteristic of the weak (or the weaker) that they like to have decisions made by committees, wherein power matters less, rules matter more, and supportive coalitions can sometimes be engineered. Canadians have understood the logic of their place.

Their preference found its most transparent expression in Canada's objectives during the period when the post-war international order was being created. They favored global over regional approaches to the maintenance of international peace and security. They also supported the extension of the multilateralist principle into the so-called "functional" areas of international cooperation. A regional approach would expose them too directly, and without the safety of numbers, to the blandishments of their American counterparts. Institutions of wider compass, it was assumed, would be more comfortable.

The vigor with which Canadian officials supported both the creation of the United Nations system and the proliferation of specialized agencies within it was in substantial degree a reflection of this preoccupation. So also was the "middle power" doctrine by which they attempted to claim a special entitlement to participation in decision-making on politico-security issues, and along with it the "functional principle" upon which they sought to legitimize their pursuit of leading roles within such organizations as were charged with Canada-pertinent agendas. If a country has a lot to do with aircraft, they argued in effect, it ought also to have a lot to do with the International Civil Aviation Organization. If it is a major supplier of food, it ought also to be a major force in the Food and Agriculture Organization.

This affection for multilateralism, and the related demand for guaranteed, even privileged, access to multilateral decision-making institutions, was evident also in Canada's subsequent support for a transoceanic and heavily institutionalized response to new perceptions of the Soviet military menace. Like the Europeans, but for reasons of their own, the Canadians preferred an "Atlantic Vision"[2] to a unilateral American guarantee of Western European security, and if the North Atlantic Treaty Organization (NATO) could be broadened to include non-military as well as military functions, so much the better.[3]

Later, the territory of North America itself was to become a potential target of Soviet attack, and a joint command with the United States seemed essential to the task of securing an appropriately swift and coordinated capacity to respond. The North American Air Defense Command (NORAD) Agreement ensued. The Canadians insisted on describing it, however, not as a mechanism for bilateral military management, but as a component of NATO. The claim rang hollow -- a fiction to which others need pay no attention save the courtesy of listening to it -- but it reflected well enough the Canadian preference: bilateral if necessary, but not necessarily bilateral.

The same multilateralist disposition could be found in Canadian policy with respect to the creation of the International Monetary Fund, the World Bank, and the ill-fated International Trade Organization, along with its eventual surrogate, the General Agreement on Tariffs and Trade (GATT).[4] In economics, as in politico-security affairs, it seemed best to operate abroad from a house of many rooms, particularly at a time when the Canadian economy was showing itself to be increasingly (but not hopelessly) interlocked with, and dependent upon, that of the United States.

This general commitment to the construction of multilateral institutions was complemented by a recurring pattern of diplomatic practice. In times of crisis the Canadians revealed a marked preference for collective forms of response, whether through the United Nations, the Commonwealth, NATO or some other multilateral contrivance. Multilateral arenas made it possible to collaborate with others in modifying the potential excesses (as the Canadians sometimes thought them to be) of the greater powers. They could also be used to provide polarized adversaries with opportunities for backing out of inconvenient corners. And they could promote more broadly that fluidity of circumstance that liberal pluralists habitually regard as the prerequisite for the orderly, i.e., bloodless, resolution of political conflict.

The behavior, both actual and potential, of the United States was not (it needs once more to be said) the only stimulus to these calculations. But it may well have been the leading contributor, and it certainly set the strategic context for Canadian action.

Having said that, it must be conceded as well that the issues with which the United Nations, the North Atlantic alliance, the Commonwealth and the Bretton Woods system were concerned were far from being defined by the Canada-U.S. relationship. They were driven instead by a wider -- in some cases a global -- politics. Canadian-American relations might be profoundly affected by them, and certainly they were included within them, but the issues themselves had a larger compass.

What, then, of the United States as an identifiable source of **bilateral** problems for Canada? Was this not a matter to b e strategically addressed by means less circumspect than those embodied in multilateralist inclinations?

Strategy 2: Diversification

This question brings us to the second of the strategic premises of Canadian policy. It, too, can be succinctly expressed: *Wherever possible, diversify.*

The diversification strategy was not unrelated to multilateralism, in the sense that multilateral institutions were often perceived as one of the vehicles through which the strategy could be pursued. But it rested nonetheless on a somewhat different set of political calculations. Its primary purpose was to reduce, in relative terms, the significance for Canadian policy of the superiority of American power (in whatever field that power might be expressed, and however it might be measured) by cultivating supplementary linkages with additional players overseas. In its most passive conception, this was thought to have advantages akin to those expressed in the classic injunction of the experienced farmer: "Don't put all your eggs in one basket." An issue might go badly wrong with the United States, but alternatives would still survive. Canada's vulnerability to American pressure (or to American error) could thus be diminished by the cultivation of other options. If the elephant rolled over, the mouse could escape to another bed.[5]

Viewed more aggressively, of course, the diversification strategy could be regarded as a means of enhancing Canada's bilateral bargaining power. The mouse could return, as it were, with a more attentive and supportive elephant in tow. In theory, if not so easily in practice, the strategy of diversification could in this way improve on the potential for "countervail," an objective as attractive to the conduct of statecraft abroad as it is endemic to the politics of pluralism at home.[6]

In the early years of the post-war period, the diversification strategy was more implicit than explicit in Ottawa's behavior. Nonetheless, it was reflected very clearly in Canadian policy with respect to the United Kingdom, Western Europe and (to a somewhat lesser extent) the Commonwealth. Canada's financial contributions to British and West European economic recovery in the mid-to-late 1940s were in some measure governed by it, and the concept itself had considerable staying power. In July 1957, for example, Prime Minister John Diefenbaker, convinced that "with an expansion of Commonwealth trade it would be possible for Canada to lessen its dependence on the United States and in that way to guard against surrendering control of its economic affairs,"[7] observed almost casually at a press conference on his return from a Commonwealth Prime Ministers' meeting that it was his "government's planned intention to divert 15 per cent of Canada's purchases from the United States to the United Kingdom."[8] As it turned out, the initiative had not been "planned" at all, and the proposal itself was impracticable,[9] but it nonetheless demonstrated the continuing appeal of diversification as a congenial strategy for a leader preoccupied with the problem of moderating American influence over Canadian affairs.

As a prominent feature of declaratory policy, however, the strategy received its most elaborate expression somewhat later in the rhetoric and initiatives of the Trudeau government during its first decade in office. The first of the six pamphlets that emerged from the government's 1968-70 foreign policy review observed that "the constant danger that sovereignty, independence and cultural identity may be impaired [by American influences] will require a conscious effort on Canada's part to keep the whole situation under control. Active pursuit of trade diversification and technological co-operation with European and other developed countries will be needed to provide countervailing factors."[10]

Elsewhere in the *Foreign Policy for Canadians* series, this theme was further reinforced. It was noted, for example, that Canada was seeking "to strengthen its ties with Europe, not as an anti-American measure but to create a more healthy balance within the North Atlantic community and to reinforce Canadian independence."[11] Similarly, "[c]loser relations with Latin American countries ... would enhance Canadian sovereignty and independence ... enrich Canadian life ... augment Canada's capacity to 'pay its way' in the world ... [and] ... enhance Canada's capacity to play an independent role in international affairs."[12]

Under the impetus of the Nixon surcharge "shock" of August 1971, these passing references were to blossom within two years into a full-dress exposition. In the autumn of 1972, the Secretary of State for External Affairs, Mitchell Sharp, released a document entitled *Canada-U.S. Relations: Options for the Future*,[13] in which the implications of the American presence in Canadian military, political, economic and cultural life were analyzed at length. Three policy choices were examined. The first (the "purely pragmatic course" represented by the status quo) and the second (greater integration through free trade or a customs union) were both rejected. The nod went to the third. It was summarized as a "comprehensive, long-term strategy to develop and strengthen the Canadian economy and other aspects of our national life and, in the process, to reduce the present Canadian vulnerability."[14] In practice this was to entail a variety of "nation-building" initiatives in both the cultural and economic fields at home, and attempts to promote countervailing linkages with countries other than the United States abroad. Of the latter, the most visible was the conclusion in 1976, of a four-year negotiation leading to the establishment of a "contractual link" with the European Community.[15] It was followed later in the same year by a similar agreement with Japan.[16] In both cases, the practical significance turned out to be more symbolic than real, but the purpose was nonetheless transparently clear: to find safety in North America through diversification overseas.

Thus described, of course, both of the foregoing strategies have their roots in the distribution of power as modified by geography. They came naturally, that is, to the successive governments of a relatively small country isolated in the amiable but unequal embrace of an adjacent superpower. Confronting similar relational circumstances, school children behave in much the same way. So do pressure groups. The realist explanation "works."

It may be worth noting, however, that the strategies also accord with the precepts that come from a liberal pluralist conception of politics, a conception in which political behavior is thought to be most reliably explained and constructively understood by reference to the pursuit of interest, and in which a just distribution of the spoils requires among other things that the acquisitive capacities of those involved in the hunt be kept in reasonable balance. Among Canada's post-war political leaders, Pierre Trudeau was philosophically the most self-conscious. It may be no coincidence that he once reduced his theory of political action to a simple essence: "create counterweights."[17] If so, Canada's selection of strategies for coping with the omnipresence of the United States may have to be attributed not only to its place in the international system, but also to its political culture as expressed in the "operational codes" of its leadership.[18]

Both of the strategies discussed thus far operate at some considerable distance from the day-to-day conduct of Canadian-American relations *per se*. Indeed, the purpose of the first is to convert Canada-U.S. issues into something else, and the objective of the second is to make them (relatively) less important. But significant bilateral relations obviously remain. Can anything general be said about the way they have been managed? Are there preferences to identify, or patterns to expose?

Strategy 3: Executive Pluralism

While there have been many examples of deviations from the norm, it is certainly possible to discern in the post-war period a number of practices that have been persistently evident in the daily management of the Canada-U.S. relationship. Some of them have been explicitly supported by government authorities in both countries as a sensible way of doing business. In Canada, if not in the United States, they have occasionally become objects of public controversy and debate. For reasons to be discussed below, a few of them have come under stress in recent years, but as in the previous cases it may be helpful to concentrate first on the patterns that emerged during the early years of the post-war era.

For want of a better term, the *praxis* at issue can be described as a kind of "executive pluralism," an approach to the management of conflict which favors attempting to solve problems at the administrative level, and settling conflicts by reference to pragmatic criteria. This has entailed among other things an understanding (more widely prevalent in the bureaucracy than elsewhere, perhaps) on both sides of the border that "linkage" is to be avoided, and that items on the bilateral agenda are best settled on an issue-by-issue basis. Any attempt to engage in "trade-offs" -- to bargain one issue-area off against another -- is likely to raise the political stakes, intensify the level of conflict, encourage the intrusion into the negotiating process of emotional, untutored, and otherwise inflexible representatives of particular interests, and force the negotiators to spend as much or more of their time and energy developing (and defending) their position at home as in advancing it at the bargaining table. Disputes in such circumstances will have little chance of being settled "on the merits" and will become prey instead to an "irrational" politics that is given more to escalating tensions than to diminishing them.

One of the corollaries of this preference for administrative-style "problem-solving" was the belief that there was value in being discreet. Public displays were to be avoided because public uproars were inimical to compromise and measured debate. Open diplomacy may have been a popular Wilsonian objective of the First World War, but it did not survive a week at the Paris Peace Conference. Covenants, once negotiated, can be -- in a democracy should be -- open, but this need not apply also to the process by which they are arrived at. "Quiet diplomacy" was thus the preferred route, and when in the middle 1960s, a former Canadian ambassador to the United States and a former American ambassador to Canada were asked to consider how best to conduct relations between the two countries, their report offered both examples and argument in its favor.[19]

On the Canadian side, these general dispositions were sustained by a fairly broad consensus among senior members of the foreign policy community. Evidence of it can be found not only in the "Heeney-Merchant Report", but also in the reflections and ruminations of many of the Canadian diplomatic practitioners of the day.[20] They seem also to have been supported by comparable attitudes in Washington. A Canadian academic observer, on the basis of a series of interviews conducted in 1969 in Washington and Ottawa, reported that "bureaucrats often felt it was to their advantage not to let all of their problems be resolved at the highest political level." When relations at the top were "strained ... they tried to isolate their policy sectors and ways of doing things." There was evidence, in short, of a common "diplomatic culture" which "placed great emphasis on consultation, exchange of information, personal friendship, informal communication, and easy access to points of decision."[21]

There were exceptions, of course. Serious differences could not always be concealed from public view, and the practices of executive pluralism did not appeal equally to all players. Prime Minister Diefenbaker, for example, delighted in mocking senior officials in the Department of External Affairs as "Pearsonalities", and sometimes operated by different rules.[22] There were times, moreover, when public outrage, carefully cultivated, had leverage potential. But in the context of an ongoing and fundamentally cooperative working relationship, such stratagems could be deployed only rarely -- and even then with considerable caution -- if the health of the relationship itself was not to be placed in jeopardy.[23]

The practice of executive pluralism also had a certain advantage in lending virtue to necessity. For the extraordinary range and scope of the issues on the Canada-U.S. agenda, when taken together with the physical proximity of the two countries and the congenial familiarity of the relations between their governing elites, resulted in a vast array of government departments and agencies (to say nothing of individual states and provinces) being directly involved in transborder discussions. The latter were often conducted quite independently of the Departments respectively of External Affairs and of State.[24] In the absence of a pervasive process of centralized coordination, attempts to engage in the systematic linking of issues would have been administratively difficult even if they had been considered strategically desirable. For reasons already indicated, observers in Canada could be forgiven if they concluded that this was a blessing in disguise, even if Canadian officials were occasionally inconvenienced or embarrassed by the bureaucratic chaos that ensued. As it was, any linkage of issues could be expected to drive the "Canada" agenda up the American administrative ladder, thereby conferring upon it a higher political profile than it would otherwise enjoy, and lending greater weight to the disparity of power as a determinant of individual outcomes.[25]

Bilateral institutions, it may be observed, have not been included among the prominent vehicles for managing the Canada-U.S. relationship in the post-war period -- even in specific issue areas. In 1974, Kal J. Holsti and Thomas Allen Levy were able, in fact, to identify eighteen of these, all created between 1909 (when the International Joint Commission was founded) and 1967 (when the Canada-United States Technical Committee on Agricultural Marketing and Trade Problems and the United States-Canada Civil Emergency Planning Committee both emerged from the woodwork).[26] But many of them had fallen into disuse. Others lacked significant authority. And the exceptions, for the most part, were concerned with highly technical matters of an apolitical sort, or alternatively enjoyed no more than advisory power. The conclusion to which the authors were drawn was clear: "the eighteen institutions, some of which remain in a state of suspended inanimation, do not handle the bulk of Canadian-American relations."[27] The two countries shared, it seemed, a preference for dealing from sovereign lairs -- the Americans, perhaps, because they were reluctant to subject their options to the confinement of standardized procedures and rules, and the Canadians because they feared the prospect of being dominated by a larger partner from within a bilateral institutional embrace.

Limits, Flaws and Weaknesses

There were weaknesses, of course, in the three components of this strategic edifice -- constructed, as they were, only partly from careful calculation and deliberate intent, since they were composed also of pragmatically patterned responses to persistent circumstances. Operating in a multilateral context, for example, can certainly reduce the exposure that would otherwise be involved in dealing bilaterally with a superpower. But not all issues are amenable to multilateral approaches, and multilateral institutions are not always hospitable to Canadian interests or amenable to Canadian influence. The superpower, moreover, must be willing to play the multilateral game, a disposition that will survive only if the consequent negative impact on what it perceives to be its interests (including its freedom of maneuver) is marginal, or is outweighed by countervailing benefits. The price for the superpower cannot be too high; hence the advantage for the smaller power cannot be too great.

Similarly, the rewards that accrue to strategies of diversification are limited by the architecture that engineering by the state is capable of creating. The success of such strategies depends not only on the cooperation of third parties including other governments, non-governmental organizations (NGOs) and private sector enterprises, but often also on forces of history (or of the market) that lie beyond the state's control. Prime Minister Diefenbaker might command a diversion of trade from the United States to the United Kingdom, but implementing his directive in a liberal political environment, and in opposition to the dictates of economic "rationality", was not a challenge that the public service, however faithful, could hope to meet. The American connection, in any case, is not the only external source of constraints on Canadian behavior. Other connections, even "countervailing" connections, generate them, too.

Executive pluralism poses the same problem. It confers costs as well as benefits. Some have argued, for example, that it carries for Canada a serious risk of executive co-option. Once Canadian officials come to think of their American counterparts, not as the representatives of a foreign power, but as "partners" in the amicable management of a continental polity, they may begin to treasure the congeniality of the relationship itself more than the specific interests they are assigned to protect. They may even lose some of their capacity to recognize, much less to pursue, an independent Canadian purpose. By either route (so the argument has gone) they may be led too easily to compromise, or to an unquestioning acceptance of the American view. A diplomatic culture held in common is just that -- held in common.[28]

This problem -- if it is thought to be a "problem," from a normative perspective -- can be compounded by organizational factors. As indicated earlier, Canadian-American relations are conducted in practice by a vast array of departments and agencies at more than one level of government. The diplomatic culture that Holsti discovered in 1969 was thus complemented by close, sometimes collaborative, working associations between the counterpart bureaucracies of the two countries, associations that were often far removed from the daily operations of the foreign service *per se*.[29] These extensive "transgovernmental" connections gave organizational buttressing to executive pluralism as a pervasive practice. But their prevalence could also be viewed as inimical to effective leadership and control at the political level and to the preservation of meaningful forms of public accountability. They compounded, in effect, the "management" problem that perpetually confronts the federal government and those who are assumed to have both the power and the responsibility to lead it.

Transformational Stresses

Whatever one thinks of these various questions -- and it is important to emphasize that they have normative as well as empirical dimensions -- it is clear that the edifice as a whole was beginning by the late 1960s to come under stress, and that the process of change accelerated thereafter. Some of the forces involved were triggered by specific events. Others reflected transformations of a more fundamental character. Keeping in mind that we are dealing with a kaleidoscope of untidy and uncertain phenomena, and not with an orderly progression of coherent historical forces, it may be useful to consider them here. They feed into the evolution at different times, occasionally work at cross purposes with one another, and exert their influence by processes at once intangible and difficult to measure. But their overall effect is beginning nonetheless to be highly visible. It may be most convenient to discuss them in relation to each of the three basic strategies in turn.

In the case of the multilateralist strategy, the stresses have resulted most fundamentally from changes in the membership of some of the more pertinent multilateral institutions. The proliferation of new states, particularly in the context of the United Nations during the 1960s and after, had the effect of diverting much of the multilateral agenda to North-South issues. These were issues in which Canada certainly had an interest, and in relation to which Canadian diplomats could sometimes launch useful initiatives. But they had relatively

little bearing on the conduct directly of Canadian-American relations
(except to the extent that they provided the occasion for differences to
surface between Ottawa and Washington on the question of the most
appropriate Northern response). With regard to some of the matters
arising in reference specifically to the Law of the Sea, Canadians were
able to coalesce with other parties in common (and sometimes
successful) cause against the American position. But opportunities of
this kind were rare. To the extent that the United Nations became
absorbed in North-South politics, Canada and the United States were
ultimately entrapped in the same net.

A comparable erosion of Canada's diplomatic assets occurred in the
North Atlantic alliance, although here the cause was not so much a
proliferation of new players as a resuscitation of old ones. In symbolic
and military terms alike, the Canadian contribution to NATO in the
early 1950s was substantial. By the 1960s, however, the recovery of the
greater European powers, when combined with the increased cost of
contemporary weapons technology, was seriously eroding the military
salience of the Canadian role -- so much so that it began to come under
attack at home, first by critics outside of government, and then from
within government itself.[30] The irony was that the critics now
regarded the alliance as a mechanism for the American entrapment of
Canadian policy, rather than as a vehicle for amplifying Canada's
influence over the United States. The eventual result, as reflected in
the force reductions announced in 1969, was a substantial diminution of
the membership dues that the Canadians were prepared to pay.

More recently, of course, the utility of NATO as a multilateral
vehicle for the conduct of a part, at least, of Canadian foreign policy
has been called further into question because the alliance itself, with
the apparent demise of the Soviet threat, has lost its primary purpose.
While weakening further in their resolve to pay their way, Canadians
still cling, of course, to the NATO game, as they cling to their other
multilateral involvements in Europe (e.g., in the Conference on Security
and Cooperation in Europe [CSCE]). But the spectacle has about it an
air of desperation and defeat, as if they know their participation has
no point save to divert their attention from a new reality that they do
not wish to confront.

These apparent futilities notwithstanding, there is other evidence,
too, that the search for multilateral shelters for Canadian diplomacy
will be slow to die. It was at the heart, for example, of the somewhat
artificial initiative entailed in the launching of a "North Pacific
Cooperative Security Dialogue" in 1990.[31] Its traces can be discerned as
well in the 1990 consummation of Canada's prolonged flirtation with

membership in the Organization of American States -- although here the balance in the contest between bilateral realities and multilateral architecture was obviously more delicate.[32]

Canada's enthusiasm for multilateral vehicles within which to conduct Canadian foreign policy thus appears unabated. But the viability and effectiveness of such instruments for facilitating Ottawa's management of what might be called the "America problem" are much less clear. New realities challenge the relevance of old solutions.

In relation to the diversification strategy, too, the range of helpful possibilities, never very great, seems steadily to have diminished. As already indicated, the 1976 contractual link with the European Community was a diplomatic success but an economic failure. The substance did not follow the rhetoric. The same was true of the agreement with Japan. Similarly, the Third World (which the Trudeau government had regarded for a time as having countervail potential) proved not to be a viable diversification alternative. Things could be done there. Initiatives could be taken there. But they would do nothing to lessen Canada's vulnerability to American wish, or to American accident. Certainly they were not an alternative to the United States as a partner in the generation of wealth. Bluntly put, the regionalization of Europe, the regionalization of the Pacific, the impotence of the Third World, and the responsiveness of the private sector to market conditions beyond the power of the Canadian government to control have together profoundly weakened Canada's capacity to engineer artificial linkages overseas as a means of offsetting its more natural linkages with the continental United States.

The severity of the problem has been compounded, moreover, by the fact that the continental linkages themselves have become ever more pervasive and deeply rooted. This in turn has had an intricate and subtle, yet deeply significant, series of impacts on the executive pluralism approach to the management of the bilateral relationship. More specifically, it has intensified the pertinence of Canada-U.S. relations to the conduct of domestic politics in both countries, a development which has weakened the ability of the executive branch of government in each case to confine the management of items on the Canadian-American agenda to the professional bureaucracy, and to deal with them both discreetly and without the direct involvement of constituency "publics."

This is not, we need to remind ourselves, a new phenomenon. It was the subject of considerable academic attention even in the early 1970s.[33] From a normative perspective, it can be regarded either favorably (in the sense of the early advocates of European unity, who supported functional integration as a mechanism for inhibiting the all-too-natural hostilities of autonomous nation-states) or unfavorably (in the sense of Canadian nationalists, who implicitly accepted the cause-and-effect premises of the functional integration argument, but feared its consequences for Canadian independence in the context of what came to be described as a "disparate dyad"[34]). But for good or ill, it is now clearly a "force of history," and it has led to the direct participation in the Canada-U.S. relationship of a wide array not only of bureaucratic interlopers (which would not in itself be inimical to the executive pluralist strategy), but also of their respective domestic constituents. On the Canadian side of the border, where the principle of responsible government makes the executive branch the preferred target of lobbyists, this has resulted in the expansion and refinement (even in "foreign" policy) of symbiotic connections between the public service (including the foreign service) and organized interests.   On the American side, where the principle of the separation of powers diverts the lobbyist's attention more to the Congress, it has drawn the legislative branch of government ever more insistently and vociferously into the process.[35]

From the Canadian point of view, the resulting complications have been compounded by a decline in Canada's importance to the United States in relation to national security, and by an increase in its importance in terms of economics. In effect, Canada needs to be treated less gingerly, and hence less gently, than in the past from the security point of view, but has become a much more inviting target of American attack from the economic point of view. This dilemma may have more to do with the weakening of the United States (relatively speaking) in the global economy at large than with Canada's economic position *per se*, but the result is the same. Hence the "shock" of the August 1971 surcharge, which for the first time made it clear that Canada could not always expect an automatic exemption from the full force of American commercial policy.

Strategic Adjustments

As already indicated, executive pluralism had been the subject of considerable criticism in Canada as an approach to the management of Canadian-American relations as early as the middle 1960s. The concern was not that it was ineffective or inefficient, but that it was "value-loaded" in the sense of having integrative, rather than counter-integrative, implications. By the 1970s, however, there were indications that it was coming under serious stress, even on its own terms. In 1974, Peter Dobell, the Director of the Parliamentary Centre for Foreign Affairs and Foreign Trade and a former Canadian foreign service officer, drew attention to the need to pay more attention to Congress in an article published in *International Organization,* and he re-stated his developing position with even greater vigor six years later.[36]   Similar themes emerged in a 1975 report on Canada-U.S. relations by the Canadian Senate's Standing Committee on Foreign Affairs (in the writing of which the Parliamentary Centre was involved).[37] By the turn of the decade the problem was becoming the subject of considerable academic comment.[38]

Perhaps the earliest visible indicator of a change of emphasis from within the Canadian government itself, however, came in the form of a change in diplomatic style at the Canadian embassy in Washington during Allan Gotlieb's tenure as ambassador in the early 1980s. Acutely aware of the congressional "problem" and of the sometimes capriciously unpredictable lobbies that give rise to it, he undertook to target the legislative as well as the executive branch of government in the representational priorities of his mission.[39] By 1983, he was receiving modest additions to his budget in support of congressional lobbying initiatives.[40] The change was to some extent a matter of degree rather than of kind.   Canadian representatives had talked to congressional committees, for example, on frequent occasions in the past -- although almost always with State Department approval, and sometimes even at State Department behest.   But it altered the game nonetheless.   It was a form of politics, certainly, that the executive pluralist model had eschewed.   And it carried risks.   Diplomats who play in the domestic politics of the countries to which they are assigned -- even where such play might be defended on the ground that the constitutional practices of the host make it unavoidable -- expose themselves to the potential for backlash from an audience made resentful by the spectacle of foreign interference in their internal affairs.

Notwithstanding the hazards, however, the identification of domestic targets for diplomatic attention was a natural corollary (in the Washington context, at least) of the increasing domestication of the foreign policy agenda itself.   The addition of "political" maneuvering to the traditional "administrative" ones was the inevitable result, together with such consequences for the *praxis* of executive pluralism as might follow.   "To link," as John Holmes once observed in oblique reference to a pair of contested issues in Canadian-American relations, "is human, and senators inevitably get border television...mixed up with convention expenses."[41]

But the principal manifestation of fundamental change in the management of the Canada-U.S. relations was far more than a mere adjustment of diplomatic practice. It was instead a new departure in Canadian public policy -- namely, the negotiation of the Canada-U.S. Free Trade Agreement (CUSFTA).

The importance that can be attributed, in the present context, to CUSFTA results not, as might be expected, from the terms of the agreement itself, the true effects of which are essentially unknown (and probably unknowable). A great deal is happening to the Canadian economy. Some of it may be due to the further relaxation of barriers to Canada-U.S. trade, and to the press of American competition (and of American opportunity). But most of it would probably have occurred anyway, spurred on by the global forces driving the contemporary international economy.

CUSFTA's real significance thus lies less in its economic substance than in the simple fact that it exists. The process by which it was negotiated was triggered in a climate in which Canadian governing elites, politicians and public servants alike, had concluded, in effect, that multilateralism was marginally useful but not centrally sufficient, that diversification probably would not (and could not) be made to work, and that Canada might as well put all of its Grade A eggs in the American basket because the other baskets were either too small, beyond repair, or out of reach. Canadians, in short, lived in North America, and had nowhere else to go. Given the protectionist inclinations of a lobby-susceptible Congress, it seemed wise to institutionalize the relationship in a way that would tame its politics not through the ad hoc and culture-dependent devices of executive pluralism, but through clearly defined rules sustained by politically detached procedures for resolving disputes.

It might be said that this is to make too much of too little, and that CUSFTA is about economic exchange alone, and not about anything else. The complaint would be well taken, but for the fact that "economic exchange" has itself assumed such prominence on the Canadian agenda. A careful reading of the evolution of thinking in the Department of External Affairs -- from the previously mentioned "options paper" of 1972 (in which the free trade option was explicitly rejected on both economic and non-economic grounds) through the 1983 discussion paper on Canadian trade policy (in which sectoral bilateral trade agreements with the United States were advocated as a complement to the traditional multilateral approach through the GATT)[42] to the documentation published by the Department in 1986, as background to the bilateral talks with the United States (in which it was argued, *en passant*, that a comprehensive "bilateral treaty could be a better guarantee of our sovereignty than the gradual uncontrolled drift toward integration now taking place")[43] -- a careful reading of such documentation reveals very clearly the shift in the government's sense of "what matters," and in its view of how "what matters" ought to be pursued. "Bilateralism, rather than multilateralism," as Professors Granatstein and Bothwell have put it, "became the watchword of the day. The third option was quietly and unobtrusively trundled off to the attic."[44]

It is important to stress once again that we are not dealing here with total transformations or revolutionary watersheds. Multilateralisms are still pursued. Diversifications are still sought. And much of Canada-U.S. diplomacy is still conducted by public service professionals in discreetly pragmatic spirit. But there is not the confidence that there once was that Canada has genuine options outside the North American milieu for limiting the intrusion into Canadian affairs and Canadian interests of the American fact. For powerful reasons easily understood, Canada's leadership has, in that respect, thrown in the towel (although it may not be willing to concede the point, even to itself).

Questions

It is still possible that this is not a permanent condition, and that future evolutions of the global economy will reopen overseas options. But in the meantime Canadians would do well to ponder three questions: (1) How should Canada go about dealing with the United States now that it is clearly, perhaps unavoidably, housed in continental confinement? (2) Does the involvement of Mexico in a trilateral free trade arrangement increase, diminish, or leave unaffected such opportunities as remain for enhancing Canada's position in relation to the United States? and (3) Could the eventual inclusion of other actors from the Western Hemisphere provide an alternative to multilateralist and diversification remedies that Canada has traditionally pursued?

These, of course, are Canadian questions. Mexicans would put them differently. Americans might not put them at all. But the answers will be of interest to all three.

Notes

1. For an excellent treatment see Tom Keating, *Canada and World Order: The Multilateralist Tradition in Canadian Foreign Policy* (Toronto: McClelland and Stewart, 1993).

2. The phrase is Lester B. Pearson's, and it titles the third chapter of *Mike: The Memoirs of the Rt. Hon. Lester B. Pearson*, Vol. 2, 1948-1957 (Toronto: University of Toronto Press, 1973), p. 37.

3. Hence, in particular, the Canadian insistence on Article II of the NATO Treaty, which provides that "The Parties will contribute toward the further development of peaceful and friendly international relations by strengthening their free institutions, by bringing about a better understanding of the principles upon which these institutions are founded, and by promoting conditions of stability and well-being. They will seek to eliminate conflict in their international economic policies and will encourage economic collaboration between any or all of them." The United States appears to have agreed to the provision as the harmless price of Canadian entry.

4. See Tom Keating, *Canada and World Order*, especially pp. 48-73, for a carefully crafted review.

5. It was Prime Minister Trudeau who first likened Canada's relationship with the United States to sleeping with an elephant. The mouse, as metaphor for Canada, was added by the press. See J.L. Granatstein and Robert Bothwell, *Pirouette: Pierre Trudeau and Canadian Foreign Policy* (Toronto: University of Toronto Press, 1990), p. 51. No one seems to have remembered that elephants are reputed to be terrified of mice!

6. The parallel between the various "balance of power" models that proliferate in the "realist" literature of international politics and the discussions of interest group behavior that emerge from pluralist interpretations of liberal democratic politics may warrant further study.

7. H. Basil Robinson, *Diefenbaker's World: A Populist in Foreign Affairs* (Toronto: University of Toronto Press, 1989), p. 12.

8. *Globe and Mail* (Toronto), July 8, 1957, quoted in Trevor Lloyd, *Canada in World Affairs, 1957-1959* (Toronto: Canadian Institute of International Affairs, 1968), p. 66.

9. Robinson, *Diefenbaker's World*, p. 14; Lloyd, *Canada's World Affairs, 1957-1959*, pp. 66-73.

10. Canada, Department of External Affairs, *Foreign Policy for Canadians*, (Ottawa: Queen's Printer, 1970), "Foreign Policy for Canadians" pamphlet, p. 24.

11. Ibid. "Europe Pamphlet, p. 14.

12. Ibid., "Latin America" pamphlet, pp. 6-7.

13. Published as a special issue of the journal *International Perspectives* (September-October 1972).

14. Ibid., p. 13.

15. For an overview of these discussions, see Granatstein and Bothwell, *Pirouette*, pp. 162-72. An earlier analysis is contained in Robert Boardman's "Initiatives and Outcomes: The European Community and Canada's 'Third Option'," *Journal of European Integration*, Vol. 3, No. 1 (September 1979), pp. 5-28.

16. This came much more easily. See Granatstein and Bothwell, *Pirouette*, pp. 172-175.

17. I am indebted to Bruce Thordarson for this observation. See his *Trudeau and Foreign Policy: A Study in Decision-Making* (Toronto: Oxford University Press, 1972), p. 77. The reference is from Pierre Elliott Trudeau, *Federalism and the French Canadians* (Toronto: Macmillan, 1968), p. xxiii.

18. There is not room here to explore this possibility in depth, but the literature written by veterans of the Canadian foreign policy community is now so voluminous as to render such an inquiry both tempting and feasible even on the basis of secondary sources. Doctoral candidates should take note.

19. A.D.P. Heeney and Livingston T. Merchant, *Canada and the United States: Principles for Partnership* (Ottawa: Queen's Printer, 1965). The report gave rise to considerable public debate, and Mr. Heeney later felt obliged to defend it in a number of publications. See, for example, his "Dealing with Uncle Sam" in J. King Gordon, ed., *Canada's Role as a Middle Power* (Toronto: Canadian Institute of International Affairs, 1966), pp. 87-100, and *The Things that are Caesar's: Memoirs of a Canadian Public Servant* (Toronto: University of Toronto Press, 1972), especially pp. 190-200.

20. Of these, on this and related subjects, the most engaging are contained in the myriad writings of John W. Holmes. See in particular his collections of lectures and essays, including most notably *The Better Part of Valour: Essays on Canadian Diplomacy* (Toronto: McClelland & Stewart, 1970); *Canada: A Middle-Aged Power* (Toronto: McClelland & Stewart, 1976), and *Life with Uncle: The Canadian-American Relationship* (Toronto: University of Toronto Press, 1981).

21. These summary quotations are from Kal J. Holsti and Thomas Allen Levy, "Bilateral Institutions and Transgovernmental Relations between Canada and the United States," *International Organization*, Vol. 28, No. 4 (Autumn 1974), p. 883. Professor Holsti's original study appeared under the title, "Canada and the United States," in Steven Spiegel and Kenneth Waltz, eds., *Conflict in World Politics* (Boston: Winthrop, 1971), pp. 375-96.

22. For an engaging discussion of the nuances involved, see Basil Robinson, *Diefenbaker's World* especially pp. 312-320. Consider also Peyton V. Lyon, *Canada in World Affairs, 1961-1963* (Toronto: Oxford University Press, 1968), especially Chapter 3.

23. Most of the available examples illustrate the problem. In April 1951, for instance, Lester Pearson gave a speech in Toronto on "Canadian Foreign Policy in a Two-Power World," during the course of which he commented that "the days of relatively easy and automatic political relations with our neighbour are over." The observation reflected among other things his concern with General Douglas MacArthur's apparently uncontrollable interventions in the higher politics of the Korean War. An uproar ensued, complicated by the fact that General MacArthur was relieved of his command on the same day, and the Minister felt obliged to explain himself at some length to his own Ambassador in Washington. (For the text of his address, see his *Words and Occasions* (Toronto: University of Toronto Press, 1970), pp. 100-108. His communication with the Ambassador, Hume Wrong, is reproduced in *Mike*, Vol. 2. Even greater complications developed in the wake

of the suicide in 1957, of the Canadian Ambassador to Egypt, E. Herbert Norman, a tragedy which was assumed to have resulted from charges in the United States Senate Sub Committee on Internal Security to the effect that Norman had Communist associations. Pearson made public the representations of the Canadian government, but the language of diplomatic protest was not sufficient to satisfy the righteously indignant. See James Eayrs, *Canada in World Affairs, 1955-1957* (Toronto: Oxford University Press, 1959), pp. 153-60. Prime Minister Diefenbaker, too, found that public diplomacy could be a difficult game to balance. Consider, for example, his tribulations in connection with nuclear weapons policy, as discussed in Lyon, *Canada in World Affairs, 1961-1963 especially* pp. 154-73.

24. This phenomenon produced a flurry of academic inquiries in the early 1970s. For a brief review, see Levy and Holsti, "Bilateral Institutions and Transgovernmental Relations," especially pp. 881-885.

25. It should be conceded here that some studies indicate that Canada has done very well in negotiations at the highest level. See, for example, Joseph S. Nye, Jr., "Transnational Relations and Interstate Conflicts: An Empirical Analysis," *International Organization,* Vol. 28, No. 4 (Autumn 1974), pp. 961-96. Part of the reason is that American presidents tend to be more interested in the overall amity of the relationship than in the outcome of any specific dispute. Members of Congress, however, usually have more parochial preoccupations.

26. Holsti and Levy, "Bilateral Institutions and Transgovernmental Relations," pp. 877-8.

27. Ibid., p. 881.

28. This concern was at the heart of a debate in Canada in the 1960s and early 1970s over the merits of "quiet diplomacy." Brought to a head in part by the Heeney-Merchant report, the argument was played out most starkly in a book of essays edited by Stephen Clarkson under the title, *An Independent Foreign Policy for Canada?* (Toronto: McClelland & Stewart, 1968). The book was partly responsible for the initiation of a discreet review of foreign policy -- the so-called "Robertson Review" -- in the final months of the Pearson government.

29. For a variety of explorations on this theme in the Canada-U.S. context, see the special issue of *International Organization,* entitled "Canada and the United States: Transnational and Transgovernmental Relations," Vol. 28, No. 4 (Autumn 1974).

30. Perhaps the first full-dress critique came from the CBC's radio correspondent in Washington. See James M. Minifie, *Peacemaker or Powder-Monkey: Canada's Role in a Revolutionary World* (Toronto: McClelland & Stewart, 1960). Consider also some of the essays in Clarkson, *An Independent Foreign Policy for Canada?* The intra-governmental debate was triggered by the Trudeau government's foreign policy review. See Thordarson, *Trudeau and Foreign Policy.*

31. The official rationale included other ingredients, too. See Rt. Hon. Joe Clark "Canada and Asia Pacific in the 1990's," Victoria, British Columbia, July 17, 1990, also External Affairs and International Trade Canada (EAITC), *Statement 90/40.* The initiative appears less prominently, but, from the vantage point of the diplomatic and strategic culture described more generally in this paper, even more

pertinently, in a *tour d'horizon* offered by the Minister two months later. See "Canada in the World: Foreign Policy in the New Era," Notes for a speech by the Right Honorable Joe Clark, Secretary of State for External Affairs, on the Occasion of the 66th Meeting of the Canadian-American Committee of the C.D. Howe Institute, Ottawa, Ontario, September 13, 1990, EAITC, *Statements and Speeches 90/11.*

32. See Rt. Hon. Joe Clark, "Canadian Policy Towards Latin America," Calgary, Alberta, February 1, 1990, *Statements and Speeches 90/2.*

33. The Autumn 1974 issue of *International Organization* was the leading example.

34. The phrase enjoyed a brief vogue among Canadian academics in the late 1970s and early 1980s. See, for example, Peyton V. Lyon and Brian W. Tomlin, *Canada as an International Actor* (Toronto: Macmillan, 1979), p. 117. In this intriguing volume, Chapters 6 ("Canada-U.S. Integration") and 7 ("Canadian-American Relations") bear directly on themes raised in the present paper.

35. The Congress had already been stimulated to greater intervention in foreign affairs, of course, by the Vietnam war and other executive-led adventures "gone wrong." But in the case of the "Canada" agenda, the motivations have more to do with "meat and potatoes" than with "blood and iron."

36. See Peter C. Dobell, "The Influence of the United States Congress on Canadian-American Relations, International Organization, Vol. 28, No. 4 (Autumn 1974), especially pp. 927-29; and his "Negotiating with the United States," International Journal, Vol. XXXVI, No. 1 (Winter 1980-1), pp. 17-38.

37. See *Canada, Standing Senate Committee on Foreign Affairs, Canada-United States Relations, Volume I, The Institutional Framework for the Relationship,* December 1975.

38. The leading voice was probably that of Stephen Clarkson, as expressed most notably in his *Canada and the Reagan Challenge: Crisis in the Canadian-American Relationship* (Ottawa: Canadian Institute for Economic Policy, 1982). See also his contribution a few years later in the form of a chapter on "Canada-U.S. Relations and the Changing of the Guard in Ottawa," in Brian W. Tomlin and Maureen Molot, eds., *Canada Among Nations - 1984: A Time of Transition,* pp. 149-63.

39. For a full account of Mr. Gotlieb's understanding of the old, and the new, "rules" for conducting the relationship, see his "Canada-U.S. Relations: The Rules of the Game," *SAIS Review,* No. 4 (Summer 1982), pp. 177-88.

40. See Clarkson, in *Canada Among Nations -- 1984,* p. 150.

41. John W. Holmes, *Life with Uncle: The Canadian-American Relationship* (Toronto: University of Toronto Press, 1981), p. 55. These 1980-81 Bissell Lectures offer much by way of balanced wisdom on what their author describes (on p. 107) as "the persistent paradoxes of life with a superpower.

42. See Canada, Department of External Affairs, *Canadian Trade Policy for the 1980s: A Discussion Paper* (Ottawa: Minister of Supply and Services Canada, 1983).

43. Canada, Department of External Affairs, *Canadian Trade Negotiations: Introduction, Selected Documents, Further Reading* (Ottawa: Supply and Services

Canada, 1986), p. 32.

44. Granatstein and Bothwell, *Pirouette*, p. 332. The change in   emphasis resulted in part from the victory of the trade wing of the Department over the traditionalists. But the fact that it *had* a trade wing was itself a reflection of a government reorganization launched in pursuit of different priorities. The tale is engagingly told *ibid.*, Chapter 8.

5

Managing Bilateralism: The Evolution of United States-Mexico Relations

Stephen J. Randall

Introduction

What has been called the "Salinas Opening" to the North may represent a fundamental reorientation of Mexican foreign economic policy. Such a reorientation is, nonetheless, only at the early stages of what will be a lengthy process of adjustment. That process will be shaped not only by current political, cultural and economic realities but also by the historical relationship between the two countries, their very different approaches to foreign policy, and differing traditions in their respective relations with the rest of Latin America and the Caribbean. One of the dramatic realities of the post-Cold War world is the growing acceptance of interdependence between the United States and the other nations of the hemisphere. Although in the past the relationship between the United States and Mexico has tended to be one of U.S. hegemony and Mexican dependency, the contemporary reality is one of asymmetrical interdependence, that is interdependence in which status and power are unequal.[1]

Mexico's acceptance of a new economic and political reality represents a departure from the basic orientation of Mexican foreign policy since the revolution. Mexico has consistently since the 1910s sought to pursue a foreign policy distinct from that of the United States, although the assertion of such "independence" of approach has been more intense during some periods than others. Significantly, no Mexican government since 1920 has been entirely able to escape the realities of Mexican-U.S. interdependence on economic, strategic and political issues. What has changed in the past decade as Mexico joined the General Agreement on Tariffs and Trade (GATT), put its economic house in order under the auspices of the international financial regime, and initiated a broad program of reform that included privatization and the North American Free Trade Agreement (NAFTA), was a more broadly based acceptance in Mexico of the reality of interdependence.

The basic premises of Mexican foreign policy in this century have included: support for the multilateral resolution of international conflicts, non-intervention in the internal affairs of other nations, and national self-determination. This orientation derives in large measure from differences in size and power with the United States, as much as from differing philosophical premises, although the latter have been a factor as well. This basic orientation is unlikely to change; what has dramatically altered, however, is the shift from a view of the U.S. as opponent to interdependent partner in trade and economic development.

The United States, for its part, has pursued policies toward Mexico that have been characterized by periods of benign neglect interspersed with periods of often intense and not especially benign interest. Like Mexico, U.S. policy has been driven by a blend of national self-interest and ideology.[2] U.S. policy-makers have been influenced in their approach to Mexico not only by the immediate problems between the two nations but also by the broader geopolitical and strategic dilemmas that have confronted the United States globally and regionally, especially since the Second World War. To a greater degree than Mexican policy, that of the U.S. has seemed more changeable, often varying from administration to administration, sometimes depending on the personal level of interest in Mexico on the part of the president.[3] Yet, there have also been consistent themes in the American approach to Mexico. The United States has sought, for instance, consistently to reduce the threat of Mexican nationalism to the security of supply of raw materials, particularly petroleum; to protect private American property holdings within Mexico against expropriation; to stem the movement of illegal migrants into the U.S.; to prevent the importation of illegal narcotics from Mexico; and to open Mexican investment and financial markets to U.S. capital.

The most intense periods of friction in the bilateral relationship since 1900 have occurred when there was a convergence of American concern over those broader global issues with a perceived Mexican deviation from the desired U.S. position. Mexican nationalism, especially economic nationalism, appeared to threaten broader American geopolitical goals in the context of World War I, the

Bolshevik Revolution, and the Cold War era, especially after the Cuban Revolution. Hence, U.S. administrations reacted with hostility to the Mexican Revolution, the nationalistic provisions of the 1917 Constitution, and the nationalization of most of the foreign oil companies in 1938. During the Cold War, U.S. administrations were disturbed by the softer line Mexico adopted toward the Cuban Revolution and Salvador Allende's socialist government in Chile in 1973, the Central American crisis in the 1980s, or Mexican criticism of the U.S. military actions in Grenada and Panama during that decade.

To focus on the peaks of conflict or the troughs of indifference in the bilateral relationship, however, distorts the reality of relations between the two countries. Even when there have been strong differences of policy and perspective between them, the United States and Mexico have maintained an active dialogue. The institutional linkages (discussed later in this paper), which have evolved over past decades have also served to provide a degree of stability to the relationship, a variety of fora within which both day-to-day and longer term issues have been addressed. In part because of geographic proximity, in part because of shared agenda and concerns, the dialogue on several levels between the two nations has been constant. Managing the issues that arise from the extensive shared extensive border -- from narcotics and water supply to migration and environmental concerns -- has been a matter of daily contact between the two countries. The importance of these issues has given rise to an extensive bureaucracy in both nations that often transcends formal diplomacy. Indeed, it is one of the fundamental features of the bilateral relationship that there is a remarkable breadth of interests and sometimes interference that cannot be contained within normal diplomatic bounds, whether it is the involvement of Congress, of citizens' groups, of business interests, or of a multiplicity of city, state and federal agencies concerned with everything from air and water pollution along the border to job security in the context of debate over NAFTA.

Evolution of a Mexican Foreign Policy Tradition

The Mexican revolutionary nationalism which has been a factor in Mexican-American relations was the product of a variety of historical developments. These included the devastating loss of territory to the United States as a result of the Mexican-American war in the mid-nineteenth century; French military occupation under Archduke Ferdinand Maximilian and the lengthy resistance by Benito Juarez's forces; the high level of foreign economic penetration of the nation under the governments of Porfirio Díaz until the revolution began in 1910; and subsequent efforts by United States interests to determine the direction of Mexican economic development. That nationalism has transcended class lines in Mexican society and been an instrument for Mexican governments to employ in policies pertaining to the United States. The institutionalization of a revolutionary party (now known as PRI) following the revolution, and effectively a one-party state until recently, also provided Mexico with the structural basis for a higher degree of consistency in its policies toward the United States than characterized American policy toward Mexico.[4]

In general, Mexican policy has consistently sought to maintain a cautious distance from the United States, achieving independent economic development, generally through import substitution programs, state-owned and controlled corporations, and strict supervision of foreign investment and trade, as well as the strong preference noted earlier for multilateralism. Given that historical tradition, the Mexican move in the 1980s toward a position of closer harmony and free trade with the United States is a significant shift in policy. Although Mexico has not lost sight of its previous sense of mission to lead in Latin America (and the free trade overtures to Chile in the context of the post-NAFTA agenda reinforce that orientation), the governments of Miguel de la Madrid and Carlos Salinas de Gortari have placed economic relations with the United States above traditional ties with the Caribbean and Latin America.

The de la Madrid and Salinas reorientation of Mexican policy toward the North represents not only a belated acceptance by Mexican leaders of the degree of Mexican-U.S. interdependence but a willingness to place that interdependence very publicly on the Mexican foreign policy agenda. Yet, in spite of the lengthy Mexican tradition of anti-Americanism and economic nationalism, the Salinas opening is based on an equally important and lengthy tradition of bilateral cooperation in which the mutual interests of the two nations were recognized. Indeed, the basic reality of the bilateral relationship has been one of growing interdependence and economic integration over the past half-century.

The second World War acted as a particularly important catalyst in pushing the two nations together for economic and military cooperation. One authority has concluded that "Wartime cooperation between Mexico and the United States signaled the beginning of a new era in diplomatic relations,"[5] with Mexico under President Avila Camacho seeking foreign investment to stimulate a drive to industrialization, thus moving away from the strict economic nationalism and socialist policies that had characterized the presidency of

Lázaro Cárdenas in the 1930s. The war and early Cold War years also witnessed the conclusion of the *bracero* program between the two countries, under which U.S. manpower shortages were to be partially alleviated through the acceptance of thousands of Mexican workers in the American West and mid-West, including in the railroad industry, manufacturing and agriculture. By 1945, there were approximately 58,000 Mexican workers in agriculture and another 62,000 in the railroad industry. With occasional interruptions and modifications the *bracero* program continued until 1964, when it was replaced by the development of the *maquiladora* program -- the in-bond, largely border, manufacturing operations that were designed to provide investment and employment opportunities within Mexico, in part to alleviate the Mexican migration pressure on U.S. border states.[6]

United States preoccupation with Cold War issues and increasing absorption in the Vietnam War in the 1960s and early 1970s, left Mexican affairs very much on the back burner. The American focus on other matters combined with Mexican concentration on policies of import substitution and continued restrictions on foreign investment made Mexico of marginal importance to the United States, ironically given the Kennedy administration's overtures to Latin America in the establishment of the Alliance for Progress.

Years of Transition in Mexico, 1968-1982

Several features of Mexican politics and society altered from the late 1960s, with considerable significance for relations with the United States. The first was the international condemnation and domestic reaction to the police and military repression and killings of Mexican students in 1968. That violent confrontation seemed symptomatic of much deeper contradictions and social tensions in a Mexican society which appeared to have lost touch with its own revolutionary heritage. The need to answer critics and to rebuild societal balance and consensus contributed to a shift in policy in the subsequent decade to the "shared development" approach of the Luis Echeverria and López Portillo presidencies (1970-1982), during which there were efforts to make the political process more pluralistic and to involve people directly in decisions that affected their communities.

Echeverria also sought to redirect Mexico's industrial policies away from the traditional import substitution of the previous decades, although restrictions remained and continued to discourage U.S. investment. Echeverria further attempted to balance the U.S. influence in Mexican foreign relations by broadening Mexico's international ties.

To that end his government concluded trade agreements with Canada, Japan, China, the Soviet Union and other East European countries. In contrast to the United States, Echeverria was supportive of Castro's Cuba, frequently traveling to the island, supported Salvador Allende in Chile and denied recognition to the military junta that replaced him in 1973. Following the coup that brought down Allende, Mexico became a haven for Chile's political and intellectual refugees.[7]

The collective impact of these economic and foreign policy initiatives may have been marginal, but they reflected the continuing desire of Mexicans to assert their separate identity from the United States. Economically, although there was a shift of investment away from U.S. sources during the 1970s, the new investment policies seem to have increased Mexican dependency on multinational corporations as well as on imported technology and industrial goods.[8]

With the discovery and development of the massive oil deposits in the Gulf of Campeche in the late 1970s, Mexico's quest for self-sufficiency and a fiercely independent foreign policy appeared to be realizable. The Cold War had intensified with the Soviet invasion of Afghanistan in 1979; the United States was confronted in the same year with its second major oil shock in fewer than ten years with the Iranian revolution, driving up prices and creating massive shortages once again. The close proximity of Mexican resources to the U.S. and the relative security of transport increased the strategic importance of Mexico to the United States. Even before the second oil shock in 1979, a report prepared in 1977 for Senator Henry M. Jackson's Committee on Interior and Insular Affairs, entitled *The Geopolitics of Energy*, urged that the United States reduce its involvement in the Persian Gulf and seek resources closer to home, including "special relationships" with Canada, Mexico and Venezuela. In a statement that anticipated developments in the 1980s, the report concluded that "should the Mexicans reject assistance in oil development, there are a whole host of additional Mexican interests which could be addressed in a special relationship -- trade, investment, labor issues ... A special relationship of this sort must necessarily cover areas other than energy raw materials, and the cost to the United States may therefore be higher than a straight oil arrangement. Making such a relationship politically acceptable to Mexico may prove even more difficult ...."[9]

The Emerging Crisis

Three major developments contributed to a crisis in Mexican-American relations in the 1980s and created the preconditions that made the Salinas opening politically feasible and economically essential. The first crisis tended to divide the two nations; that was growing estrangement over United States Central American policy following the Sandinista revolution in Nicaragua and the fall of the Somoza dynasty. The second and concurrent crisis, conversely, underlined Mexico's economic interdependence with the United States; that was the debt crisis that faced Mexico with the decline of oil prices, after the brief euphoria that followed the development of the Campeche offshore resources. A third major source of friction also served to remind the two nations of their interdependence; that was the escalation of narcotics trafficking across the Mexican border into the United States, as Colombian narcotics cartels sought alternate routes into the American market.

Even during the favorable environment of the Carter administration, which hosted President López Portillo as its first foreign visitor, Mexico's foreign secretary, Jorge Castañeda, was highly negative about Washington's perspective on its southern neighbor. In a 1979 address in Washington, Castañeda expressed pessimism about the capacity of the United States to rediscover any "good will, sympathy or moral considerations" toward Mexico. "Its past history with us, its present day arrogance, selfishness and conservative mood will not allow for a change. Great powers will act as great powers. The nature of our mutual relationship depends essentially on Mexico's attitude and conduct."[10]

With the inauguration of the Reagan administration and the deepening economic crisis in Mexico, tensions escalated. The economic boom associated with Campeche was brief and an interlude between the crisis of the mid-1970s and that of the mid-1980s. In the mid-1970s, the country had suffered high levels of inflation (30% in 1976), an accumulated debt of $20 billion (U.S.), devaluation of the peso, and a decline in foodstuff production. Before the development of the Campeche and Tabasco reserves in southern Mexico, the country had already been faced with an austerity plan imposed by the International Monetary Fund. By 1981, the United States was trading Mexican debt for Mexican oil deposited in the U.S. strategic petroleum reserve. In 1982, the U.S. arranged a billion dollar payment into the Strategic Petroleum Reserve; and in fiscal 1983, it provided through the Commodity Credit Corporation almost $2 billion for grain, oil, and seeds, among other commodities.[11]

Further deterioration in oil prices and the ensuing debt crisis forced President de la Madrid into another austerity program,[12] notably the Baker Plan in 1985, with export earnings applied to the Mexican external debt, and with a vigorous privatization program under both presidents, in which hundreds of state-owned enterprises have been sold to the private sector. Privatization included the Cananea copper mine, which had been one of the symbols of early Mexican economic nationalism because of its previous American ownership and labor strife. Other prominent state enterprises that went on the auction block included Nacional Hotelera, Vehiculos Automotores Mexicanos, Aerolineas Mexicanas, and a major foundry in Monterrey. In 1985, as world oil prices continued to decline, the International Monetary Fund and World Bank raised the stakes in addressing Mexico's debt crisis, with economic reforms and Mexico's growth rate tied to the level of loans from the international agencies.

It is evident that there was considerable concern in the Reagan administration at this stage that Mexico's economic crisis would translate into political destabilization. The de la Madrid government, it should be noted, shared the concern over destabilization, which was aggravated by the impact of refugees from Central America in southern Mexico along with guerrilla activity in the southern border area, although because of their largely domestic nature, these issues were of more concern to the Ministry of Government than to the Foreign Ministry.[13] On the U.S. side, political and economic stability were seen as two sides of the same coin. Following the 1988 election that brought the pro-American, U.S.-trained economist Carlos Salinas de Gortari to power, the U.S. extended a $3.5 billion loan. Two years later the United States renegotiated the Mexican public debt to major international commercial banks.[14]

What added particular volatility to these developments was their coincidence with the Reagan administration's determination to reassert American hegemony, generally in foreign policy and in the global economy, in response to the perceived declining position of the U.S. in the world. It had clearly lost the pre-eminent status it had enjoyed in the 1945-1960s years and by 1982, was suffering from a trade deficit of $32 billion. The Reagan administration sought to redress that balance, as well as win the Cold War, and this orientation added a particular edge to U.S.-Mexican policies.[15]

Mexican deviations from U.S. preferences may have been an irritant prior to the election of Ronald Reagan as president, but under Reagan they were seen as serious defections. This applied especially to Mexico's position on Central America during both the López Portillo and Miguel de la Madrid presidencies.

The Mexican position on Nicaragua was a source of serious bilateral tension. From the outset, Miguel de la Madrid's government viewed the

Central American situation as an internal conflict generally unrelated to the East-West struggle on which the Reagan administration was fixated. Mexico broke relations with Anastasio Somoza's government in 1979; the following year it withdrew its ambassador from San Salvador as the right wing death squad activity intensified and the FMLN (Faribundo Marti National Liberation Front)-government conflict escalated. In 1981, Mexico went so far as to support the recognition of the FMLN, and shared that position with France.[16] Convinced that the issue was political pluralism and self-determination for the countries of the area, de la Madrid's government urged -- including before the United Nations Security Council -- a negotiated settlement rather than military solution, withdrawal of external forces from the area, and the continuation of economic relations with Nicaragua. In 1983, Mexico joined Colombia, Venezuela, and Panama to form the Contadora group, which for the next several years pressed, along with the Central American presidents, for a negotiated settlement, albeit with little encouragement from Washington and reticence in Managua.[17]

Important as the Central American situation was, when Secretary of State George Schultz, Commerce and Treasury secretaries Malcolm Baldridge and Donald Regan met with their Mexican counterparts (Sepulveda, Hernandez and Silva Herzog), and President de la Madrid, in Mexico City in April 1983, the bilateral agenda was considerably broader. Their discussions ranged widely over the debt crisis, foreign investment, American efforts to boycott Mexican tuna, the Simpson-Mazzoli bill on immigration, and tourism; the following year when President de la Madrid visited Washington for talks, a major issue was Mexican agricultural export subsidies.[18] In 1985, meetings between Schultz and Sepulveda, narcotics was high on the agenda, as were tuna, trade, investment, and sanitation on the southern California border, but it was the Mexican economic crisis that was the critical catalyst in altering the bilateral relationship.[19]

Managing Bilateralism: The Institutions

The Central American issue illustrates the fact that what most characterized the bilateral relationship, even in crisis, were ongoing consultations. As suggested earlier in this chapter, by the 1980s, Mexico and the United States were driven closer together by a convergence of interests; some of those changes derived from alterations in the international regime; some were products of U.S. security interests, which acquired an increasingly broad definition in the 1980s; other developments were the result of Mexico's altered circumstances and the emergence of a political elite that saw clear advantage in a reorientation of Mexican policy toward the United States. The Salinas opening was made possible by both a long historical tradition of consultation and by the altered realities of the 1980s. As early as the 1940s, United States policy-makers spoke in terms of a "special relationship" between the two nations. By the 1980s, there was a basic irony in Mexico's orientation toward the United States. On the one hand, the Central American crisis made Mexicans more skeptical of U.S. foreign policy goals in the region and more likely to accept the notion advanced in 1948 by Frank Tannenbaum of Mexico as the anvil of U.S.-Latin American diplomacy.[20] Yet, on the other hand, the realities of interdependence forced the two nations to overcome their mutual suspicions and antagonisms.

The reorientation of Mexican policy in the 1980s, was facilitated by the well-established institutional mechanisms for consultation between the two countries. Bilateral institutions constituted a critically important base on which the North American free trade discussions and program could be established. As early as 1889, the two countries established the International Boundary and Water Commission, which was under the jurisdiction of the respective foreign ministries. Mexico took the lead in 1959 in approving legislation authorizing its legislators to participate in annual discussions with their U.S. counterparts; the U.S. followed suit in 1960, an initiative that was supported by then Senators John Kennedy and Lyndon Johnson. In the 1960s, the Mexico-United States Interparliamentary Group contributed to the settlement of the Chamizal dispute, which pertained to the channel of the Rio Grande between Ciudad Juarez and El Paso. The group also facilitated passage of the Colorado River Salinity Settlement in 1974, which was designed to improve the quality of water in the lower Colorado river.[21]

When Jimmy Carter assumed the presidency he and President Luis López Portillo agreed to establish more effective mechanisms to treat the routine and emergency issues that arose. It was not, however, until 1981 that the Reagan and López Portillo administrations created the Binational Commission. The title was misleading; in practice, the commission was technically only the two foreign secretaries and their staffs, although, because of the high level of importance attached to economic questions, normally the main economic representatives at cabinet level participated in meetings. For the United States this meant Treasury, Commerce and the U.S. Trade Representative.[22]

United States Agencies

The Carter administration sought to put American policy formation toward Mexico on a more streamlined footing. In 1977, the State Department commissioned a review of Mexican policy by David Ronfeldt and Caesar Sereseres. The next year National Security Adviser Zbigniew Brzezinsky requested the National Security Council to review relations with Mexico. It was in this context of review of the bilateral relationship and conduct of policy that the Carter administration created the Office of Coordinator for Mexican Affairs. The office was based in the State Department, and its incumbent held ambassadorial rank.[23] Although the notion was in itself a positive signal to Mexico of the seriousness of American intent, the initiative likely caused as much confusion as certainty, in particular by making unclear the relationship between the Coordinator's office and the ambassador in Mexico City. The coordinator appears to have worked relatively effectively with State, Interior, Health, Housing, and Justice, but the U.S. trade representative and the Treasury were less pliable. For these and other reasons, the Reagan administration abandoned the office.[24]

Although American policy has been nominally centered in the White House and the State Department, the high level significance in the bilateral relationship of narcotics, immigration/migration, the environment and trade have made those agencies and departments of the U.S. government inevitably involved. If one needed a lesson in the complexity of managing the cross-border relations, it came with the controversy surrounding the torture and death of Drug Enforcement Agency agent Enrique Camarena in 1985 and the U.S. perception of Mexico's slow and inadequate response. The controversy led to congressional hearings in Washington under Senator Jesse Helms. Those hearings cast Mexico in such negative light that they provoked a diplomatic incident. Yet, out of the controversy also came a renewed vigor in narcotics enforcement and, in 1987, the bilateral agreement, Operation Vanguard, which involved more thorough investigation following aerial spraying of marijuana and poppy crops.[25]

Mexican Institutions

Mexico is by nature a more centralized and autocratic state. Nonetheless, the presidential office and Foreign Ministry have experienced many of the same problems of bureaucratic proliferation and either conflicting or overlapping jurisdictions that their American counterparts have faced in recent decades. As in the United States there has also been a relative decline in the power of the Foreign Ministry because of the ascendancy of trade, investment, narcotics, environment and migration issues. The existence of several other Mexican ministries with divisions with international relations responsibilities has further complicated the bureaucratic maze. The Ministry of Commerce and Industrial Development, to cite one example, has an International Affairs Bureau, a Foreign Trade Service Bureau, a Border Affairs Bureau, and a Foreign Investment Bureau. Certainly all of these activities are the ultimate responsibility of the Foreign Ministry, but this structural arrangement almost invites dispute. There have also been considerable inter-ministry differences of approach on key issues. In addition, although the federal executive is constitutionally empowered to conduct foreign policy, local, regional and state leaders have also been active in determining cross-border relations with the United States.[26]

Mexico has also recognized over the past decade the need to attempt to influence U.S. congressional and public opinion. Examples of such efforts include the U.S. tour in 1985, by the head of the Mexican Public Information Agency, and similar focused efforts in 1991,[27] and later to influence key sectors of the American public on NAFTA.

The broad proliferation of congressional, executive, state and city entities and agencies in both countries that have some responsibility for cross-border relations is both curse and blessing. On the negative side of the ledger it is impossible to coordinate all of their activities to ensure consistency of overall policy. On the other hand, as Joseph Nye has suggested for the United States,

> These miniature foreign offices that domestic agencies have developed for dealing with the international aspects of issues with which they are concerned are not merely bureaucratic nuisances. They are needed in the management of interdependence issues that are both domestic and foreign. As the entire government becomes involved in "international" affairs, it becomes more difficult to reserve a separate section of the agenda for the State Department.[28]

Whether or not Nye's optimism that bureaucratic proliferation provides as much opportunity as dilemma is well-placed, the establishment under NAFTA of more formalized bilateral trade dispute settlement mechanisms will be a positive development. Such mechanisms will in themselves, however, do little to alter the respective images of Mexico and the United States in the other country.

Conclusion

In final analysis the international relations dynamic in the western hemisphere is in transition. That transition has been fueled by the lost decade and debt crisis of the 1980s in Latin America as well as by the twin realities of historical trends toward closer integration and the contemporary thrust toward regional free trade, investment liberalization, and privatization. It is within that context that Mexican-U.S. relations have evolved in the past decade.

The challenge that lies before both nations is to find the most effective institutional mechanisms available to depoliticize trade, investment, migration, narcotics, labor and environmental disputes between the two countries. If history is an accurate guide, the future holds considerable promise, balanced with acute challenges, as two very different cultures attempt to come to terms with the realities of living with one another in an ever smaller global environment. U.S. policymakers have erred in the past by failing to understand that Mexico's acceptance of U.S. predominance and the necessity of close ties with its northern neighbor has not negated Mexican nationalism, its adherence to national self-determination, or its own agenda in the hemisphere. As much as the Salinas opening is a sharp move toward the neo-conservative agenda that dominated the United States, Canada and Great Britain in the 1980s, an older, more traditional Mexico remains, with other preferred models of development and approaches to the United States. The Chiapas uprising represents at least one component of that other Mexico. It is a reminder to U.S. and Mexican leaders alike that Mexico has many voices. The narrow victory of President Clinton's forces in Congress in support of NAFTA is another reminder that Americans as well remain ambiguous about the U.S. relationship with Mexico. Thus, NAFTA may improve and strengthen the formal mechanisms for managing the bilateral relationship. The question is, will these mechanisms be able to deal with the asymmetrical interdependence that characterizes relations between the two societies.

Notes

1. Louis Perez, "Dependency," in Michael Hogan and Thomas Paterson, eds., *Explaining the History of American Foreign Relations* (Cambridge: Cambridge University Press, 1991).

2. Michael H. Hunt, *Ideology and United States Foreign Policy* (New Haven: Yale University Press, 1987).

3. Peter H. Smith and Osario Green, eds., *Foreign Policy in U.S.-Mexican Relations* (San Diego: University of California Center for U.S.-Mexican Studies,

1989), p. 2.

4. Green and Smith, (p. 7) appear to accept uncritically George Kennan's notions that U.S. policy is characteristically lacking in realpolitik. For Kennan's views see George F. Kennan, *American Diplomacy 1900-1950* (Chicago: University of Chicago Press, 1951). For a corrective to Kennan, see Michael Hunt, *Ideology and United States Foreign Policy*; Thomas J. McCormick, *America's Half-Century: United States Foreign Policy in the Cold War* (Baltimore: Johns Hopkins University Press, 1989).

5. W. dirk Raat, *Mexico and the United States: Ambivalent Vistas* (Athens: University of Georgia Press, 1992), p. 150.

6. Ibid., pp. 150-52. Robert Pastor, former National Security Adviser for Latin America in the Carter administration incorrectly suggests that Mexicans "first began journeying north to the United States in very large numbers" in the early 1960s. See Pastor, "NAFTA as the Center of an Integration Process: The Nontrade Issues," *Brookings Review* (Winter 1993), pp. 40-45. Pastor fails to understand the earlier integration impact of World War II and the Cold War and the large scale migration that began with the development of irrigation in the Southwest U.S. early in the century and the curtailment of European immigration by American law in the 1920s, which created substantial demand for both Mexican and Canadian (often French Canadian) labor.

7. Raat, *Mexico and the United States*, pp. 156-57.

8. Ibid., p. 159.

9. Melvin A. Conant and Fern R. Gold, *The Geopolitics of Energy* U.S. Senate, Committee on Interior and Insular Affairs (Washington: U.S. Government Printing Office, 1977), pp. 138, 146.

10. Castañeda cited in Cathryn Thorup, "U.S. Policy Toward Mexico: Prospects for Administrative Reform," in Green and Smith, *Foreign Policy in U.S.-Mexican Relations*, p.140.

11. Department of State. Background Briefing on U.S.-Mexican Binational Commission, April 17, 1984, *American Foreign Policy Current Documents*.

12. Miguel Ramirez, "The IMF Austerity Program, 1983-1987: Miguel de la Madrid's Legacy," *Occasional Papers in Latin American Studies*, University of Connecticut, July 1989.

13. Jorge Chabat, "The Making of Mexican Policy Toward the United States," in Green and Smith, *Foreign Policy in US-Mexican Relations*, p.76.

14. Raat, *Mexico and the United States*, pp. 162-66. On the narcotics issue see Carlos Rico, "The Making of US Policy Toward Mexico: Should we expect coherence?" in Green and Smith, *Foreign Policy in U.S.-Mexico Relations*, pp. 113, 116-117.

15. Rico, "The Making of US Policy Toward Mexico," p. 113.

16. Green and Smith, *Foreign Policy in US-Mexican Relations*, p.11.

17. Claude Heller, "U.S. and Mexican Policies Toward Central America," in Green and Smith, *Foreign Policy in U.S.-Mexican Relations*, pp. 172, 174, 177, 201. Stephen J. Randall, "La Política Exterior de Los Estados Unidos de América y el futuro de la democracia en Centro-América," in Monica Verea Campos and José Luis Barros Horcasitas, eds., *La Política Exterior Norteamericana hacia*

Centroamérica: reflexiones y perspectivas (México: Miguel Angel Porrua, 1991), pp. 379-94.

18. White House, Office of the Press Secretary, Background Briefing on the Visit of President de la Madrid, May 14, 1984, *American Foreign Policy Current Documents.*

19. Department of State, background Briefing on U.S.-Mexican Relations, March 11, 1985, *American Foreign Policy Current Documents.* Significantly, in terms of the relevance of Canada to the U.S.-Mexico bilateral relationship, the two parties on that occasion noted that the U.S. had just concluded a salmon treaty with Canada and that the lessons learned in that instance might be applied to the tuna dispute. In fact, the tuna dispute eluded bilateral resolution, and the GATT found in favor of Mexico.

20. There is an insightful discussion of the "special relationship" in David Ronfeldt and Caesar Sereseres, "The Management of U.S.-Mexico Interdependence: Drift Toward Failure?" in Carlos Vásquez and Manuel García y Griego, eds., *Mexican-U.S. Relations, Conflict and Convergence* (Los Angeles: University of California, 1983), pp. 43-108; see also Mario Ojeda, *Alcanes y limites de la política exterior de México* (México D.F.: El Colegio de México, 1976). The impact of the Cuban revolution on U.S.-Mexican relations is examined in Olga Pellicer de Brody, *México y la revolución Cubana* (México D.F.: El Colegio de México, 1972). For the anvil metaphor, see Robert Quirk, "Mexico and the United States," in Curtis Wilgus, ed., *The Caribbean: Mexico Today* (Gainesville: University of Florida Press, 1963), pp. 193-98.

21. *The Mexico-United States Interparliamentary Group, A sixteen Year History,* a Report by Sen. Mike Mansfield, Majority Leader, U.S. Senate, to the Senate Foreign Relations Committee (Washington: U.S. Government Printing Office, 1976).

22. Department of State, Background briefing on Secretary Schultz's Trip to Mexico, July 24, 1985, *American Foreign Policy Current Documents.*

23. Cathryn Thorup, "U.S. Policy Toward Mexico", pp. 140-45.

24. Carter appointed Robert Krueger to the office.

25. Richard Craig, "U.S. Narcotics Policy Toward Mexico," in Guadalupe Gonzalez and Marta Tienda, eds., *The Drug Connection in U.S.-Mexican Relations* (San Diego: University of California at San Diego Center for U.S.-Mexico Studies, 1989), p. 76.

26. Jorge Chabat, "The Making of Mexican Policy toward the United States," in Green and Smith, *Foreign Policy in U.S.-Mexican Relations,* pp. 74-75, 80, 84, 94, 100-103.

27. Chabat, "The Making of Mexican Policy," p. 79.

28. Joseph S. Nye, Jr., "Independence and Interdependence," *Foreign Policy* (Spring, 1976), p. 138.

6

Convergent Paths Toward Integration: The Unequal Experiences of Canada and Mexico

Gustavo del Castillo

Introduction

Mexico and Canada are separated by distance. But more than that, they are separated by the specific characteristics of what lies between them -- the United States -- and the particular relationship each country has maintained with this intervening entity. The asymmetrical bilateral relationship that both Canada and Mexico have with the United States has impeded fundamental understanding between these two distant neighbors. This asymmetry has a long history, and it is likely to endure for some time to come.

The underlying precept of this work is that this imbalanced relationship has forced Canada and Mexico to ignore each other, and to focus instead on their respective relations with the United States. The attacks and defeats suffered from Fort York to San Jacinto compelled these two weaker nations to contend with their stronger neighbor. This chapter will explore whether Canada and Mexico have bases other than this prevailing asymmetry on which to establish a relationship, or whether through increasing integration this fundamental historical trend can be broken. If the latter is true, then both Mexico and Canada will witness a historic reversal which might indeed change the North American continent. This in part is what has driven many Mexican "integrationists" to support the North American free trade area as a first step in what undoubtedly will be many measures needed to bring these two nations together. Paradoxically, while the United States has been the factor separating these countries, it may also be the factor that facilitates their integration.

The Nature of Asymmetry in North America

To understand why Canada and Mexico disregarded one another from the beginning of the nineteenth century to the end of the twentieth, one has to comprehend the nature of asymmetry as it exists in North America. Until the early twentieth century, Canada was in no position to dictate how it would articulate with its common neighbors because of its colonial status. On the other hand, the independent status of Mexico helps to explain its nineteenth century fortunes and developing dependency on the United States. You can't win for trying. Still, the United States' monopoly over North Atlantic trade during the nineteenth century (as of 1812 the United States had the largest merchant marine in the Western Hemisphere) made possible a process of capital accumulation which fostered that country's early industrialization. Canada's wealth found an intermediary in Great Britain.

Mexico, meanwhile, held an ongoing debate for much of the nineteenth century over the best means to foster accumulation, and in the process engaged in a fratricidal conflict between liberals and conservatives. One important factor to be kept in mind is that the hegemonic position of the United States with respect to Caribbean and North Atlantic trade effectively isolated Mexico and forced Canada to turn to its parent country. In this respect, Mexico had to look inward as a strategy for development. When both Canada and Mexico gazed outward, they focused on the United States. It was fortunate for Canada that manifest destiny never looked north, and that the United States' national consolidation was achieved at Mexico's expense.[1] If Mexicans had burned the White House in 1812, the United States would have reached the same detente with Mexico as it did with Great Britain. Under the protection of Great Britain, Canadians could settle the land between the Atlantic and the Pacific in peace, while Mexicans developed a persecution and inferiority complex resulting in a wall as protective and daunting as the Great Wall of China. From 1847 on, Mexicans distrusted and avoided Anglo-Saxons; when this outlook gave way in 1991, it signified a revolution as meaningful and profound as the Mexican Revolution of 1910. Unfortunately, the Mexican wall had blocked the view to Canada as well as to the United States. As neighbors we are now peering over that wall and discovering what we have been missing. How U.S., Canadian and Mexican relations have developed since the nineteenth century has to do with each country's respective power positions, in both continental and global terms. The U.S. hegemonic position, combined with Britain's domination over Canada, left Mexico in a decidedly weak and inferior situation on the continent, inwardly oriented and capital starved because of internal warfare.

Thus, while both Canada and Mexico were fundamentally agrarian societies, they were distinguished by the position each occupied vis-à-vis the dominant centers of power at the time. Canada faced grain export surpluses, while Mexico remained a subsistence economy. Those regions of Mexico that were able to generate surpluses immediately found international markets for their products: cotton from the Comarca Lagunera went to Union forces during the Civil War; hemp from Yucatan supplied the U.S. Navy and merchant marine. Export performance in these industries created regional economic elites (in Torreón-Saltillo-Monterrey and Mérida) and an incipient capitalism which made possible early regional industrialization, with its concomitant need for planning.[2]

The Canadian experience differed markedly from that of Mexico; the most significant difference being the relationship between Canada and Great Britain. Whatever protection Canada had from U.S. encroachment was due to Great Britain's enormous power in a unipolar world during the second half of the nineteenth century. American efforts during this period were aimed at breaking this link in order to gain access to Canadian resources. Canadian-U.S. trade at this time already indicated the future directions that this relationship would follow. By 1886, 44 percent of Canadian trade was with the United States, 46 percent by 1921, and 68 percent in 1982.[3] Nevertheless, because of the industrialization process taking place simultaneously in Great Britain and the United States, agricultural and wood export prices gained in Canada, and there was always an influx of capital from Great Britain. Canadian policy thus had to focus, not only on a central power across the Atlantic, but also on the United States. While focusing on the latter, Canada tried to obtain the advantages of free trade through the Treaty of Reciprocity in 1854. During this time:

> The average farmer's export of wheat doubled from 45 bushels in the 1840s to 80 in the 1850s, and went as high as 135 bushels in the 1860s. Improved transportation on the St. Lawrence-Great Lakes with the completion of the canal system lowered transport costs and reduced insurance rates, all helped to increase Canadian exports.[4]

Still, Canada's exports and its growing trade relationship with the

United States would have been all the more difficult if Great Britain had not put faith in Adam Smith's free trade and implemented such policies as the repeal of the restrictionist Corn Laws. The province of Canada was allowed to choose its own foreign economic policy, whatever its results might be. Fortunately for Canada, the United States abrogated the 1854 Treaty of Reciprocity in 1866, forcing the issue of Canadian identity and nationality,[5] not to mention the development of a domestic industrial policy. From 1866 to 1911, when the United States proposed a bilateral trade agreement with Canada, both countries fostered their national industrialization projects through the imposition of trade barriers and tariffs.

Since 1776, when Benjamin Franklin proposed the union of English-speaking peoples in all the British colonies of North America, the United States has fixed on gaining access to the raw materials of Canada and Mexico. The 1854 Treaty of Reciprocity focused entirely on Canada's raw materials; no manufactured products being included. Yet, when a similar reciprocity trade deal was negotiated between Mexico and the United States in 1883, the exchange was unequal: the U.S. was to receive Mexican raw materials in exchange for American manufactured products.

The 1883 Reciprocity Treaty admitted thirty Mexican products into the United States duty free and underscored that no manufacturing would be involved, e.g., hule *sin manufacturar*, madera *sin labrar*, paja *sin manufacturar*, pieles de chivo *sin curtir*, tabaco en rama *sin manufacturar*, etc. (emphasis added). On the other hand, Mexico would admit seventy-four such U.S. products:

> Arados y sus rejas, bombas para incendios y bombas comunes para riegos, casas completas de madera ó hierro, instrumentos para las ciencias, instrumentos de acero, hierro, bronce, ó madera, locomotoras, máquinas de vapor, máquinas de coser, máquinas y aparatos de todas clases para la industria, la agricultura, la minería, las ciencias y las artes, y sus partes sueltas ó piezas de refacción, etc.

In his evaluation of the treaty, the Mexican chief negotiator, Matias Romero wrote, "If we judge by the actual exchange between the United States and Mexico, it would be just to admit ... that the benefits from free trade are in favor of our northern neighbor."[6] The House of Representatives' Ways and Means Committee report on the agreement acknowledged, "It is true that machines and apparatus of all sorts for industry, agriculture, mining, the sciences and the arts, and parts for repairs are included in the list of free trade products but," it observed, "what kind of market exists for these goods in a country that doesn't use them and doesn't need them?"7 Why would any country want to establish commercial relations with a nation such as Mexico when (a friendly) Treasury Agent J.F. Evans, sent to Mexico to report on conditions in the country, wrote back:

> The Mexican people are not at all progressive. With their variety of climates, lands, and other advantages, they have nothing but the more rudimentary arts, they have no literature nor school system; they have no modern agricultural machinery, or for that matter, they have no knowledge of their people since they have never taken a population census, and they have only one kind of food for seven eighths of their population .... Mexico is not a republic in the true sense of the word, it is a military despotic system, based on the bayonets of soldiers recruited in the jails.8

Between concluding the Treaty of Reciprocity with Canada in 1854 and signing the Reciprocity Treaty with Mexico in 1883, the United States suffered through a civil war and began the long process of industrialization and national consolidation. While raw materials had been a priority in its nation-building process, the selling of manufactured products took on a new priority by the end of the nineteenth century. The cancellation of the Treaty of Reciprocity with Canada reflected the changes in the U.S. economy as well as the belief that if Canadians wished to continue trading with the United States after the cancellation of the agreement, they would be enticed (forced) to join the Union. If a favorable agreement could be had with Mexico, it would reinforce the changes in the U.S. economy; and, if Mexico ever developed, it would represent a large export market, much different than the limited Canadian market. In this context then, the United States employed a consistent two-track approach: protectionism toward Canada, and free trade with Mexico. Although the agreement with Mexico was negotiated in 1883, in 1886, the implementing legislation still had not been drawn up in the U.S. Congress, because of opposition from sugar and tobacco industries. These industries felt they needed protection against what could have been major export surges from Mexico once capital investments began flowing into this resource rich country.

The pattern of U.S. foreign economic policy in the nineteenth century and Canada's isolation from Mexico clearly resemble the "hub and spokes" model outlined in the discussions over the North American Free Trade Agreement (NAFTA) in the early 1990s.9 The isolation of these two countries did not reflect an intentional disregard for one another, but rather the structural outcome of their respective relationships with the United States. In sum, the structure developed in North America during the nineteenth century was the outcome of the consolidation of U.S. hegemony on the continent, made possible by detente between the United States and Britain, by the lack of integration and the development of national economies in Mexico and Canada. Also, both Canada and Mexico undertook national development plans under the guise of mercantilism, effectively closing their economies, and their foreign economic policy followed these steps. From this zero-sum perspective, both of these economies would secure benefits only from their main trading partner; they gave no heed to the possible benefits that might emerge from economic interaction between the two minor members of the triangle.

Contemporary Asymmetry and Relations
between Canada and Mexico

From the first bilateral approaches that Canada and Mexico made toward the United States, the aim of both countries was to deal with the most relevant regional actor. At the end of the twentieth century, this hegemonic regional actor is itself being transformed by the end of the Cold War, by the processes of global production, by the evolution of international trading organizations such as the General Agreement on Tariffs and Trade (GATT), and by the commitment of Canada and Mexico to a new found bilateralism. These transformations are significant enough to alter the nature of economic relations in North America and require that mechanisms be found to address these changes.

I suggest that NAFTA, as well as the Enterprise for the Americas Initiative (EAI), represent the response of the United States to the challenges posed by Japan and the European Union as it seeks to preserve the economic hegemony it gained after the Second World War.[10] At a first glance, this seems like a simple proposition (or an extension of dependency theory), but in fact it involves new approaches to the management of capitalist production, generalized throughout the world since the collapse of the Communist alternative.[11]

The conflict over new approaches to capitalist evolution arises because of the Republican party's slow but determined forging of an ideology in the United States beginning with the election of Richard Nixon in 1968 and persisting through the presidency of George Bush. The Republican party's domination of the White House for a third of a century led to the diminution of the state as a relevant social actor. This resulted from the rediscovery of Adam Smith's faith in market forces as the determining factors in economic exchange, allocation, and distribution of wealth in a society. Because the process of European integration has necessitated active state intervention in defining social and economic welfare in all the countries involved, and because of a different historical tradition, the state continues to be an important social actor.[12] The Japanese experience in regaining economic development and the rise of new regional economic actors such as Korea, Taiwan, and China have involved the active participation of the state in the management and definition of capitalist practices and strategic economic goals.

Relating this perspective to the processes of economic integration in North America, it can be seen that what is at stake, at least from the perspective of the United States, is whether Canada and Mexico -- who have asked for preferential trading status -- will play by U.S. rules. In other words, the price for the Canada-U.S. Free Trade Agreement (CUSFTA) or NAFTA to succeed is whether the countries involved agree with the ideology that now relegates the state to the role of manager. Should this ideology prevail, the United States would benefit in several ways:

1. Accepting the "state as manager" principle obviously advances this ideology over the "interventionist" approach existing in the European Union and Japan.

2. It consolidates North America, and the rest of Latin America, within the U.S. camp. And, having been successful in this endeavor,

3. It brings thirty some nations to put pressure on the multilateral system (the GATT) to adapt the international trading rules to the ideology now being fostered by the United States.

In this context, CUSFTA and NAFTA take on strategic significance for the United States. If that country persists in its belief that the state is irrelevant, the trading nations that receive preferential treatment will have to operate within strict parameters, and any deviation could be very costly. That is to say, maintaining this system of beliefs by operationalizing it through a formal trade agreement -- be it CUSFTA or NAFTA -- will produce a trading system in competition with that being developed by the European Union or the trading practices of Pacific Basin countries. Because system maintenance would have taken on strategic importance, countries that involve the state to any significant degree -- for example, through the application of subsidies or the feeble application of sanctions against intellectual property violators -- will now not just violate U.S. trade law, they will threaten the trading system being developed. Violators will be harshly sanctioned.

I believe that this perspective has other consequences, which have not been discussed by North American specialists. Since I have argued that system maintenance will be of primary importance, then mechanisms already in place which may threaten the system will have a short life span. It is in this context that we have to consider the successful operation of Chapter 19 of CUSFTA and the possible application of Chapter 20 of NAFTA, concerning the resolution of trade disputes. The bilateral CUSFTA dispute settlement panels operating to date have questioned the administrative procedures through which U.S. trade law is implemented, and reversed Commerce Department decisions. Therefore, I would argue, there will be enormous constituency pressure on Congress to modify or nullify panel decisions in order to maintain the trading system developing from the signing of CUSFTA.[13] In other words, transnational actors in the form of these panels have put in question the actions of national actors intent on reinforcing the hegemonic nature of U.S. power.

The fact that transnational actors have some relevance in the management of U.S. trade law will be increasingly unacceptable to American domestic actors, both public and private. This is particularly meaningful because of the global context in which the U.S. economy must now operate. That is, an increasingly competitive global economy and the declining participation of the United States, especially in comparison to the highly competitive Japanese economy and that of the European Union, have resulted in increased protectionism in the United States (trade surpluses by other countries are galling to the United States, just as are the achievements resulting from successful high research and public development outlays, the European Airbus being a notable example). In this context, it should be expected that calls for neoprotectionist policies will be heard at times when the United States suffers from some type of cyclical economic downturn, and when a strong U.S. dollar hinders export possibilities. At such times, global trade reform in the U.S. context tends to mean managed trade, where the United States will gain some advantage -- usually some type of quota or voluntary export restriction -- giving some breathing room to affected domestic industries. It should be noted that these types of neoprotectionist (and anti-GATT) policies become operationalized through bilateral agreements.[14]

Within the present context of NAFTA, the most obvious instrument of control that the United States has imposed on its trade with Mexico is the side agreements on import surges, thought to be possible because of the foreign direct investment (FDI) which supposedly will flow to Mexico to take advantage of low labor costs in the production of goods to be exported to the U.S. market. If FDI to Mexico were limited to U.S. multinationals, it would be less certain that this form of managed trade would be imposed. But the real fear of both the United States and Canada is that FDI will come from Europe and the Far East, using Mexico as a back door into North American markets (even though such exports may meet NAFTA rules of origin).

The United States is not the only country within NAFTA that is utilizing and introducing some form of protection into the agreement. Canada has sought protection from transnational institutions infringing in domestic politics by not accepting the environmental sanctions and procedures of the environment commission and the panel findings, instead insisting that Canadian courts handle all sanction questions applying to Canada.[15] Yet this Canadian exemption from the agreement differs from U.S. practices within the context of the argument that I am making here. That is, whereas U.S. retaliation and protection occur because of the desire to maintain the system and structure of trade being developed in North America, while retaining the status quo influence of domestic actors, Canadian protection is aimed at maintaining only the predominance of domestic actors through the rejection of the sanction procedures on environmental issues. It is important to note that this Canadian position has evolved since CUSFTA was negotiated, when Canada sought protection from U.S. unilateral decisions by pushing hard for the Chapter 19 procedures. Now it seems that the acceptance of transnational actors in Canadian life is somewhat diminished, with Canada opting instead to return toward provincialist nationalism.

Thus, the evolutionary steps that North America is taking are composed of at least three elements. First, there is the U.S. position that North America engage in trade practices that are congruent with the Republican belief in the operations of market forces, while diminishing the role of the state. Second, both Canada and the United States appear to be content with the status quo operations of internal actors, and oppose the transnationalization of conflict resolution procedures. Finally, the opposition to the increased participation of transnational actors has reinforced continued nationalism.

Given these elements, the principal question becomes, how can the two marginal nations, Mexico and Canada, influence a trading bloc ideology developed out of the loss of U.S. economic hegemony, the globally uncompetitive position of many manufacturing firms in the continent, and the debt ridden nature of the countries of North America?[16]

The range of influence -- that is, the number of dimensions which would have to be touched in U.S. society, economy and government -- is certainly not small given the complex nature of the United States and the myriad forms through which individuals, forms of production and private and public institutions are interwoven.[17] Also of concern are the forms and mechanisms utilized by either Canada or Mexico to influence and determine policy outcomes in the United States. Yet as the interaction and the intensity of tripartite relationships increase, two additional concerns about U.S. influence loom on the horizon. The first is the possible entry and expansion into Canada and Mexico of political processes prevalent in the United States that follow from the adoption of similar public institutions. The second is the importance that U.S. *intermestic* policies will have for the rest of North America. (Intermestic policies refer to domestic policy decisions that affect other countries' internal politics.)

In the process of negotiating international trade agreements, North America has developed institutions and processes that are alike in function, occupy roughly similar positions within the trade bureaucracies, and are answerable to parliamentary bodies. One of the clearest cases of institutional diffusion is the development of private sector trade advisory groups (TAGs) in the United States and their later appearance in Canada and Mexico. These trade advisory groups are the mechanism utilized by these three nations to relate the private sector to trade policy makers during international trade negotiations and during each country's respective legislative process.[18] The structuring of TAGs in the United States during the early 1960's and in Canada at the time of the free trade negotiations with the United States represents an attempt to formalize and limit the impact of lobbyists on trade policy. These initial premises have not been met in the United States, since TAGs have become an integral part of the Washington political process and indispensable actors which the U.S. Trade Representative and Congress must consult. In Canada the International Trade Advisory Committee (ITAC) and the Sectoral Advisory Groups on International Trade (SAGITs) are now also an integral part of the trade process, unmovable actors that have to be consulted.

The institutionalization of the ITAC and SAGITs has gone further in Canada than in the United States, and certainly much more so than in Mexico, where the Coordinadora de Organismos Empresariales de Comercio Exterior (COECE), organized as a private institution and invited to play an advisory role in the NAFTA negotiations -- a good example of the patronizing role of the Mexican government -- has no formal linkage function joining the private sector to the legislative process. In other words, a structure similar to those existing in the United States and Canada was set up in Mexico, but it plays a much different role than its counterparts in the rest of North America. The argument that I would like to make is that the institutionalization of such structures in democratic societies such as Canada and the United States represent rational options which respond to a democratic political process, while the Mexican COECE is a structure absent of process.

The question to be asked is whether structures such as the TAGs, which are being created to address specific problems of policy-making, can, in the long run, also affect the political process as well. Put differently, do structures operating within specific political systems begin to operate similarly, transforming and "harmonizing" the different political systems that have adopted them? Some would argue that trade practices or trade policies as reflected in different trade agreements are certainly not the measures to transform political systems. Nevertheless, historical experience seems to indicate differently: the case of the European Union demonstrates how trade practices involving fiscal and monetary harmonization and harmonized custom procedures lead systems to look the same -- to the point where the most intransigent believers in national policies or national autonomy (Thatcherism) argue against the loss of sovereignty, while political systems burdened by corrupt business-governmental alliances, such as the Italian case, have been forced to restructure politically.[19] The limited experience of North America along these lines cannot be held up as an example of a valid counterproposition. What is certain is that in the European integration experience none of the countries involved wield the hegemonic power of the United States, which may be the greatest roadblock to North American integration.

When David Ronfeldt wrote about the nature of intermestic politics in the United States he was not thinking of how such politics would affect the process of economic integration. If anything, the nature of intermestic politics posed problems for the bilateral relations of the United States with other countries.[20] Because of the hegemonic power that the United States exercises in North America, the effects of intermestic politics were conceptualized to run in one direction -- from the center hub toward peripheral countries like Mexico and Canada. I would argue that given an increasingly integrated region, these effects can be bidirectional, affecting the hub as well as the periphery. Also, as integration progresses to dimensions other than the economic, intermestic politics will also affect the social and political life in the countries of North America; that is, intermesticity will diminish nationality.

This presents a paradox in that the domestic policies of each of the countries of North America will increasingly encroach on the internal politics of other national actors. But since the process of integration will be on the rise and the costs of withdrawal from the emerging economic system too high, structures will have to be found to regulate the dominions of intermesticity. Because these structures cannot be unilateral, the hypothesis put forward here is that national actors would opt, in the long run, for some form of transnational institutions to act as arbiters between the countries of North America.

I believe that the paradox facing Canada and Mexico is that having to deal with the United States imposes issues of integration which are markedly different from those facing the European Union. The European experience has demonstrated that integration can proceed incrementally. This incrementalism is the product of long historical traditions, which has resulted from the existence of many and diverse nation-states. North America, on the other hand, is composed of a limited number of young nation-states, although it suffers from the presence of the most resilient of them all, the United States. In this context, the most rational proposition would be that integration and the construction of transnational institutions will be hindered by the dominance of the United States and that integration will be a very long, conflictive, and drawn-out process. Yet the nature of intermesticity in North America can be conceptualized as an accelerator of integration.

Nevertheless, the question remains, whose intermestic affairs will demand the most responses in the North American context? If we work from the premise that U.S. policy and process will remain unchallenged, then both Mexico and Canada will continue to feel the impacts of and react to U.S. intermestic policies. There can be only one response in an integrating North America: both Canada and Mexico must develop national policies that are inherently intermestic so as to challenge unilateral U.S. policies and at the same time force the United States to seek mechanisms to lessen the impact of these intermestic politics. The only resulting mechanisms in an intermestic North America are transnational institutions for conflict resolution and rule-making. In this sense, the remaining regional power of the U.S. will bring about a more rapid process of integration in North America than anyone expects, and will not follow the linear, incremental nature of the European experience but will take quantum leaps. In this respect, our minds will have to be ready to prognosticate these changes and be ready to adapt to rapidly changing conditions, be they the result of public policy failures or successes.

Notes

1. There is no doubt that the U.S., from the time of the Continental Army under George Washington until the aftermath of the War of 1812, always looked north, hoping to increase its territory and revolutionary converts. Having obtained part of the old province of Quebec, it let territorial conquest rest. Manifest destiny was always applied to what U.S. Anglo-Saxons considered inferior peoples, such as Mexicans and the different indigenous groups living in what is now the United States, but it did not include British born Canadians or French Canadians.

2. For a discussion of the relations between the U.S. and Yucatán, and elite behavior see, Gilbert M. Joseph. "The United States, Feuding Elites and Rural Revolt in Yucatán, 1836-1915" in Daniel Nugent, ed., *Rural Revolt in Mexico and U.S. Intervention* (Center for U.S.-Mexican Studies: University of California, San Diego, 1988).

3. Data appears in Gordon T. Stewart "Three Lessons for Mexico From Canadian-American Relations" in *Frontera Norte*. Vol. 3, No. 6 (July-December 1991).

4. R. Douglas Francis, Richard Jones and Donald B. Smith. *Origins: Canadian History to Confederation*, (Toronto: Holt, Rinehart and Winston, 1988), p. 273.

5. It is reported that when Henry David Thoreau visited Montreal he asked a bookseller for books published locally and was told that there were none. Most were bought in the United States, with the exception of textbooks. See Randall White, *Fur Trade to Free Trade. Putting the Canada-U.S. Trade Agreement in Historical Perspective* (Toronto: Dundurn Press, 1988).

6. Matias Romero. *Reciprocidad comercial entre México y los Estados Unidos* (Oficina Tip. de la Secretaría de Fomento. México, D.F. 1890), p. 19 (author's translation).

7. Ibid, p. 24.

8. Ibid. p. 34.

9. See, Ronald J. Wonnacott, "U.S. Hub and Spoke Bilaterals and the Multilateral Trading System," C.D. Howe Institute, *Commentary* No. 23, October 1990. See also, Richard Lipsey, "Growth, Erosion and Restructuring of the Multilateral Trading System," Paper presented at the Annual Meetings of the American Economics Association, Atlanta, Georgia. December 1989.

10. For a discussion of the rise of protectionism in the United States as a consequence of the diminished power of the U.S. hegemon, see Helen Milner, "Trading Places: Industries for Free Trade," in John S. Odell and Thomas D. Willett, eds., *International Trade Policy Gains from Exchange Between Economics and Political Science* (Ann Arbor: University of Michigan Press, 1993).

11. Lester Thurow. *Head to Head. The Coming Economic Battle Among Japan,*

Europe, and America (New York: Warner Books, Inc. , 1992).

12. E.V.K. Fitzgerald. "The Restructuring of the Mexican and U.S. Economies: A European View," Paper prepared for the meeting of the "Chapultepec Group," Stanford University, November 1980.

13. This perspective would seem to be contradictory -- change or destroy the system in order to maintain it. Yet, from an American perspective it has all the logic in the world. Consider President Johnson's position on Vietnam - destroy it so it can be saved. American history is made up of multiple examples of pyrrhic victories.

14. Good examples of this are the quota agreement on microchips from Japan and the voluntary export restrictions on automobiles, also from Japan. The steel industry cases have evolved over time, first appearing as voluntary export restrictions and changing to anti-subsidy or dumping cases due to eagerness of the Commerce Department.

15. *Inside U.S. Trade.* August 20, 1993.

16. See Gustavo del Castillo. "El tratado de libre comercio y las empresas manufactureras mexicanas." *Comercio Exterior.* Vol. 41. No. 7 (July 1991). Also see, Gustavo del Castillo and Gustavo Vega. "Perspectivas sobre el libre comercio: Un estudio comparado de empresas mexicanas y canadienses." *Frontera Norte,* Vol. 3, No. 6 (July-December 1991).

17. There is a rich intellectual tradition which attempts to analyze the problems of influence, class, and policy outcomes in the United States. Four texts which stand out are those of Gabriel Kolko, *Wealth and Power in America. An Analysis of Social Class and Income Distribution* (New York: Praeger Publishers, Inc. , 1962); G. William Domhoff, *The Powers That Be: Process of Ruling Class Domination in America* (New York: Vintage Books Edition, 1979); Manuel Castells. *The Economic Crisis and American Society* (Princeton: Princeton University Press, 1980). More recently see Kevin Phillips, *The Politics of Rich and Poor: Wealth and the American Electorate in the Reagan Aftermath* (New York: Harper Perennial, 1990). These authors depart from the classic work by Robert H. Dahl, *Who Governs?* (New Haven: Yale University Press, 1961) in that the premises of democratic institutions and government are seriously questioned, leading to conclusions radically different than those arrived at by Dahl.

18. For an in-depth treatment of the subject of the different trade advisory groups in North America see, Gustavo del Castillo "Private Sector Trade Advisory Groups in North America: A Comparative Perspective." Unpublished manuscript.

19. In the U.S. debate over NAFTA, two of the most outspoken critics, Pat Buchanan and Ross Perot, argued against the loss of sovereignty implied in the agreement.

20. See David Ronfeldt and Caesar Sereseres. "The Management of U.S.-Mexican Interdependence: Drift Toward Failure?" RAND Corporation, Santa Monica, CA, January, 1978. Also see, Bayless Manning. "The Congress, the Executive and Intermestic Affairs: Three Proposals." *Foreign Affairs.* Vol. 55, No.2 (January 1977), pp. 306-324.

PART THREE

Perspectives on
North American Integration

7

Mexico, Latin America
and the Group of Three
in the Context of NAFTA

Gustavo Vega Canovas

Introduction

This chapter analyzes the factors that led Mexico to negotiate the North American Free Trade Agreement (NAFTA) and explores the relevance of this initiative for that country's future relationship with Latin America, especially with Colombia and Venezuela, within the so-called Group of Three (G3). It argues that NAFTA was part of a broader Mexican strategy of fostering Latin American economic integration in order to diversify its trade and investment relations and to reinforce its commercial autonomy. The complementarity of Mexican, Venezuelan and Colombian interests make the G3 the most promising avenue for pursuing this goal. The chapter is divided into three parts. Part one discusses the factors that led Mexico to open up its economy and to negotiate NAFTA. The second section summarizes the main provisions of the agreement and their relevance for Mexico's economic relations with Latin America. The final part considers the origins and evolution of free trade discussions of the G3 and the goals of the three countries.

Mexican policy in the G3 is guided by three fundamental principles, namely, the search for new markets, the diversification of exports, and the strengthening of economic cooperation with Central America. The capture of new markets has been an important objective of Mexican trade policy since the 1960s, when the Latin American countries in general, and the Central American countries in particular, accelerated their economic integration, establishing such mechanisms as the Latin American Free Trade Association (LAFTA), the Central American Common Market (CACM), and the Andean Pact. This objective was strengthened during the 1970s, when the discovery of big petroleum deposits and the failure to reach an agreement with the United States on the sale of natural gas, the so-called "gas fiasco", made the Mexican government adopt a deliberate policy of reducing Mexico's dependence on the American market. As part of this policy, Mexico decided not to sell more than 51 percent of its petroleum exports to a single country, and to look for alternative markets for its trade. The goal of diversification regained prominence soon after the fall of oil prices, in 1981, and their virtual collapse in 1986.

Mexico's Economic Opening

Mexico's decision to restructure its economy and seek free trade with the United States (and eventually with Canada) was a result of a number of internal and external factors, among the most important of which was the shift to an outward-led development strategy in the mid 1980s. For over 40 years, Mexico's approach had emphasized growth based on the internal market. However, the weakness of world oil prices and the scarcity of external funds following Mexico's debt crisis caused the Mexican government to break with tradition in its import substitution policies, and to seek more revenues through exports. The failure of the import substitution model was not only that it had created an inefficient industrial structure but also that, to a large degree, it had been unable to generate a process of capital formation and accumulation to finance Mexico's industrialization.

Beginning in 1985, Mexico adopted liberalization policies that have made its economy one of the most open in the developing world. Mexico became a member of the General Agreement on Tariffs and Trade (GATT) in 1986, and the maximum Mexican tariff fell from a level of 100 percent to 20 percent between 1985 and 1990. The country also significantly liberalized its policies in such areas as foreign investment and intellectual property rights. For instance, in June 1991, Mexico passed a new law on intellectual property and the transfer of technology which included provisions: (1) increasing the patent term to 20 years, similar to that used by a number of developed countries; (2) offering product patent protection for products and processes not previously subject to protection; and (3) strengthening its trade secrets law. Mexico, in short, had a law that met many of the international standards sought by countries that export intellectual property goods and services.

Mexico's main policy objectives were to achieve rapid economic growth, reduce inflation and restore the confidence necessary to win back flight capital, and to service its large external debt. Economic policies emphasized fiscal and monetary stringency, deregulation, privatization, and further liberalization of trade and investment policies. Mexico was, therefore, serious about looking for new ways to integrate more efficiently into the global economy. Its active participation in the Uruguay Round of GATT and its interest in a free trade agreement with the United States and Canada formed part of that strategy. Since the Mexican government had already instituted substantial liberalization, the measures required to decrease protectionism in a NAFTA would have a less traumatic effect on the Mexican economy.

Mexico was also disturbed by the rise of protectionism in industrial states, so that its interest in a NAFTA was partly defensive in nature. For instance, the consolidation of the European Community (EC) that would take effect in January 1993, threatened to induce a considerable amount of trade diversion, particularly if the Uruguay Round were unsuccessful. Mexico, like Canada, saw a free trade agreement as an "insurance policy" against U.S. protectionism and as a means of gaining more assured access to its largest export market. Mexico and Canada compete in exporting various automotive, textile and apparel, furniture, petrochemical and other products. To prevent Canada from gaining a margin of preference through the Canada-U.S. Free Trade Agreement (CUSFTA) Mexico concluded that it too had to pursue the free trade option.[1]

The concern over trade diversion that would result from CUSFTA was but one problem facing Mexico. An immediate concern in 1990, after the collapse of the communist regimes in Eastern Europe, was that capital flows would be directed towards those countries and that in the competition for foreign direct investment (FDI) Mexico would lose. After attempts to attract such capital in Europe and Japan, President Salinas concluded that the most promising source would be the United States and Canada through a general free trade agreement.

NAFTA: A Model for the Rest of the Western Hemisphere?

The NAFTA agenda was broad and ambitious, including not only traditional issues like border barriers and unfair trade practices, but also new issues such as services, intellectual property and investment,

TABLE 7.1   NAFTA Negotiating Groups
_____

1.   Market Access
     -   Tariff and non-tariff barriers
     -   Rules of origin
     -   Government procurement
     -   Automobiles
     -   Other industrial sectors

2.   Trade Rules
     -   Safeguards, subsidies and trade remedies
     -   Standards

3.   Services
     -   Principles for services
     -   Financial
     -   Insurance
     -   Land transportation
     -   Telecommunications
     -   Other services

4.   Investment (Principles and Restrictions)

5.   Intellectual Property

6.   Dispute Settlement
_____
Source: Secretaría de Comercio y Formento Industrial (SECOFI)

together with dispute settlement and environmental rules. Table 7.1
shows a complete listing of the groups into which the negotiation was
divided.
     In general terms, NAFTA is an improved version of CUSFTA in that
it requires Mexico to establish equal or, in some cases, even higher
levels of trade liberalization.   NAFTA also tackles some unsettled
issues between Canada and the United States, including the protection
of intellectual property rights and provisions that distort investment,
such as the rules that require a minimum local and export content.
Under NAFTA, for example, tariff barriers and most non-tariff barriers
will be phased-out over a 10 year period, although for some sensitive
products, such as corn and beans, the phase-out period will be 15 years.[2]
Furthermore, NAFTA extends to Mexico the benefit of the dispute
settlement process of CUSFTA, and includes provisions concerning trade
in services, investment and agriculture.[3]

NAFTA's Accession Clause

NAFTA has been structured in such a way that it could become the vehicle for attaining regional plurilateralism, which would generate a coherent group of regional agreements, by means of the so-called "accession clause". Although the specific terms of this clause have not yet been clearly defined, it is important to explore the next steps towards trade liberalization. The goal of the United States is supposedly to establish free trade throughout the Western Hemisphere.[4] The question now is what will Mexico have to do to attain this goal.

The accession clause will allow NAFTA itself to be the vehicle for greater trade liberalization, that is, to provide an open door for other Latin American and Caribbean countries to enter the free trade club. The main advantage of this provision is that it will preclude the development of a pattern of "hub and spoke" agreements.[5] If NAFTA were not accessible, the United States would negotiate with countries on an individual basis or in sub-regional groups. For example, the trilateral NAFTA could be followed by a free trade agreement between the United States and Chile, which in turn would be followed by a pact with the MERCOSUR countries (Argentina, Brazil, Paraguay, and Uruguay). Mexico, Chile and the MERCOSUR countries would all benefit from free access to the United States market, but not to markets of the other U.S. partner countries. By contrast, a NAFTA which would be open to all countries of the region would lead to a more integrated and equal market in which trade would flow freely in all directions. The accession clause notion is welcomed by many Latin American countries, since there is a widespread belief that a relatively simple formula could simplify future free trade agreements. These expectations, however, could exaggerate the importance of such a provision, since an accession clause cannot "depoliticize" negotiations.

In the beginning, Mexico's interests in this clause were contradictory. Mexican negotiators were not against the accession clause notion, as demonstrated by the fact that the Mexico-Chile Economic Complementarity Agreement includes an accession clause under which other Latin American countries may join. Entry into NAFTA, however, was a completely different question. For Mexico, the U.S. market was much more important than the Chilean market or even all of the South American markets.

Mexican negotiators expected to gain special access to the U.S. market, and they preferred a bilateral rather than a trilateral negotiation which would include Canada. They were also disappointed when, in June 1990, President George Bush proposed the

Enterprise for the Americas Initiative (EAI). If, as expected, the initiative is continued by the Clinton administration and if it is successful, it will gradually erode the margin of Mexican preferences in the U.S. and Canadian markets. Nevertheless, Mexican negotiators had sound reasons not to reject the accession clause. Should the United States decide to launch further free trade discussions in the region, Mexico would be in a better position by having a place at the negotiating table. Mexico's dilemma in this respect is identical to that of Canada in 1990, when NAFTA was proposed and it was forced to participate in order to defend its interests.

There are some issues of principle and procedure concerning the accession clause which still have not been clarified. The most important of these refers to the specific terms that Latin American countries would have to comply with in order to enter NAFTA. Entry into NAFTA should be as fair, transparent, consistent and automatic as possible. The accession clause should specify the conditions of eligibility as well as the principles, practices and procedures which NAFTA members are required to observe. As well, and in order to minimize the politicization of the process, the clause should include a fast-track procedure similar to that used in the United States' legislative process.

Mexico, Latin America and the Group of Three

Mexican interests in the G3 negotiations must be seen in the context of that country's overall approach toward Latin America, which is a priority region in economic and political terms, not only for reasons of cultural identity and common heritage, but also because Latin America is a natural market for Mexico. However, for several reasons that cannot be discussed here in detail, Mexico's trade with Latin America is characterized by very low volumes in absolute terms, a relative concentration of Mexican imports and exports in a limited number of countries of the region, and by recurrent balance of payments difficulties between Mexico and the other Latin America countries.[6]

To foster a higher degree of integration, Mexico has proposed and promoted a new negotiation strategy in the region in accordance with the demands of the competitive global environment and the new politics of liberalization. The strategy tries to overcome the limitations of previous agreements and trade negotiations based on the following measures: (1) the negotiation of trade agreements that cover a wide range of products in order to eliminate sectorial distortions that hinder the optimum allocation of resources; (2) the determination of a maximum tariff among the countries negotiating an agreement, and the working out of a tariffs phase-out schedule, so that a clear tendency towards an effective liberalization, wide enough to enhance trade flows, is defined from the beginning; (3) the total elimination of non-tariff barriers for all products, except for some highly sensitive items, to guarantee that the agreed protection and its gradual phase-out are fully transparent; (4) a commitment to eliminate export subsidies and discriminatory and unequal tax charges to ensure a fair cost structure; (5) the removal of obstacles to foreign trade in transportation to reduce trade costs; (6) the drawing-up of clear and strict rules of origin to avoid triangulation; (7) the creation of transparent mechanisms for transitional safeguards; (8) the provision of fast and impartial procedures for disputes settlement; (9) the creation of sound and permanent programs of trade and investment promotion, and the gradual liberalization of services and investment, as well as an adequate protection of intellectual property; and, (10) the establishment of regional economic arrangements in accordance with the spirit of multilateralism.[7]

Based on these principles, Mexico has advanced in its negotiations with various Latin American Integration Association (ALADI) members. The first result has been the signature of a free trade agreement between Mexico and Chile. The treaty provides for the gradual removal of tariffs and the elimination of non-tariff barriers in bilateral trade. Almost all products have been grouped into two schedules: one, which includes the majority of goods, provides for the total phasing-out of tariffs by 1996; the other, which includes a very small number of products, contemplates the total liberalization by 1998. It has been proposed to apply the same sort of agreement to other Central and South American countries. In the next section the negotiations that Mexico has carried out within the G3 will be analyzed.

The Group of Three

The G3 is an offshoot of the Contadora Group, which was originally formed by Colombia, Mexico, Panama, and Venezuela to promote peace and political stability in Central America. The Contadora Group countries were not only concerned about the future of their Central American neighbors but also about the repercussions that political uncertainty and confrontation in Nicaragua and El Salvador could have for themselves.[8] The G3, created soon after the ministerial meeting of February 1989 and ratified in June of that same year, had as its main goal the completion the work of the Contadora Group. But after the conflicts in those two nations were resolved by means of elections in Nicaragua and through peace negotiations in Salvador, the G3 turned to issues of common interest, particularly those of an economic nature.

It should be borne in mind that, although the G3 has accelerated its economic agenda, its members' political and geopolitical interests in Central America and the Caribbean region still exist, especially in connection with Cuba and Haiti. The particular interests of each member may be different, but they all agree on the need to foster political stability in the region, especially since the end of the Cold War. The "pragmatic and economic" interests of G3 countries are also explained by their desire to benefit from the Enterprise for the Americas Initiative which the new government of President Clinton has committed itself to continue, although perhaps with some variations.

It appears that the most attractive issue for the G3 concerning the EAI is that of hemispheric trade, in which a regional free trade area in the hemisphere may be created, by means of bilateral or multilateral agreements.[9] Mexico as the country that has already concluded NAFTA with Canada and the United States, and a pact with Chile, could become the bridge through which Colombia and Venezuela could access the U.S. market. The three countries are also interested in increasing intra-regional trade among themselves.

The G3 has already created high level working groups in the areas of energy, trade, telecommunications, maritime and air transportation, finance, culture, tourism and cooperation with Central America and the Caribbean; and finally, a group to promote economic development in Central America.

Mexico Within the G3. Mexico's interest in trade liberalization agreements within the G3 is guided by the following objectives:

1. To improve its trade balance with Venezuela, and maintain the existing favorable level with Colombia.
2. To gain access, via the G3, to trade with the Andean Pact countries of Latin America, or with other nations with which Colombia and Venezuela may negotiate trade agreements.
3. To increase investments and economic relations with Central America, especially in the energy field, through the establishment of a major electric complex that will link Colombia, Venezuela, the Central American countries and Mexico. This project could also satisfy Mexico's energy

requirements and would increase its sales of technology to the
other countries.

4. To avoid excessive concentration of economic ties with NAFTA
   countries, especially the United States. This is particularly
   important for Mexico's concern in maintaining sovereignty and
   autonomy in its commercial policy. Alternative groupings, like
   the G3, would help to increase Mexico's political and economic
   influence in Latin America, and would also give it more
   negotiating leverage with the United States, because of the
   weight it might acquire within Latin America.

5. To expand the market for products already demanded by
   Colombia and Venezuela, or potential demands for chemical and
   petrochemical products, automobiles and auto parts, transport
   machinery, oil industry equipment and materials, basic
   electrical and electronic items, and home appliances.

In short, Mexican policy towards the G3 and Latin America is
dominated by an evident pragmatism and is the result of a shift in its
development strategy towards export led growth and a search for
foreign investment. However, there are also strong political reasons for
the integration of the G3, including concern for the political stability of
Cuba, Haiti, and Central America, which are considered as a matter of
national security for Mexico. Equally important is the need to maintain
Mexican autonomy in commercial policy towards third markets. The
Mexican government's rejection and opposition to the Torricelli Act,
which imposed limits to the commercial activities of the subsidiaries
of American companies abroad, is a clear proof of Mexico's interest in
maintaining a margin of independent action in its foreign economic
policy.

For Latin America, NAFTA represents the beginning of a more
ambitious hemispheric free trade area. It is also a model that other
countries of the region wanting similar agreements with the United
States will have to follow. Therefore, a key element of any trade
liberalization agreement will be the integration of countries in
subregional free trade blocks, such as the MERCOSUR, the Andean Pact
and the G3, before it is possible to attain an hemispheric trade
integration.[10]

Colombia and Venezuela Within the G3. Currently, the G3 appears
to be the most viable option for Colombia and Venezuela as well as for
Mexico, to establish a regional trade and investment agreement within
Latin America. Although Colombia and Venezuela have negotiated

TABLE 7.2   Intra-Regional Trade in the Americas (percent)

Exporter	Year	Total Exports ($millions)	Share of Total Exports to Regions	United States	ALADI	Andrean Pact
Colombia	1988	5,026	56.6	39.3	11.1	7.1
Mexico	1987	22,532	73.6	64.6	1.5	3.9
Venezuela	1986	8,613	65.6	52.9	3.7	4.4
U.S.A.	1988	303,380	35.1		21.5	11.2

Source: Refik Erzan and Alexander Yeats, "U.S.-Latin America Free Trade Areas: Some Empirical Evidence," in Sylvia Saborio, ed., *The Premise and the Promise: Free Trade in the Americas* (Washington: Overseas Development Council, 1992). Reprinted with the permission of Transaction Publishers.

similar   agreements within the Andean Pact and ALADI, several economic and political factors suggest that the G3 represents a better option.

First is the degree of economic restructuring that Colombia and Venezuela have undertaken compared to Ecuador and Peru, the other members of the Andean Pact, who have very reluctantly made slow progress in achieving trade and investment liberalization.[11] It is clear that, within the Andean Pact, Colombia and Venezuela are the major players and, not surprisingly, their aim in completing an agreement within the pact is to preserve and increase their influence over the other three countries.[12] However, in spite of the influence of Colombia and Venezuela in the Andean Pact, and the relative importance of Colombian trade with other Latin American countries (see Tables 7.2, 7.3 and 7.4), Mexico, Colombia and Venezuela have advanced rapidly in negotiating trade liberalization and economic cooperation, as is evident in the tariff agreements and the Mexican commitment to purchase Colombian coal.

The second factor that makes the G3 a better option is the importance of a durable economic agreement in ensuring macroeconomic stability. Colombia, Mexico and Venezuela seem to better fulfill this requirement than other Latin American countries.[13]

The third reason is that NAFTA can bring additional gains to the G3 in goods, services, capital and technology trade. Even though NAFTA will generate a certain degree of trade diversion of food, agricultural and manufactured goods from some Latin American countries, it appears

TABLE 7.3   Product Composition of Intra-Regional Trade in the G3 and the United States (percent share of all products exported to the Americas)

Exporters & destination Products	Colombia		Mexico		Venezuela		USA	
	Canada & USA	Other America	Canada & USA	Other America	Canada & USA	Other America	Canada & USA	Other America
Food and Feeds	29.5	7.3	17.2	2.4	2.3	2.6	2.9	10.9
Agricultural Materials	8.1	5.3	1.0	3.2	--	0.2	1.5	3.2
Coal and Petroleum	42.8	5.6	32.0	42.7	89.2	62.3	2.1	3.5
Ores and Metals	0.6	0.2	5.5	4.1	3.3	6.4	2.6	2.2
All Manufact. Goods	18.1	67.0	44.2	47.5	5.2	28.5	68.9	76.1
Exports to the Americas ($ millions)	2,037		13,577	1,580	4,482	764	65,287	40,793

Source: Extracted from Table 7.2

TABLE   7.4   Total Exports from ALADI Countries by Destination
                (Percentage with respect to the world total)

Destination	Year	Colombia	Mexico	Venezuela	ALADI
Developed countries	1988	70.7	87.3	67.2	69.9
	1989	76.1	89.7	68.6	n.d.
U.S.A.	1988	34.3	64.7	44.6	35.1
	1989	40.8	69.0	46.5	n.d.
EC	1988	25.5	13.3	11.9	23.5
	1989	25.7	11.9	13.4	n.d.
ALADI	1988	11.9	4.1	5.5	11.1
	1989	9.2	3.2	6.4	n.d.

Source: Juan Gonzola Zapata G., *El Grupo de los Tres: punto intermedio entre el Pacto Andino y la Iniciativa para las Américas* (Bogota, Colombia: FESCOL, April 1992).

that it will not particularly affect Colombian and Venezuelan products,[14] thereby leaving considerable potential for those countries' exports to the United States (see Table 7.5).   Moreover, trade within the G3 could increase the exports of Venezuela and Colombia to Mexico, as Mexico increases its economic growth, which is to be expected with the ratification of NAFTA.

A fourth reason propelling the G3 negotiations is the complementarity that the three countries can achieve in the energy field.   One of the most advanced working groups is the one in energy, where the G3 seems to be making rapid progress in the areas of natural gas, coal, hydroelectricity and the construction of an electric complex.

A final factor that makes the G3 a better option is the degree of economic integration that Colombia and Venezuela have already achieved in the last few years through a variety of agreements on trade liberalization, tariff reduction, investment, and the opening of borders.   This integration facilitates the G3 negotiations by eliminating obstacles between two of the three member countries.   G3 viability, compared to the Andean Pact and ALADI, is evident in the progress it has made during its brief existence.   Created in 1989, in just a

TABLE 7.5   Latin America: Exports Displaced by a NAFTA
                   (U.S.$ thousands)

Exporter	Foods & Agriculture Materials	Energy Products	Ores & Minerals	All Manufactures	TOTAL
Argentina	-743	-188		-270	-1201
Bolivia	--	-1		-18	-19
Brazil	-9834	-209	-1	-8263	-18308
CACM *	-3856	-25	-1	-3406	-7288
Chile	-509	--	-240	-46	-795
Colombia	-419	-464	--	-484	-1368
Ecuador	-190	-458	--	-22	-669
Paraguay	-9	--	--	-2	-11
Peru	-22	-293	-55	-78	-448
Uruguay	-1	--	--	-164	-165
Venezuela	-192	-4278	--	-608	-5078
Subtotal (in the region)	-15775	-5916	-296	-13361	-35350*
World Total	-35027	-22391	-1843	-381374	-440636

* Central American Common Market
Source: See Table 7.2

year the G3 managed to agree to create nine high level working groups, and reach several agreements such as the electric complex.

Trade in Goods and Trade Balance Within the G3.   It is clear that the interest of any country in achieving free trade agreements is driven by a desire to improve its economy. This applies to all countries although the potential risks, advantages and losses for each nation are a function of its particular level of development as well as its capacity to penetrate international markets.

Within the G3, the evolution of the three member countries' trade balances is an important motivating factor in their search for a free trade agreement.[15] Mexico had a favorable balance of trade with Colombia and Venezuela for the periods 1983-84 and 1987-88, even though in the last period the positive balance declined, reaching a slight deficit with regard to Venezuela in 1991 (Tables 7.6 and 7.7). Venezuela's trade balance had more fluctuations, with both negative

TABLE 7.6   Mexico: Total Values of Its Exports and Imports with
               Colombia and Venezuela and Trade Balance with Both
               Countries   (U.S.$)

| | Exports | | Imports | | |
	Total	%	Total	%	Trade Balance
Colombia	151'485,687	55.8	45'421,104	25.55	106'064,583
Venezuela	119'994,408	44.2	142'361,308	24.45	-12'366,900
Both	271'480,095	100.0	177'782,412	100.00	93'697,683

Source: See Table 7.1

TABLE 7.7   Group of Three and ALADI: Trade Balance
               (U.S.$ thousands)

| | | Destination | | | |
Origin	Years	Colombia	Mexico	Venezuela	ALADI
Colombia	83-84		72,415	218,601	605,728
	87-88		149,342	1,437	259,871
Mexico	83-84	-90,291		-54,986	-723,209
	87-88	-154,478		-113,765	-431,985
Venezuela	83-84	-286,579	43,473		-729,106
	87-88	-89,580	-78,960		745,245
ALADI	83-84	-715,342	625,742	378,730	
	87-88	-207,589	434,316	-533,462	
World	83-84	-1'519,514	1'298,235	9'021,074	34'104,949
total	87-88	476,847	6'270,455	-780,802	23'256,383

Source: See Table 7.1

and positive balances, although the deficit worsened in 1987-88.
Colombia has had a negative trade balance in almost all cases, with
Mexico, the ALADI, and Venezuela (see Table 7.7).
    It could be argued that the wish to improve their trade balances is
the driving force of the G3 member countries in reaching an agreement.
Such an improvement could result from an expansion of exports within

the group, and the enhancement of its penetration in the U.S. market. Surely, Colombia would be the most interested in enlarging the amount and number of its exports to the G3 and to other countries, because of its trade balance situation.

It is important to discuss the trade profiles of Mexico, Venezuela and Colombia, by product and export destination, in order to be able to assess the potential effect that trade liberalization agreement could have on them. There is no question of the weight of the U.S. in the three countries' trade. The United States is the most important exporter to the G3 countries and to ALADI countries in general. The volume of American exports to the ALADI countries is proportionally higher than Colombian, Mexican, and Venezuelan exports to the region as a whole; 21.5 percent of ALADI imports come from the United States, compared with 16.3 percent from the G3. Even more important is the U.S. role as destination for the exports of the region, especially for the G3, since the ALADI and G3 countries export proportionately more to the United States than to any other country (see Table 7.2), Mexican exports being the most heavily concentrated on that country.

The European Union (EU) is the second most important destination of Colombian, Mexican, and Venezuelan exports, though in a much less proportion than to the United States. Although this trend is similar among the three countries, Colombia's exports to the United States double Mexico's and Venezuela's combined exports to the EU (Table 7.4). The three countries have a very small trade with the ALADI nations, although here again Colombia accounts for the highest proportion of exports. Trade within Latin America is only about 0.25 percent of that of developing countries of South and Southeast Asia;[16] in 1989, the intra-American trade share did not reach 10 percent in the case of Colombia, which is the country with the highest level of exports to the region.

In a product by product analysis of the G3 members' trade, the differences among their exports to the United States and Canada combined, and to all other countries in the Americas, seem more evident in the cases of Colombia and Venezuela than of Mexico. This is so because the former export a higher share of their manufactured goods to Latin America than to the United States. Colombia, one of the most dynamic countries, has 67 percent of its exports in this category. It is also the higher exporter of coal and petroleum to the same countries (Table 7.3). This means that Colombia has a potential market in the region, even though Mexico and Venezuela have already established themselves as exporters of machinery and transportation equipment.

TABLE 7.8   1989: Exports from Colombia and Venezuela to the United States
(U.S.$ millions)

Colombia	Value	Export % to U.S.A.	Venezuela	Value	Export % to U.S.A.
Products			Products		
Flowers	182.7	7.38	Crude oil	5,610.5	86.48
Bananas	147.1	5.53	Oil		
Coffee	284.9	11.50	by-products	--	--
Sugar	92.9	3.73	Metal		
Crude oil	935.3	27.76	products	310.0	4.78
Refined oil	245.3	9.90			
Apparel	70.0	2.82			
Subtotal	1,947.7	78.63	Subtotal	5,920.5	91.25
TOTAL	2,476.8	100.00	TOTAL	6,487.9	100.00

Source: See Table 7.4

Venezuela still seems to depend to a large extent on its exports of petroleum to the United States (almost 90 percent of its sales to that country consist of energy products). Mexico has succeeded in increasing its exports of manufactured goods, which are now higher than petroleum. This trend undoubtedly reflects the emphasis that has been placed on industrialization in the country and the dynamism of the maquiladora sector during the past decade. Colombia is still an important exporter of foodstuffs, including coffee, to the United States. But perhaps the most relevant and dynamic sector in relation to the United States is crude and refined petroleum products (see Tables 7.3 and 7.8).

The G3 members' trade has become more diversified, with the most dynamic sectors being chemical products, petroleum and manufactured goods. Chemical products were especially dynamic in the past decade, both in the exports and the imports of the three countries. In the case of manufactured products, the situation is somewhat different, although they represent a significant proportion of the G3 countries' exports. Mexico is the most integrated with Canada and the United States, something that NAFTA could accentuate to the detriment of Colombia and Venezuela. Energy products also account for an important share of the G3 exports to the United States, Venezuela being the clear leader. Colombia is the smaller exporter of energy goods to Latin America

TABLE 7.9   1991: Ten Main Products From Mexico to Colombia and
                 Venezuela
                 (U.S.$)

Product	Colombia Value-91	%	Product	Venezuela Value-91	%
Dimetil			Dimetals,		
tereftalatum	41097845	27.1	coins	10796,086	9.0
Wood			Tetraftilic		
structures	9585871	6.3	acids & salts	10334993	8.6
Tetraftilic			Pipes		
acid & salts	8564927	5.7	oil pipes	7007353	5.8
Synthetic rubber	7216124	4.8	Perforation	6958975	5.8
			pipes		
Comm. equipment					
Telephone	6401036	4.2	Isocianats	3387110	2.8
Oil extraction			Books and		
pipes	5128725	3.4	printings	3377120	2.8
Autom. machine			Dimetil		
data process.	5126806	3.4	tereftalatum	3351389	2.8
			Polietilen		
Books	3750913	2.5	tereftalatum	3283900	2.7
Electrodes	3309084	2.5	Soldering	2896701	2.4
Automobiles	2564732	1.7	Soldering	2020491	1.7
Main			Main		
products	128415328	84.8	products	58011835	
TOTAL	151485687	100.0	TOTAL	129842961	100.0

Source: See Table 7.4

which explains that country's evident interest in the sale of soft coal to
Mexico, with which it has tariff preferences.

    In sum, the internal trade of the G3 offers comparative advantages
for the three countries, although the potential competition among them
in exports of chemical, petroleum and manufactured products cannot be
ignored. Mexico appears to be the most "advanced" concerning the type
and diversity of exports, especially in chemical and petrochemical,
and manufactured products, although Colombia seems to have considerable potential in the production and export of manufactured goods (see
Tables 7.9 and 7.10).

TABLE 7.10   Ten Main Products to Mexico from Colombia and Venezuela
              (U.S.$)

Colombia			Venezuela		
Product	Value-91	%	Product	Value-91	%
Prints in					
Spanish	5743170	12.6	Fuel oil	17672291	13.4
Fungicides	5077578	11.2	Non-allied		
			aluminum	13248560	10.0
Soft coal			Dodecilbencen		
fuels	4640862	10.2	mixtures	12768185	9.7
			Meliterbutiric		
Prints	2524039	5.6	ether	11064768	8.4
Regular publicat.	2134332	4.7	Earth prods.	9325481	7.1
Gelatine	2106556	4.6	Aluminum wire	7498883	5.7
Carboximetil-			Laminated		
cellulose	1651260	3.6	products	5912879	4.5
Molibden			Other laminated		
oxides/hidróxides	1290629	2.8	products	5190208	3.9
Daily and regular			Aluminum		
publications	1250392	2.8	ingot	3363433	2.5
Parts for			Iron		
auto parts	1046782	2.3	wire	2986943	2.3
Total main					
products	40062469	88.2			
TOTAL	45421104	100.0	TOTAL	132361308	100.0

Source: See Table 7.4

G3 Areas of Negotiation

One of the factors that will probably help promote rapid progress in achieving a regional free trade agreement is the fact that the three countries have substantially reduced their tariffs in the last few years, so that they have achieved substantial similarity in their tariff schedules. This will facilitate the negotiation of tariff reductions from a similar approach.

Mexico was the first to adopt a rapid unilateral tariff liberalization process in the second half of the 1980s. From a 100 percent level in 1982, Mexico reached a maximum level of 20 in 1990 (the weighted average tariff being 9.2 percent). Most import permits have been eliminated.[17]

During the Sixth Andean Presidential Congress, Colombia and Venezuela adopted four common tariff levels of 5, 10, 15, and 29 percent. The consistency and similarity of tariff levels and tariff policies undoubtedly offer advantages for a trade liberalization agreement, which does not seem to be the case with the Andean Pact at the present time.

Energy cooperation is one of the most important issues of negotiation within the G3, and an area in which considerable progress has been made. Energy was included in the agenda of the G3 in October 1990. This interest was reinforced during the meeting of the Rio Group, where special emphasis was given to the energy area and to the creation of an energy basin -- Colombia-Venezuela-Mexico-Central America. As a result, a Committee of Energy Cooperation was created, which in turn established four technical working groups: (1) a coal group, coordinated by Colombia; (2) a gas group, coordinated by Venezuela; and, (3) and (4) hydroelectricity and electric interconnection groups, coordinated by Mexico. These working groups are a recognition of the complementarities of the three economies in this field (oil, in the case of Mexico; coal and natural gas in the cases of Colombia and Venezuela), as well as of their future electricity requirements. Trilateral cooperation in energy is making good progress. Colombia has signed several agreements with Mexico for the sale of coal, while Venezuela has signed agreements for the sale of natural gas to Colombia.[18]

Perhaps the most important issue for the future of energy cooperation within the G3 is the production of hydroelectricity and the establishment of an electric complex. The hydroelectricity working group has considered a series of hydroelectric projects in Mexico and Colombia, and a long term program in Venezuela, that would generate electricity at competitive prices for export to the other members of the G3 and to Central America. A technology transfer exchange accord among the three countries has also been envisioned.

On the other hand, the electric interconnection working group is considering several projects for the generation of non-hydroelectric electricity. The electric interconnection project is one of the most ambitious and essential undertakings of the G3. Its goal is to satisfy the future electricity needs of G3 members as well as of Central American countries. The hydroelectricity working group has requested financial support from the Interamerican Development Bank, through the United Nations Economic Commission for Latin America (ECLAC). The participants in this project are the Spanish electricity company, ENDESA, the Regional Group of Electric Integration, of the Electrification Council of Central America and the Central America Interconnection System. Clearly, the G3's cooperation in energy is one of the most ambitious initiatives, which could result in significant economic benefits and stronger political influence for Colombia, Mexico and Venezuela in the region.

Conclusion

The negotiations for a trade liberalization agreement within the G3 are perhaps the most advanced in Latin America. Although the G3's original political objectives have now been met, it has become a forum which may facilitate the idea of regional economic plurilateralism.

The interests of the G3 members towards the Caribbean, as they have been traditionally in the case of Central America, are the products of geopolitics and national security. They are also an answer to the political uncertainty of the region. For Mexico, the G3 represents, in political terms, a foundation for its independence in foreign economic policy.

Colombia, Mexico and Venezuela can indeed derive economic advantages by trading among themselves and, as the G3, by trading with other countries of the continent. The main obstacles that could limit trade within the G3 are the similarities of their economies and of their exports and imports. As noted earlier, the main products traded among the three countries are chemicals, petrochemicals, printings, and, in the case of Mexico, manufactured goods, auto parts, and oil industry machinery and equipment. Although Colombia and Venezuela can and, in fact, are increasing their exports to Mexico, NAFTA will give preference to Canadian and U.S. products in the Mexican market, thus displacing Colombian and Venezuelan future exports. Therefore, it is crucial that serious study be given to the possible accession of Colombia and Venezuela to NAFTA or the conclusion of a free trade agreement with Mexico.[19]

In the future the G3 might attract the other Andean Pact members, which could bring them considerable economic advantages, due to the potential for increasing trade in chemical and petrochemical products, as well as auto parts and machinery from Mexico; printed materials and various manufactured goods, including apparel, from Colombia, and natural gas from Venezuela. But perhaps more important is the project to establish an electrical interconnection complex among the three countries and with Central America, which would surely increase the G3's influence in the Central American countries.

Notes

This paper was translated from Spanish by Anna-Marie Peredo and Stephen J. Randall.

1. The need to address the likely discriminatory impact of the Canada-US FTA on Mexican products was discussed in Gustavo Vega C., "El Acuerdo de Libre Comercio entre Canada y Estados Unidos: Implicaciones para México y los Paises en Desarrollo," *Comercio Exterior*, Vol. 38, No. 3 (March 1988) and in Sidney Weintraub, "The Impact of the Agreement on Mexico," in Peter Morici, ed., *Making Free Trade Work: The Canada-US Agreement* (New York: Council of Foreign Relations, 1990), pp. 102-123. More precise quantitative estimates were undertaken by the government of Mexico showing that CUSFTA has had some trade diversion consequences for Mexico. In terms of 1988 trade flows, the gross trade diversion was $662 million, of which $421 million was in the automotive sector and $102 million was in consumer electronics. Offsetting the diversion was $257 million of trade creation, of which the largest component was $123 million for knitting mills. See: Staff of Economic Advisors to the Minister of Industry and Trade, *Tariff Elimination between the United States and Canada: Effects on Mexico's Trade Flows* (Unpublished report, Mexico City, 1990), Abstract.

2. NAFTA, for example, eliminates all tariffs and quotas in the regional trade of textiles and apparel. This is the first time that a developing and important supplier country finds no barriers to its products in the markets of two of the most advanced, developed countries. Also, in the agriculture sector, NAFTA removed non-tariff barriers to trade and replaced them with tariff-quotas, which will be phased-out in a 15 year period. This is unprecedented and, according to several authors, represents an important achievement considering the hurdles agricultural trade liberalization has encountered in other trade negotiations. See Gary Hufbauer and Jeffrey Schott, *NAFTA: An Assessment* (Washington: The Institute for International Economics, 1993), Chapter 1.

3. NAFTA removes a number of barriers to telecommunication services and ground transportation trade, and opens the financial sector to American and Canadian financial institutions to the year 2000. It is an important precedent for future regional and multilateral negotiations. See ibid.

4. It must be said, however, that according to recent declarations of U.S. experts, the accession clause will not be only applied to the Latin American and Caribbean countries, but also to any nation of the world, particularly to the Asian countries. Therefore, Latin American countries will be urged to take a position concerning their possible admission into the NAFTA. See *Excelsior*, October 10, 1992.

5. See Ronald Wonnacott, *The Economies of Overlapping Free Trade Areas and the Mexican Challenge* (Toronto and Washington: C.D. Howe Institute and the National Planning Association, 1991).

6. Some of the main factors that, in my opinion, explain the low volume of trade with the region are: the recession that has beset the international economy in the last few years, and its negative impact on the participation of Latin America in global trade; the lack of a proper infrastructure, both physical and financial; and the evolution of the relative real exchange rates and the strongly protectionist trade policies of almost all Latin American countries.

7. See Pedro Noyola, "El surgimiento de espacios económicos multinacionales y las relaciones de México con Europa, la Cuenca del Pacífico y América Latina y el Caribe," in Secretaría de Comercio y Fomento Industrial (SECOFI), *Hacia un tratado de libre comercio en América del Norte* (México: Miguel Angel Porrúa Grupo Editorial, 1991), pp. 141-142.

8. Juan Gonzalo Zapata G., *El Grupo de los Tres: punto intermedio entre el Pacto Andino y la Iniciativa para las Américas* (Bogota, Colombia: FESCOL, April 1992).

9. Ibid.

10. Acuerdo de Cartagena, *La Iniciativa para las Américas del presidente Bush: un desafío para América Latina y el Caribe*, September 20, 1990.

11. In recent years, Bolivia has made dramatic changes to its economic policy towards liberalization, which recall the Mexican experience during the mid-1980s. This makes Bolivia a potential member of an expanded free trade area within the G3.

12. Zapata, *El Grupo de los Tres*.

13. Ibid.

14. Refik Erzan and Alexander Yeats, "U.S.-Latin American Free Trade Areas: Some Empirical Evidence," in Sylvia Saborio, ed., *The Premise and the Promise: Free Trade in the Americas* (Washington: Overseas Development Council, 1992), pp. 117-152.

15. See the interview with the Ambassador L.A. Casas, *Excelsior*, September 19, 1992. He clearly recognized that Colombia's motive for reaching an agreement in the G3 was a desire to improve its trade balance.

16. Erzan and Yeats, "U.S.-Latin American Free Trade Areas," p. 118.

17. Mexico now has five tariff levels, of 0, 5, 10, 15, and 20 percent.

18. Jorge Valencia R., "Cooperación energética en el Grupo de los Tres," in Zapata, *El Grupo de los Tres*, pp. 30-36.

19. After this chapter was completed, Mexico, Colombia and Venezuela concluded a free trade negotiation. The agreement reached provides for the elimination of tariffs and other trade barriers over a ten year period, establishes standards for commerce, and contains a dispute settlement mechanism similar to NAFTA's. The pact is scheduled to enter into force on January 1, 1995, pending ratification by the three countries.

8

Canada and Latin America in the Shadow of U.S. Power: Toward an Expanding Hemispheric Agreement?

Maxwell A. Cameron and Brian W. Tomlin

The North American Free Trade Agreement (NAFTA) reduces barriers to trade and investment between Mexico, the United States, and Canada -- three countries of dramatically different sizes and levels of development. The asymmetries of power and interdependence in patterns of North American trade and investment are well documented and have long been a central preoccupation for policy makers in both Canada and Latin America who are used to operating in the shadow of U.S. power.[1] However, in recent years Canadian and Latin American foreign policy makers have abandoned efforts to find alternatives to closer economic integration with the United States and have joined the hemispheric free trade bandwagon.[2] The United States, first under President George Bush and then Bill Clinton, has welcomed the opportunity to pursue bilateral bargaining strategies within the hemisphere, even as its will and capacity for global leadership has been challenged by Asia and Europe.[3] With the approval of NAFTA by the U.S. House of Representatives on November 17, 1993, attention has now shifted to the prospects for an extension to include other countries in the hemisphere. In the analysis that follows, we explore this issue through an examination of the role that Canada might play in the creation of an expanded hemispheric agreement.

We argue that it is unlikely that Canada will take the initiative in the extension of the hemispheric free trade zone, and will instead follow the lead of the United States should it decide to further consolidate its regional market. Our conclusion is based on an analysis of the process through which Canada joined NAFTA. Prior to that outcome, Canada under Prime Minister Brian Mulroney adopted a closer alignment with Washington's foreign policy and a more market oriented approach to economic policy. The nationalist policies of the Trudeau era were abandoned in favor of a strategy of fostering competition by expanding and securing access to the U.S. market through the Canada-United States Free Trade Agreement (CUSFTA). When Mexico petitioned the United States for a similar agreement, Canada sought inclusion in order to prevent an erosion of the benefits of CUSFTA. The dominant concern of policy makers was to protect access to the United States market, and only secondarily to expand into Mexico and beyond.

Analysis of recent trends in Latin America reveals similar forces at work. Latin America has also undergone a major policy reorientation; policy makers throughout the region are promoting trade liberalization as the cornerstone of market reform. Under tremendous fiscal pressures, Latin American countries have engaged in a process of intense competition to attract foreign capital and secure markets for their exports. This has led to a proliferation of bilateral and sub-regional agreements to liberalize trade, and many countries have expressed a keen interest in joining NAFTA as the culmination of this process. Our analysis suggests that the successful implementation of national policies for market reform and trade liberalization will be necessary preconditions for membership in NAFTA; as a result, accession will probably proceed incrementally as various governments implement these policies, with Chile most likely to be at the front of the line for membership.

This paper is divided into four sections. The first section briefly reviews the initiative from Mexico to form a NAFTA. Mexico exemplifies the changes in policy orientation that have taken place throughout Latin America, and the section provides crucial background information on the forces leading to NAFTA. The second section reviews the changes in policy orientation and priorities in Canada, and illustrates how Canadian policy remained defensive and reactive in the face of the NAFTA initiative. This provides the basis for our assertion that Canadian policy is unlikely to be proactive in the extension of NAFTA beyond Mexico to include other countries in the hemisphere. The third section reviews changes in Latin American foreign economic policy and contrasts current bilateral and sub-regional initiatives toward economic integration with previous initiatives when the region was under the influence of a less "market-friendly" economic doctrine. The fourth and final section discusses the issues raised by the accession of other countries that want to join NAFTA.

The Initiative from Mexico

In January 1990, Mexican President Carlos Salinas de Gortari travelled to Europe in an effort to convince business and government officials that the dramatic changes taking place in Eastern Europe should not distract investors from opportunities in Latin America, especially Mexico.[4] The President did not receive an encouraging response to his efforts, however, and the "polite rebuff by the West Europeans reinforced Salinas's belief that Mexico must work with a dynamic trading partner to avoid becoming a stagnant backwater."[5]

The failure of the European initiative played a major role in the Salinas decision that closer links with the United States would be the best way of opening up Mexico to the global economy in an era of regional trading blocs.[6] This decision was consistent with the more outward-oriented economic strategy that had gained acceptance in Mexico during the decade of debt and economic stagnation in the 1980s. In February 1990, Salinas unexpectedly sent his Minister of Commerce and Industry, Jaime Serra Puche, and his chief economic advisor, José María Cordoba Montoya, to Washington to propose a free trade agreement with the United States.[7]

The United States executive quickly endorsed the Mexican proposal,[8] for geopolitical as well as economic and social reasons. President Bush, Secretary of State James Baker, and Commerce Secretary Robert Mosbacher -- the "Texas Trio" -- were immediately supportive of free trade, and the National Security Council (NSC) staff prepared the policy analysis that gave the initial green light. Some form of formal economic integration with Mexico had long been sought by the United States. The executive concluded that a free trade agreement would provide a means to "lock in" the market reforms and trade liberalization measures undertaken by the Salinas regime and to encourage Mexico to pursue a foreign policy less antagonistic to the interests of the United States.

Canada was a reluctant partner at the start of the negotiations to create NAFTA. Canadian trade and investment ties with Latin America, and Mexico, have been weak historically, providing little commercial incentive to enter into free trade negotiations with the Mexicans. In addition, the government was not eager to reopen the bruising national debate that had occurred over free trade with the United States.[9] In the end, however, Canada entered NAFTA because key policy makers believed it had little choice if it was to protect its position in the North American market.[10]

Canada's Interest in Hemispheric Free Trade

In order to address the question of Canada's interest in hemispheric free trade, three aspects of recent Canadian activities toward the region will be examined in search of evidence that would suggest whether or not a proactive policy to promote greater economic integration in the Americas is likely. In the sections that follow, we will examine: (1) Canada's 1989 long term strategy for Latin America, leading to the decision to join the Organization of American States (OAS) and become a full member of the hemispheric community; (2) the roots of the 1990 Canadian decision to participate in the negotiations leading to NAFTA; and (3) recent Canadian activities and resource commitments in Latin America and the Caribbean. Our aim is to assess the likelihood that Canada will take the initiative to promote accession to NAFTA on the part of countries in the region.

Membership in the Hemispheric Community

Canadian foreign policy in the 1980s was dominated, as usual, by relations with the United States. Secondary emphasis was placed on Europe and the Asia Pacific region. Export and investment opportunities in Asia, in particular, stood in contrast to the problems -- debt, political instability, dictatorship, corruption, rent-seeking, income inequality, byzantine regulations, and unproductive public spending -- that had plagued Latin America. Asia Pacific offered more attractive opportunities for Canadian exporters.[11] Changes in the global economy in the early 1980s sharply undermined Latin America's economic performance but not that of the East Asian countries. As a result, Latin America fell dramatically behind East Asia.[12]

Despite the weak performance of the Latin American economies, Canada's involvement in peace initiatives in the region raised its profile in Canadian foreign policy, and directly engaged the prime minister and the secretary of state for external affairs. In October 1989, the cabinet approved a new *Long Term Strategy for Latin America*, designed to move Canada closer to the region through increased participation in its affairs in a number of areas, including trade, drug control, debt management, peacekeeping, and development assistance.[13] The core element of the strategy was not enhanced commercial relations in the region, however, but instead centered on Canadian membership in the OAS.

At the same time, changes in Latin America in response to the debt crisis began to make the region more attractive to Canadian policy makers. The embrace of market solutions, combined with a trend toward democratization of political systems in the region, were seen favorably by Canadian policy makers. Canadian officials noted a more pragmatic attitude toward hemispheric cooperation on the part of the Latin Americans.[14] This would allow Canada to play an active role in the region without getting caught in deep historical conflicts between Latin America and the United States. The potential for cooperation in the region was manifested in the emerging patterns of regional integration.

Canada had considered, and rejected, joining the OAS earlier in the decade, when the Department of External Affairs, traditionally opposed to membership, convinced its minister, Allan MacEachen, that despite Prime Minister Trudeau's statement to the contrary, membership was not something whose time had come.[15] Traditional forces within External Affairs argued that joining the organization was not in Canada's interest because it would "be forced to toe the American line" on key issues or "risk Washington's wrath on issues of greater importance to Canada."[16] The government of Brian Mulroney, however, was not put off by the prospect of closer alignment with Washington,[17] and the time for membership arrived. On October 27, 1989, at the Hemispheric Summit of heads of government, Mulroney announced Canada's intention to join the OAS. Whether the summit was the opportunity, or the catalyst, for the decision is uncertain.[18]

When Secretary of State for External Affairs Joe Clark addressed the OAS Permanent Council in Washington in November 1989, he stated that Canada's decision to join the organization was a key element of Canada's new strategy for Latin America. In fact, it was probably the only element in the strategy: a little more than a year later, an External Affairs update focused almost exclusively on OAS membership in its assessment of the implementation of the strategy for Latin America.[19] That focus was about to change sharply, however, in the direction of commercial interests. The External Affairs update signalled the impending change in its discussion of the future of the strategy, focusing on the need to expand trade relations in light of the prospective trilateral free trade negotiations. But this reorientation had little to do with closer Canadian relations with Latin America, and much more to do with Canada's relationship with the United States.

The NAFTA Decision

Tracing the roots of the Canadian decision to participate in trilateral free trade negotiations provides an additional perspective on the question of Canada's interest in a broader hemispheric free trade zone. The experience suggests that, while this was an issue launched by Mexico, it was Canada's predominant relationship with the United States that determined the decision in the end.

Joe Clark, in his February 1990 speech in Calgary, noted that a large contingent of members of the Mexican cabinet had visited Ottawa in January for discussions with their Canadian counterparts.[20] Stating that "a new partnership with Mexico is key to our Latin American strategy," Clark also noted that Brian Mulroney would visit Mexico in March 1990. It was during his flight to Mexico in mid-March that Mulroney received a telephone call from Derek Burney, Canada's ambassador in Washington. Secretary of State Baker had called Burney to say that the U.S. had received a request from Mexican President Salinas for bilateral free trade negotiations with the United States. Salinas planned to inform Mulroney of his request during the Mexican visit. It was agreed that Mulroney would ask to be kept informed of developments while Canada examined the issue internally.

To conduct the examination, a small task force was created within the Department of External Affairs and International Trade Canada (EAITC) to address the implications of a Mexico-U.S. free trade agreement for Canada. By the end of April 1990, the task force had a draft memorandum to cabinet ready, and circulated it to other government departments for comment. At this stage, Investment Canada flagged the diversion of investment dollars to the U.S. as a long term problem that could arise from a separate Mexican-U.S. agreement. The memorandum was taken to cabinet on May 22, 1990, by Minister for International Trade John Crosbie. The cabinet document sketched the impact of a Mexico-U.S. FTA on various Canadian stakeholders and sectors,[21] and put forward two options for cabinet consideration. The first option, tantamount to doing nothing, called for Canada to simply monitor developments. The second, recommended by the task force, called for the government to seek agreement from the U.S. and Mexico that Canada be provided an opportunity to participate in exploratory discussions, without prejudice to any subsequent Canadian decision on whether to join the negotiations. Cabinet adopted the second option, and directed the task force to prepare a fuller report on the impact of a Mexico-U.S. free trade agreement on Canada. Canada wanted to keep its options open while it studied the issue further. As the task force continued its work during the summer of 1990, it became clear to Canadian officials that Mexico and the U.S. were committed to negotiations, and pressure mounted for a decision.

Canada's priorities continued to reflect a preoccupation with its bilateral relationship with the United States. A second memorandum to cabinet was considered by the Priorities and Planning Committee on August 29, 1990. This time, four options were presented for consideration: continue to monitor developments; seek observer status at bilateral Mexican-U.S. negotiations; negotiate a bilateral Canada-Mexico free trade agreement; or join Mexico and the United States in trilateral negotiations. The task force recommended the fourth option because it addressed all of Canada's interests in the issue: it offset the danger of investment diversion in a "hub and spoke" model; it prevented Mexico from getting preferential access to the U.S. market through a better free trade agreement than CUSFTA; and it offered access to the growing Mexican market. For the ministers, however, political considerations were also important.

Although Crosbie and his officials on the task force favored the trilateral option, the powerful Department of Finance had strong reservations, and ministers realized that a trilateral agreement would likely emerge in time to provide a contentious issue for the next federal election. On the other hand, the government needed a significant policy initiative in the aftermath of the failure of the Meech Lake Accord (an attempt to revise Canada's constitution), and free trade was one on which they had prevailed in 1988, and on which they could again join political battle with the opposition parties. In the end, ministerial combativeness, coupled with the reality that Canada could not prevent a bilateral Mexico-U.S. deal, and could influence the terms of Mexico's access to the North American market most directly by being at the table, led to the decision to seek participation in the negotiations.

Canada's decision to join the trilateral negotiations was prompted by a concern that a bilateral Mexico-U.S. agreement would give the U.S. an advantage in attracting investment as the only country with access to a continental market, and might result in preferred access to the United States market for Mexico. Once the negotiations were under way, Canada's principal objective became the negotiation of improvements to the Canada-U.S. free trade pact in areas such as rules of origin, government procurement, financial services, and dispute settlement provisions concerning the application of countervailing and anti-dumping duties. In the decision to seek participation, and in the negotiations themselves, access to the Mexican market was a secondary, although not completely unimportant, consideration for Canada. There is nothing in the experience, however, to suggest a strong Canadian interest in seeking additional free trade partners in the hemisphere.

A further, organizational indicator of the reality that, for Canada, NAFTA is primarily a Canadian-U.S. trade deal can be found in the reorganization of the Department of External Affairs and International Trade that was announced on June 22, 1993. Responsibility for the management of NAFTA implementation was assigned to the Trade Policy Bureau, in the Trade and Economic Policy Branch of the department. However, the bureau is required to work closely with the Trade and Economic Policy Bureau in the United States Branch, where John Weekes is the Senior Assistant Deputy Minister and Free Trade Agreement Coordinator.[22] There is no similar requirement for formal coordination with the Latin America and Caribbean Branch.

Government Priorities

The Canadian decisions to join the OAS and participate in the NAFTA negotiations were not accompanied by an increase in the resources directed by the government to relations, especially commercial, with countries in the hemisphere, other than Mexico. Instead, Europe remained at the center of Canada's foreign policy focus. In the period 1988-92, almost 30 percent of official visits by the minister for international trade, and over 40 percent by the secretary of state for external affairs, were to Europe.[23] This despite the fact that the European share of Canadian merchandise exports has declined over the past twenty years from approximately 20 percent to 10 percent. Moreover, in 1991-92, Canadian activities in Europe received almost 40 percent of the trade development resources of EAITC [24] and 31 percent of EAITC staff doing trade and economic relations work at Canadian missions in 1992-93, were located in Europe.[25] Despite this attention, funding for the Programme for Export Market Development (PEMD) produced only an average (Eastern Europe) to low (Western Europe) rate of return.[26] In summary, there is a heavy concentration of Canadian activity and resources in a region of declining importance, and the returns are disappointing.

The Pacific Rim compares with Europe in its commercial importance to Canada, with a 10 percent share of Canadian merchandise exports. In addition, PEMD funding produced a better than average rate of return in Asia Pacific.[27] Activity and resource figures are somewhat lower than those for Europe, however. In 1991-92, Canadian activities in Asia Pacific received almost 30 percent of the trade development resources of EAITC, [28] and 24 percent of EAITC staff doing trade and economic relations work at Canadian missions in 1992-93, were located in Asia Pacific.[29]

For Latin America and the Caribbean, the picture is mixed. With a 2 percent share of Canadian merchandise exports, and a very high rate of return on PEMD funding, the region received only 5-6 percent of the trade development resources of EAITC in 1991-92.[30] Furthermore, Keith Christie, a senior official on the Policy Planning staff at EAITC, notes[31] that Asia Pacific and Latin America *combined* accounted for only 20 percent of official visits by the Minister for International Trade and Secretary of State for External Affairs in the 1988-92 period. On the other hand, almost 12 percent of EAITC staff doing trade and economic relations work at Canadian missions in 1992-93, were located in Latin America and the Caribbean.[32] Furthermore, over the 1991-93 period, there was a net increase of five persons in the number of EAITC staff at the Canadian mission in Mexico, all of them assigned to trade work.

Perhaps a more accurate picture of the degree of EAITC's failure to shift resources to Latin America can be found in a description of changes in the relative shares of staff doing trade and economic relations work in the various regions. Table 8.1 presents percentage shares for the period 1990-1993, as well as the percent change in the *actual* number of trade and economic relations staff between 1990 and 1993.

At a time when the total number of such staff abroad declined by 4.7 percent, Europe's relative share increased from 27.7 to 30.9 percent, and the actual number of staff engaged in trade and economic activity at missions in Europe increased by 6.6 percent. It was the *only* region to register an absolute increase over the period. Latin America and the Caribbean, on the other hand, maintained its relative share at 11.5 percent over the period while experiencing an absolute decline in economic and trade staff at missions of 4.3 percent. When the net increase in Canadian mission staff in Mexico is accounted for, however, the absolute decline in staff assigned to the remaining countries in the hemisphere is even greater.

Decisions regarding resource allocation result from many contending forces, and only imperfectly reflect relative Canadian policy priorities. They do not necessarily reflect changes in the corporate culture;

TABLE 8.1   Canada-Based Staff at Bilateral Missions Engaged in Trade
             and Economic Relations Activities, 1990-1993 (Percentages)

	1990-91	1991-92	1992-93	% change 1990-93
Africa and Middle East	14.2%	13.0%	12.3%	-17.7
Asia and Pacific	23.1	23.0	23.8	-1.6
Europe	27.7	30.1	30.9	+6.6
Latin America and the Caribbean	11.5	10.8	11.5	-4.3
United States	23.5	23.1	21.5	-12.9
	(100.0)	(100.0)	(100.0)	
Total Number	386	392	368	-4.7

Source: Government of Canada, *Departmental Estimates*, Part III (various years). Original figures were expressed in person-years for 1990-91 and 1991-92, and full time equivalents for 1992-93. There are no significant differences between the two forms of measurement.

nor do they reflect the strength of private sector interest in Latin America, which is obviously a major force driving policy in this area. Nevertheless, this analysis demonstrates that OAS membership and the NAFTA negotiations have not been accompanied by a shift of Canadian official activity and resources to Latin America. Instead, there continues to be a disproportionate concentration on Europe, a region of declining importance for Canada's trade and economic relations.

A number of Canadian officials have suggested that Canada may adopt a proactive policy to promote greater economic integration in the Americas through an expansion of NAFTA into a hemispheric free trade zone. A recent Policy Planning Paper from External Affairs and International Trade Canada argued that

> from a Canadian vantage point, we must be active in shaping the Latin American and Caribbean response to the NAFTA .... Canada should, therefore, take the initiative and actively reach out to these countries by establishing a regular trade policy dialogue at the senior officials' level that emphasizes the benefits of acceding to the NAFTA ....[33]

Stanley Gooch, Assistant Deputy Minister in the Latin America and Caribbean Branch at EAITC, referred to President George Bush's Enterprise for the Americas Initiative (EAI) as an important vehicle for economic and political transformation in the region.[34] He noted the May 1992 meeting between the presidents of the United States and

Chile which placed Chile at the head of the line to join the move toward trade liberalization, and indicated Canada was receptive to an extension of the NAFTA southward. More specifically, in a speech in Santiago, Chile in April 1993, International Trade Minister Michael Wilson stated that Canada would view an application from Chile for NAFTA membership with favor. Similarly, in Buenos Aires, Argentina, in April 1993, Wilson stated that "Canada is willing to explore ways in which Argentina and other countries can become partners in NAFTA."

Christie argues that Canada should pursue closer relations with Latin America because the region has an economic dynamism which is beginning to match that of Asia Pacific, combined with an intense interest in closer trade and economic relations with North America.[35] Christie[36] also argues, however, that there is currently a serious deficiency in the financial and human resources deployed by the Canadian government in Latin America, suggesting a lack of congruence between official rhetoric and action. Our analysis of the 1989 Latin American strategy, the 1990 NAFTA decision, and resource commitments in the region suggests that Canada is unlikely to "take the initiative" to promote greater economic integration in the Americas through accession to the NAFTA.

Latin American Interest in Hemispheric Free Trade

Whether Canada plays an active role in promoting hemispheric integration will depend critically on the strength of Canadian business interest in Latin America, and there is anecdotal evidence that such interest is rising. Gooch claims that the Canadian embassy in Mexico receives more calls from businesses seeking assistance from the government than any other Canadian embassy in the world. At one point during the NAFTA negotiations, Canadian negotiators had difficulty booking flights back to Ottawa from Mexico City due to business traffic. Business interest has not been confined to Mexico; in the early 1990s, Canada became the leading foreign investor in Chile, with much of the investment going into mining.

Canadian business interest in Latin America arises from the renewed economic dynamism in the region, and what Abraham Lowenthal calls a "consensus among economic policy makers on the main tenets of sound policy".[37] After decades of import substitution industrialization, many Latin American countries are undergoing a profound transformation toward a more market oriented framework for policy based on deregulation, privatization of state owned enterprises, liberalization of trade and investment rules, monetarist macroeconomic policies, the pursuit of flexibility in the labor market, and a reduction of social spending. In the early 1990s, this strategy seemed to be producing an economic recovery in a number of Latin American countries. Chile led the way, with 6 percent growth between 1987-1991.[38] Latin American gross domestic product (GDP) growth rates reached a total of 12.5 percent during the entire period between 1981 and 1990, and per capita growth was 8.9 percent in the same period. By contrast, in the period between 1991 and 1993, Latin American GDP grew by a total of 10.8 percent, and per capita growth was 4.6 percent.[39] For the first time since the debt crisis, Latin America experienced positive net resource transfers in 1990 -- a net inflow of capital that continued through early 1993.

The depth of the new policy consensus is unclear, and so is its sustainability.[40] By 1994, growth was sluggish again, and in some instances capital flight became a threat. Events such as the uprising in Chiapas and the assassination of Mexican presidential candidate Luis Donaldo Colosio created uncertainty in capital markets -- markets that had been boosted by inflows of largely speculative capital. In this section, we discuss the growing interest in Latin American regional and hemispheric integration, as well as the remaining challenges. Current patterns of economic integration are different from previous initiatives, and they face serious obstacles that provide a measure of the difficulties that may be associated with the extension of NAFTA to other countries. Most of the new integration proposals are driven by a competitive struggle for international investment capital and a desire for access to the U.S. market, and their success may hinge on whether the United States rewards market reform. Chile, Venezuela, Argentina, and Colombia have all signalled an interest in joining NAFTA and are pursuing a variety of sub-regional arrangements as a prelude to joining a hemispheric agreement.

Latin American Integration Initiatives

Whereas current regional integration proposals are part of a package of economic reforms designed to attract foreign direct investment and promote a more outward-oriented strategy for growth, earlier efforts to achieve regional integration in Latin America were intended to serve as vehicles for self-reliant industrialization and Latin American solidarity. They were notoriously unsuccessful for a simple reason: Latin American countries traded little among themselves. The Latin American Free Trade Area (LAFTA), created in 1961, is a good example of the earlier type of integration project. It was promoted by the United Nations Economic Commission on Latin America and the Caribbean (ECLAC) to expand the market for Latin American intermediate and capital goods in order to facilitate a broader process of import substitution industrialization (ISI).[41] However, LAFTA failed to eliminate tariffs and quotas, or to promote substantial trade in goods other than natural resources.[42] The abandonment of LAFTA -- and its replacement by the more modest Latin American Integration Association in 1980 -- reflected the lack of intra-regional trade.

Other sub-regional pacts were relatively more successful, at least in the early phases of ISI when intra-regional trade expanded rapidly.[43] This was especially true of the Central American Common Market (CACM), established in 1960, and the Caribbean Community (CARICOM), which emerged out of the Caribbean Free Trade Association in 1973. However, ISI failed to generate the level of intra-regional trade that would drive these initiatives to completion. For example, the Andean Pact, established by Bolivia, Colombia, Chile, Ecuador, and Peru in 1969, fell short of the expectations of its members. These countries never traded more than about 4 percent of their exports within the Andean Pact region. Chile abandoned the pact in 1976, after President Pinochet began to radically liberalize the economy and open it up to foreign investment. In the 1980s, other members of the pact "defected" from their obligations as trade among them declined, due to the region-wide economic contraction. Finally, territorial disputes between Ecuador and Peru created tensions within the group[44] and by 1985, the Andean Pact was "completely paralysed."[45]

The external debt crisis initially diminished the priority placed by Latin American governments on economic integration. However, new mechanisms of integration were given impetus by the shift away from protectionism toward a more outward-oriented economic strategy in Latin America after 1982. Confronted with the need to generate revenues to pay the debt, Latin American governments were eager to exploit opportunities to trade and attract foreign capital; they were also willing to rely more on market signals and competition than government intervention. The new pattern of economic integration favored rapid, across-the-board, measures rather than the gradual, sector-by-sector, approach.[46]

Competition for access to markets and to attract investment capital has undermined intra-regional solidarity.[47] According to Jeffrey Schott, trade liberalization in Latin America is like a beauty contest:

All of these countries are in competition for capital and foreign investment. So, they are trying to design the most beautiful economic policies to attract investors, their own investors and foreign investors. The capital side of the equation may be as, if not more, important than the trade side.[48]

One of the contenders, the Andean Pact, was revived in 1990. It is widely believed that the EAI gave it a new lease on life.[49] The abandonment of ISI by the countries of the Andes led to a redefinition of the objectives of the Pact: new targets were formulated, including elimination of tariffs by 1995, a Common External Tariff (CET), and liberalization of foreign investment rules. The Grupo de los Tres (G-3), another sub-regional contender composed of Colombia, Venezuela, and Mexico reached agreement in 1994.[50] In 1991 the Central American Common Market was also revitalized and expanded to include Panama and Honduras (which left after a conflict with El Salvador in 1969). The Central American countries are worried that NAFTA will result in trade distortion that will hurt their interests and cause job loss. However, they support NAFTA politically and have sought ways of integrating with the economies of Mexico and the Caribbean, hoping that will enhance their position. Similarly, CARICOM has been revitalized in recent years.

Perhaps the most important new sub-regional initiative was actually initiated before the NAFTA: the Mercado Común del Sur (MERCOSUR), which includes Argentina, Brazil, Paraguay, and Uruguay.[51] These are among the Latin American countries in which intra-regional trade is highest. Intra-MERCOSUR trade accounts for 40 percent of Paraguay's exports, 35 percent of Uruguay's, 15 percent of Argentina's, and 4 percent of Brazil's. Signed in 1991, the parties to the agreement hoped to establish a CET, eliminate all intra-regional tariffs by the end of 1994, and create a framework for the coordination of macroeconomic policy.

Despite overtures from the MERCOSUR countries, Chile declined to join any regional integration pact. In the 1980s, Chile unilaterally liberalized trade and depreciated the exchange rate, leading to a major decline in manufacturing. However, exports diversified and became the engine of rapid growth after 1986.[52] Chile entered into bilateral agreements with a number of Latin American countries, the most important of which creates a free trade area with Mexico by 1995.[53] Chile also negotiated trade deals with Venezuela, Argentina, Colombia, and other countries.[54] Likewise, Mexico has established itself as a "gateway" to North America, signing agreements with Central America and other countries. Saborio describes this pattern as "NAFTA plus a Mexico-centered hub of additional accords."[55]

Current Problems in Latin American Integration

Despite the widespread enthusiasm for trade liberalization in Latin America, serious obstacles remain. The process of integration has proven extremely difficult for the countries of the Andean Pact, where political unity has always been elusive. They were unable to agree on a CET in early 1993, and Peru abandoned the pact when it was refused special concessions.[56] The largest members of the pact, Colombia and Venezuela, seemed to be more interested in negotiating with Mexico than with Ecuador, Peru and Bolivia.

MERCOSUR, like the Andean Pact, faced serious internal obstacles, and it is unclear that it will achieve the ambitious goal of a unified market by 1995.[57] MERCOSUR countries were unable to agree on a CET in 1993:[58] MERCOSUR countries arrived at agreement on 85 percent of the products they export, however, progress was delayed by Brazil's refusal to accept a low CET on capital goods.[59] Brazil wanted a high external tariff to protect its information sector, while Argentina had no tariff in that sector. Furthermore, the United States and Brazil have a long-standing dispute over computers and patent protection.[60] Such conflicts are a major obstacle to MERCOSUR's forming part of a hemispheric free trade agreement.

Economic integration in MERCOSUR has been made more difficult by macroeconomic imbalances. Argentina's Economy Minister, Domingo Cavallo, argued that because of an overvalued currency, "under current conditions Argentina would be very hurt" by MERCOSUR.[61] Heavy inflows of capital into Argentina in the early 1990s raised fears about excessive demand and speculation. Brazil continued to struggle with inflation and macroeconomic instability;[62] this forced it to repeatedly adjust its exchange rate, causing friction with Argentina. The completion of MERCOSUR could also be held up by electoral politics. Elections are set for 1994 in Brazil and Uruguay and 1995 in Argentina.

The Brazilian policy establishment reacted with caution to the idea of hemispheric free trade. Brazil's disputes with the U.S. concern anti-dumping rules, the Export Enhancement Program, and products subject to the Multifiber Arrangement, none of which were dealt with in the Enterprise for the Americas Initiative. Moreover, hemispheric integration offers no serious debt relief.[63] MERCOSUR countries have highly diversified trade links with the rest of the world; thus, linking MERCOSUR to the United States could result in substantial trade diversion, retaliation by trading partners, and high adjustment costs.[64]

It is not surprising that Brazil proposed the first diplomatic challenge to expanding NAFTA into a Western Hemispheric Free Trade Area (WHFTA). On March 9-10, 1994, foreign ministers from the

MERCOSUR countries decided to examine the feasibility of a Brazilian proposal to create a South American Free Trade Area (SAFTA). The proposal would open the doors for accession of other South American countries to the MERCOSUR.

What was the thinking behind the Brazilian proposal? Clearly, some Brazilian officials believe that MERCOSUR should seek to expand and include other countries rather than deepen and converge with NAFTA. The result could be a competition between SAFTA and NAFTA for new members. NAFTA had what one Brazilian official called "the discrete charm of the industrialized bourgeoisie," but not all countries in South America, he argued, would be willing to pay the same high "entry fee" that Mexico paid in order to gain admittance into this exclusive club. Moreover, Mexico and Chile had political systems that are exceptional in the Latin American region. The Mexican restructuring was aided by a hegemonic party system and corporatist institutions. Chile underwent economic reform under 17 years of authoritarian rule: it emerged with an export-oriented economy, a weakened labor movement, and a disciplined party system. Other Latin American countries may be less able to legislate and implement economic reforms that impose such a painful social cost, and they may be attracted by SAFTA's faster and easier accession, lower "entry fees," minimal loss of sovereignty, and access to Brazil's huge internal market.[65]

Despite the complexities of hemispheric integration -- especially given the position of Brazil -- most of Latin America has clearly shifted to a more outward-oriented economic strategy. A total of 15 agreements were signed between Latin American countries and the United States in the period between May 1990 and December 1991, covering 30 countries.[66] These framework agreements involve few obligations, but are seen as a prelude to further formal integration. Hemispheric economic integration no longer rests on the nationalist objectives of import substitution, industrialization and Latin American solidarity. Instead, it is part of a process of economic restructuring in the region.[67] A major consequence of this restructuring process is what Lowenthal called "a growing predisposition toward pragmatic cooperation with the United States."[68] Latin American countries want closer links with the United States, and the EAI is attractive to many Latin American policy makers because it holds out the possibility of access to markets and foreign investment. In the final section we discuss Canada's interests and assess its influence over the process of hemispheric integration.

Conclusion: Canada's Role in the Hemispheric Community

In their draft Policy Planning Paper,[69] Colin Robertson and Keith Christie argue that Canada must be active in shaping the Latin American and Caribbean response to NAFTA. To leave the U.S. to take the lead would be to risk the emergence of a hub and spoke arrangement centered on the U.S. Mexico's growing network of trade agreements with countries in the region poses a similar, though lesser, risk. These concerns are reflected in Canada's initiation of the NAFTA accession clause. At the outset, Mexico resisted the inclusion of the clause, while the Americans were largely indifferent. Canada, however, wanted to avoid the need to go through another major renegotiation of its access to the U.S. market, should the need to negotiate another free trade agreement arise. In the end, Mexico came to understand this potential problem, and shifted to the Canadian position. The accession clause, however, was the product of Canada's continuing concern about protecting its access to the American market, and in preventing the diversion of investment to the U.S. as the only platform from which to serve an expanding regional market.

There is a widely shared belief in Washington that many Latin American countries are not ready for inclusion in a hemispheric free trade agreement. Jeffrey Schott testified before Congress that he did "not believe, with the exception of Chile, that any country in the hemisphere is near to the point that they could accede to a NAFTA."[70] Yet, the intense competition for capital in Latin America means that many countries will be clamoring to join. The extension of NAFTA to Chile would intensify this pressure.

Talks between the United States and MERCOSUR countries have left open the possibility of accession to NAFTA either as individual countries or as a group. Argentina has indicated it would like MERCOSUR to become part of the EAI, and Argentine President Carlos Menem promoted the idea of MERCOSUR countries joining NAFTA as a group under what he calls a "4+1" formula. One argument in favor of Menem's position is defensive: Brazil and Argentina stand to lose shares of the Latin American and United States markets if an expanding hemisphere free trade agreement excludes them.[71] At the same time, Argentine officials did not dismiss Brazil's proposal for a SAFTA.

Of all the countries in the region, Brazil is clearly the least enthusiastic about hemispheric integration along the lines of NAFTA. The limits on the scope of state activism imposed by a hemispheric free trade agreement is a problem for a country like Brazil. Unlike Brazil,

Chile responded immediately and favorably to the EAI and asked for inclusion in NAFTA. After some hesitation, President Patricio Aylwin was told by the Bush administration that there would be no discussion of further extension of NAFTA until ratification of the agreement with Mexico. In October 1990, Chile signed a framework agreement with the United States.[72] In his welcoming message to President Clinton, Aylwin repeated "our interest to open soon negotiations to sign a free trade accord between our countries."[73]

Clinton indicated that he "would be prepared to discuss immediately with Argentina, with Chile, with other appropriate nations the possibility of expanded trade relations along the NAFTA model .... I have long thought NAFTA should be a model for embracing all of Latin America's democracies and free market economies."[74] Chile is at the front of the line to join NAFTA not because of its importance as a market, but because it is a country that has consolidated market reforms and can be held up by the United States as an example for the rest of Latin America to follow. A number of policy makers in Washington have stressed that a free trade agreement with Chile is important to "send a signal" to other Latin American countries that economic reform and market liberalization will be rewarded.[75]

Chile has greater experience with trade liberalization than any other Latin American nation. As Albert Fishlow put it, "A broad based trade liberalization also has to precede negotiations for a free-trade area. It is the demonstrated capacity to compete against larger imports that will have to undergird a national consensus in favor of ever freer trade. That earlier exposure is why Mexico and Chile now are such attractive candidates."[76] Moreover, Chile's interest in NAFTA is motivated by the desire to send a signal to investors that the country remains committed to a market oriented policy framework.

Canada has no particular interest in encouraging Chile to join NAFTA. Canadian trade with Chile -- less than $100 million in exports -- is insignificant.[77] Although Canada is the largest investor in Chile, it is not among Chile's 15 major trading partners: 18.5 percent of Chilean exports are destined to Japan, and 18.4 percent go to the United States. Within Latin America, Chile trades with Brazil, Argentina, Venezuela, Peru, Bolivia, and Colombia more than with Mexico. Whereas Mexico accounts for half of all U.S. exports to Latin America, Chile accounts for under 3 percent.

Can Canada influence the process of hemispheric integration? Article 2205 of NAFTA spells out the terms for accession. But the accession clause has been called "no more than a hortatory statement" by Hufbauer and Schott,[78] who stress that it lacks "clarity of purpose and procedure, and that it will need supplementary guidance from the NAFTA Free Trade Commission (established in Article 2001) if it is to be of use to aspiring new members."[79] Nevertheless, the clause does state that each country has a veto over any new member: "Any country or group of countries may accede to this Agreement subject to such terms and conditions as may be agreed between such country or countries and the Commission and following approval in accordance with the applicable approval procedures of each country."[80] As such, accession "requires unanimous approval of prospective new members by all the existing members (i.e., a one country veto)."[81]

Chile's highest levels of government pushed hard during 1994 to encourage the U.S. administration to seek fast-track authority to negotiate accession by 1995. The Chileans indicated a willingness sign a bilateral deal with the United States or join NAFTA through the accession mechanism, depending on which route offered a better deal.[82] U.S. willingness to consider unilateral free trade with Chile elicited a rebuke from Canadian trade minister Roy MacLaren who said "The development of bilateral agreements causes real problems to the business community and government in managing trade relationships."[83]

There is nothing in NAFTA to prevent countries from entering into separate bilateral agreements with other countries outside the framework of NAFTA. It is unlikely that Canada would use its veto power to reject a country that could subsequently form a bilateral free trade agreement with the United States, thus creating the hub and spoke regime Canada seeks to avoid. And so, as with Mexico, Canada is likely to follow the lead of the United States.

Differences between Canada and the United States could emerge concerning accession by countries outside the Western Hemisphere. Canada argued for an accession clause that was not restricted to the Western Hemisphere, and subsequently championed the right of countries like Australia to join. Canada has an interest in extending NAFTA to Asia Pacific. Unlike the United States, which exports more to Latin America than to Japan, Canada exports three and a half times more to Japan than to Latin America. If other countries in Asia are added, then U.S. exports to Latin America amount to half of U.S. exports to Asia Pacific, whereas Canadian exports to Latin America are less than one sixth of Canadian exports to Asia Pacific. South Korea and Singapore were among the Asian countries reported by MacLaren to be interested in accession to the NAFTA.[84]

Brian Stevenson[85] argues that a variety of forces have brought Canada closer to Latin America since 1968. "The attempt at closer relations with Latin America emerged, first, from the recognition that this was a region with economic and diplomatic potential for Canada that would supplement, and counterbalance, the relationship with the U.S."[86] Moreover, Canadian membership in the OAS and NAFTA will probably draw Canada into a more intensive relationship in the hemisphere, while the end of the cold war and the consolidation of European integration are likely to eventually reduce the salience of Europe in Canadian foreign policy. However, Canada's OAS and NAFTA decisions do not reflect a comprehensive Canadian policy shift in the direction of greater regional integration; nor is any such change reflected in the allocation of resources among Canada's various regional pursuits. The OAS decision was the core of the government's Latin American strategy, a strategy that did not even contemplate hemispheric, let alone North American, free trade. And the decision to negotiate a North American free trade agreement was driven in large part by the Canadian-U.S. relationship. There is little in this to suggest that Canada might initiate the extension of the hemispheric free trade zone, but much to suggest that Canada will continue to follow the lead of the United States should it decide to continue to consolidate its regional market.

Notes

The authors received funding for this study through separate research grants from the Social Sciences and Humanities Research Council of Canada. They would like to thank David Pollock who read and provided comments on an earlier draft. Responsibility for the analysis rests exclusively with the authors.

1. Roughly 70 percent of Canadian and Mexican exports are destined to the United States; only 22 percent of U.S. exports go to Canada, and less than 7 percent to Mexico. See Maxwell A. Cameron, Lorraine Eden, and Maureen Appel Molot, "North American Free Trade: Co-operation and Conflict in Canada-Mexico Relations," in Fen Osler Hampson and Christopher J. Maule, eds., *A New World Order? Canada Among Nations, 1992-93* (Ottawa: Carleton University Press, 1992), pp. 175-179.

2. "Bandwagoning" contrasts with "balancing" behavior. According to Kenneth Waltz, "Internally, losing candidates throw in their lots with the winner. Everyone wants someone to win ... In a competition for the position of leader, bandwagoning is sensible behavior where gains are possible even for the losers and where losing does not place their security in jeopardy. Externally, states work harder to increase their own strength, or they combine with others, if they are falling behind. In a competition for the position of leader, balancing is sensible behavior where the victory of one coalition over another leaves weaker members of the winning coalition at the mercy of the stronger ones." (Kenneth Waltz, *Theory of International Politics* (Reading, Massachusetts: Addison-Wesley,

1979), p. 126. The end of the cold war has raised the priority of economic competition, leading to balancing among economic regions and bandwagoning within regions.

3. James Baker, III, "The Geopolitical Implications of the U.S.-Canada Trade Pact" *The International Economy*. (January/February, 1988).

4. "Mexico Offers 'Strategic Opportunity' for European Investors President Salinas Tells E.C. Leaders During Tour." *Mexico: Economic Newsletter* (Spring 1990), p. 4; Robert Graham, "Salinas hopes to sell a country come of age," *Financial Times*, January 30, 1990.

5. George W. Grayson, "Mexico Moves Toward Modernization" *Current History*, Vol. 90, No. 554 (1990) p. 109.

6. In late 1989, Salinas made a portentous observation: "Look at the blocks that are being created: Europe in 1992, the Pacific Basin countries, the United States and Canada. I don't want to be left out. We, by geographical happenstance, are neighbors. But by political will we want to get the best from the relationship. We want to participate in the biggest market in the world. If we give our investors the certainty of access to the U.S. market, investment in Mexico will grow substantially." "Mexico's New Partnership," *Newsweek*, October 16, 1989, p. 52.

7. "Free Trade Talks With U.S. Set off Debate in Mexico," *New York Times*, March 29, 1991.

8. Although, as events in the summer and autumn of 1993 would demonstrate, the Congress would be another matter altogether.

9. G. Bruce Doern and Brian W. Tomlin, *Faith and Fear: The Free Trade Story* (Toronto: Stoddart, 1991), pp. 205-42.

10. Michael Hart, *A North American Free Trade Agreement: The Strategic Implications for Canada* (Ottawa: Institute for Research on Public Policy, 1990), pp. 131-136.

11. The development paths of the newly industrializing countries (NICs) of Latin America and East Asia showed marked contrasts. See Fernando Fajnzylber, *Unavoidable Industrial Restructuring in Latin America* (Durham: Duke University Press, 1990); Gary Gereffi, "Paths of Industrialization: An Overview," in Gary Gereffi and Donald L. Wyman, eds., *Manufacturing Miracles: Paths of Industrialization in Latin America and East Asia* (Princeton: Princeton University Press, 1990); Stephan Haggard, *Pathways from the Periphery: The Politics of Growth in the Newly Industrializing Countries* (Ithaca: Cornell University Press, 1990); Fernando Fajnzylber, "The United States and Japan as Models of Industrialization," in Gereffi and Donald L. Wyman, *Manufacturing Miracles*. Although both regions experienced rapid economic growth during the post-war years, they combined export-oriented industrialization (EOI) and import-substituting industrialization (ISI) in different sequences. The East Asian NICs shifted from ISI to EOI in the early phases of development, and then used a successful export drive to promote further industrialization. The Latin American NICs persisted in ISI in the 1970s without achieving export competitiveness.

12. In 1987, per capita income was higher in the NICs of East Asia than Latin America. Per capita income in Latin America declined in relation to 1981 levels. Whereas South Korea grew from a $3 billion to a $121 billion economy between

1965 and 1987, Mexico grew from a $20 billion to a $142 billion economy - even though its population was twice the size of South Korea, Gereffi, "Paths of Industrialization," p. 9.

13. As identified by Secretary of State Joe Clark in a speech at the University of Calgary on February 1, 1990. No official description of the "Long Term Strategy," as approved by cabinet was ever released.

14. Cameron, Maxwell A., "Canada and Latin America," in Fen Osler Hampson and Christopher J. Maule, eds., *After the Cold War: Canada Among Nations, 1990-91* (Ottawa: Carleton University Press, 1991), pp. 110-114.

15. John Best, "Canada's Membership in the OAS Could Go Either Way," *Vancouver Sun*, April 30,1983.

16. As the argument "against Canada becoming involved more extensively in Latin America" was described by Joe Clark in his Calgary speech on February 1, 1990.

17. As Joe Clark expressed it in his Calgary speech, "It is perverse to argue that, whenever Canada *agrees* with Washington, we are doing so for *American* reasons. Canadian interests do not automatically coincide with those of the United States. But neither do they automatically conflict."

18. Brian J.R. Stevenson, *Domestic Pressures, External Constraints and the New Internationalism: Canadian Foreign Policy Towards Latin America, 1968-1990* (Doctoral Dissertation, Department of Political Studies, Queen's University, Kingston, Ontario, 1992), p. 367. See also James Rochlin, *Discovering the Americas* (Vancouver: University of British Columbia Press, 1994), pp. 190-202.

19. External Affairs and International Trade Canada, *Canada's First Year in the Organization of American States: Implementing the Strategy for Latin America,* (1991).

20. At the time of the Mexican visit, one Canadian official said "Ottawa doesn't believe that anything will come of the interest expressed by some U.S. politicians in signing a free trade agreement with Mexico." Drew Fagen, "Ottawa hopes Mexicans' visit will expand trade opportunities," *Globe and Mail*, January 22, 1990.

21. The Task Force secured impact analyses from a variety of other government departments, including Energy, Mines and Resources; Agriculture; and Industry, Science and Technology. The agriculture and textiles sectors were the only ones singled out as specific problem areas. In general, the impact analyses indicated that Mexican access to the Canadian market posed no threat, although in the longer term Mexico would provide moderately serious competition for Canada in the U.S. market.

22. Weekes previously had been Chief Negotiator in the Office of North American Free Trade Negotiations, as well as Assistant Deputy Minister, Trade Policy Branch.

23. Keith H. Christie, "Different Strokes: Regionalism and Canada's Economic Diplomacy." External Affairs and International Trade Canada, *Policy Planning Staff Paper* No. 93/08, p. 10.

24. Ibid.

25. Government of Canada, *Departmental Estimates*, 1993-94.

26. Christie, "Different Strokes," p. 10.

27. Ibid., p. 19.

28. Ibid., p. 19.

29. Government of Canada, *Departmental Estimates*, 1993-94.

30. Christie, "Different Strokes," p. 19.

31. Ibid., p. 20

32. Government of Canada, *Departmental Estimates*, 1993-94.

33. Colin Robertson, and Keith Christie, "Canada in the Americas: New Opportunities and Challenges," p.13. See also Keith Christie, "The Day After: An Agenda for Diversifying Free Trade," Department of Foreign Affairs and International Trade, *Policy Staff Paper* No. 94/04.

34. "Canada and Latin American Integration," Presented to the Colloquium on Trade Liberalization Arrangements in the Western Hemisphere, Toronto, May 31 - June 2, 1992, p. 10.

35. In their discussion of the EAI, Berry, Waverman and Weston argue that Canada's interest in hemispheric free trade lies in the potential for significant economic gains from an expansion in the currently very low level of trade and investment activity, and in the prospect for a multilateral regional trading area with institutions and rules-based mechanisms to prevent the exercise of unilateral power by any country. Al Berry, Leonard Waverman, and Ann Weston, "Canada and the Enterprise for the Americas Initiative: A Case of Reluctant Regionalism," *Business Economics*, Vol. 27, No. 2 (1992).

36. Christie, "Different Strokes," p. 19.

37. Abraham F. Lowenthal, "Latin America: Ready for Partnership?" *Foreign Affairs*, Vol. 72, No. 1 (1993), p. 75.

38. Sebastian Edwards, "Latin American Economic Integration: A New Perspective on an Old Dream," *The World Economy*, Vol. 16, No. 3 (1993), p. 333.

39. See Economic Commission for Latin America and the Caribbean, *CEPAL News*. (September 1993).

40. Albert Fishlow, "The Latin American State," *Journal of Economic Perspectives*, Vol. 4, No. 3 (1990), pp. 61-74. See also Lowenthal, "Latin America." It was argued by the late ECLAC economist Fernando Fajnzylber that by concentrating exclusively on the need to open domestic markets some countries may actually intensify the problems they face in strengthening their entrepreneurial sector and achieving a diversified and competitive economy. Fajnzylber, Fernando, "The United States and Japan," p. 349.

41. Víctor L Urquidi and Gustavo Vega, "Resumen General y Conclusiones," in Urquidi and Vega, eds., *Unas y otras integraciones: Seminario sobre integraciones regionales y subregionales* (Mexico: El Colegio de México and Fondo de Cultura Económica, 1991), p. 42.

42. Edwards, "Latin American Economic Integration," p. 320.

43. Sylvia Saborio, ed., *The Premise and the Promise: Free Trade in the Americas* (New Brunswick: Transaction Publishers, 1992), p. 16.

44. Urquidi and Vega, Rusumen General y Concluskones," pp. 47-8.

45. Edwards, "Latin American Economic Integration," p. 324.

46. Saborio, *The Premise and the Promise*, p. 17.

47. Economic integration may no longer be an expression of nationalism and solidarity, but of a more market-oriented competitiveness. For a discussion of nationalism and integration in Latin America, see Rómulo Almeida, "Reflexión Acerca de la Integracion Latinoamericano," and Felipe Herrera, Felipe, "Hacia una América Latina Integrada," in Urquidi and Vega, *Unas y otras integraciones*.

48. U.S. Congress, *Beyond the Northern American Free Trade Agreement: Chile, the Caribbean, and Administrative Views (Part I and Part II)*. Hearings Before the Subcommittee of International Economic Policy and Trade and Western Hemisphere Affairs of the Committee on Foreign Affairs, House of Representatives, One Hundred and Second Congress, p. 113.

49. Pascó-Font and Sylvia Saborio, "U.S.-Andean Pact Free Trade," in Saborio, *The Premise and the Promise*, p. 233.

50. See, in this volume, chapter 7 by Gustavo Vega Canovas.

51. The MERCOSUR dates to 1986, when Argentina and Brazil launched a Program of Economic Cooperation and Integration.

52. Trade accounts for 72% of GDP in Chile. See Andrea Butelmann and Alecia Frohmann, "U.S.-Chile Free Trade," in Saborio, *The Premise and the Promise*, p. 181.

53. *El Financiero*, February 12, 1991.

54. Butelmann and Frohmann, "U.S.-Chile Free Trade," pp. 182-183.

55. Saborio, *The Premise and the Promise*, p. 20. In addition, a series of other less significant bilateral proposals have flourished. Bolivia was turned down in its bid to integrate with MERCOSUR, which would have linked the Southern Cone countries with the Andean Pact. Colombia has sought an agreement with Paraguay that would give it access to the MERCOSUR market. And Ecuador has negotiated a free trade agreement with Venezuela. Multilateral institutions have not been completely ignored in this process. For instance, Ecuador joined the GATT in 1993. Ecuador clearly joined the GATT with the same motive as Mexico in 1986 - as a point of departure for subsequently dealing directly with the United States. As soon as it joined the GATT, Ecuador stated it would begin preliminary negotiations with the United States.

56. Peru was expected to resume membership in 1994.

57. International Trade Reporter, "Southern Cone Leaders Support MERCOSUR: But Economists Doubt It Will Open by 1995," *Current Reports*, Vol. 9 (July 22, 1993), p. 1257.

58. Paraguay proposed a maximum CET of 10 percent, Uruguay wanted 15 percent, Argentina 20 percent and Brazil 25 percent. In addition, there was a proposal for each country to have a list of exceptions that would carry a 35% tariff. A compromise was agreed to in principle, by which after six years all tariffs would be in the 0-20% range. A 35% CET may be placed on highly sensitive items as determined by individual countries. "MERCOSUR Meeting on Common Tariff Delayed," *Inter-American Trade Monitor*, June 18, 1993.

59. "Major Setback on External Tariff," *Latin American Research Review*, November 25, 1993, p. 542.

60. Roberto Bouzas, "U.S.-Mercosur Free Trade," in Saborio, *The Premise and the Promise: Free Trade in the Americas*, p. 259. Brazil's Foreign Minister,

Fernando Henrique Cardoso, complains about being cast by the United States as the "bad guy" in Latin America, especially for its intellectual property legislation. "Latin America Called Vital to U.S. Economic Strategy," *EAI News: The Bulletin on Integration in the Americas,* May 12, 1993.

61. "Bolivia to Integrate with MERCOSUR, But Pact in Doubt," *Enterprise for the Americas Initiative Bulletin,* December 18, 1992.

62. Edwards, "Latin American Economic Integration," pp. 326-328.

63. Alcides Costa Vaz, "The Enterprise for the Americas Initiative Under the Brazilian Perspective" Paper presented at the XVII International Congress of the Latin American Studies Association (LASA), Los Angeles, September 24-27, 1992, pp. 13-18.

64. Bouzas, "U.S.-Mercosur Free Trade," pp. 265-267.

65. This analysis of SAFTA is based upon remarks by Brazilian government officials and analysts in a workshop on "Brazil and Canada in the Hemispheric Community," held at Carleton University, Ottawa on May 26-27, 1994. The participants spoke on a "not for attribution basis." A rapporteur's report on the workshop was written by Richard Till Heyde, to be published later in 1994 by FOCAL.

66. Saborio, *The Premise and the Promise,* p. 20.

67. Ricardo Grinspun, "NAFTA and the Neoconservative Transformation: The Impact on Canada and Mexico." *Review of Radical Political Economics,* Vol. 25, No. 3 (1993), pp. 14-29.

68. Lowenthal, "Latin America," p. 75.

69. Robertson and Christie, "Canada in the Americas: New Opportunities and Challenges."

70. *Beyond the Northern American Free Trade Agreement,* p. 99.

71. Bouzas, "U.S.-Mercosur Free Trade," p. 264.

72. Francisco Rojas Aravena, "Chile y la iniciativa para las americas," in *La Respuesta a la Iniciativa para las Américas,* Santiago: FLACSO-Chile, forthcoming.

73. *Enterprise for the Americas Initiative Bulletin,* January 22, 1993.

74. *Inter-American Trade Monitor,* July 2, 1993.

75. *Beyond the Northern American Free Trade Agreement,"* p. 122,136.

76. Albert Fishlow, "Beyond the Rhetoric," *Hemisfile,* Vol. 2, No. 3 (1991), p. 11.

77. Nevertheless, Canada signed a framework agreement with Chile on trade and investment in 1991, and it is possible that Canada could expand its exports to Chile in the areas of mining equipment, services and technology.

78. Hufbauer, Gary Clyde and Jeffrey J. Schott, *NAFTA: An Assessment* (Washington, D.C.: Institute for International Economics, 1993), p. 5.

79. Ibid., p. 111.

80. External Affairs and International Trade Canada, *North American Free Trade Agreement,* Ottawa, September 6, 1992.

81. Hufbauer and Schott, *NAFTA: An Assessment,* p. 115.

82. Kelly McParland, "Chile Advances its NAFTA Drive," *Financial Post,* May 4, 1994.

83. Drew Fagen, "U.S.-Chile Talks Opposed by MacLaren," *Globe and Mail*, March 14, 1994.

84. Peter Morton, "Countries Lining up to Enter Agreement," *Financial Post*, May 12, 1994. It should be noted that Ottawa, unlike Washington, did not draw up a list of countries whose application for accession to NAFTA it would view favorably.

85. Stevenson, *Domestic Pressures*, p. 370.

86. As well, Stevenson maintains that pressure from the growing Latin American constituency in Canada also produced closer relations.

9

The U.S. "North American" Trade Concept: Continentalist, Hemispherist, or Globalist?

Alan K. Henrikson

The debate in the United States over the North American Free Trade Agreement (NAFTA) has been described by President Bill Clinton as a "battle of ideas." I concur that it was an ideological contest, even more than a clash of political and economic interests. As Assistant Secretary of State for Inter-American Affairs Alexander Watson interpreted the NAFTA controversy of 1993, "The essence of the debate is as old as the Republic itself: whether we do better to engage with the world or to insulate ourselves from it."[1] On the day of the decisive 234-to-200 House of Representatives affirmative vote on the issue, a *New York Times* editorial agreed with this characterization of "what the NAFTA vote is ultimately about: whether the country is willing to move forward or retreat into economic isolation."[2]

Recognizing that there was indeed a protectionist temptation among many American workers who felt their jobs were threatened by the North American Free Trade Agreement, particularly its permitted increase of imports from labor-inexpensive Mexico, I posit that the debate over NAFTA as a policy issue was not actually about isolationism versus internationalism -- that is, between "retreating" and "competing," as President Clinton himself repeatedly posed the question. To the extent that genuine policy concepts, rather than popular attitudes, were at stake in the NAFTA controversy, I suggest that the "battle of ideas" was a reflection of a basic divergence of thinking about the nature of internationalism itself in the modern world.

There were three distinct versions of internationalism vying for influence during the NAFTA debate. These were *continentalism, hemispherism,* and *globalism.* More particularly, the question was whether the emphasis in national trade policy should be placed on (1) developing the North American continent as a truly unified market, (2) enlarging the area of limited Canadian-U.S.-Mexican economic cooperation to cover the entire Western Hemisphere, or (3) promoting the example and influence of the North American Free Trade Agreement globally, thus liberalizing the entire world trading system. In the following analysis, I propose to do three things. First, I shall elaborate upon the concepts of continentalism, hemispherism, and globalism as interpretive lenses through which the meaning of the North American Free Trade Agreement can be more easily perceived. Second, I shall attempt to identify the factors that could determine which level of international trade cooperation will dominate. Third, I shall offer a concept as a basis for a more general theory that may help to explain the future development of the North American economy, and perhaps other economic groupings elsewhere in the world.

In the context of the post-Cold War world economy, from which many trade-distorting political obstacles already have been removed, the distinguishing element of the proffered theory is the decisive role of economic *regions,* defined here as "natural economic zones." These areas, though sometimes indefinite at their margins, are usually unmistakable at their cores, which are often metropolitan centers. Kenichi Ohmae has called them "region states," a term which rightly indicates that the inhabitants of these natural economic regions can have political wishes and weight though it inaccurately suggests such "states" having a formal character or governmental status.[3]

Although they pose no direct or immediate threat to existing international borders, these community-forming spheres of commercial and other human exchange are nonetheless reorganizing the world. Some of these vibrant regional zones of activity are internal to countries, but many of them surrounding major (or even minor) cities are forming close connections with contiguous and even noncontiguous metropolitan-based regions in other countries.[4] The "nation-state" is simply no longer the only appropriate level for the analysis of international relationships. "For the Clinton administration," Ohmae has reflected, "the irony is that Washington today finds itself in the same relation to those region states that lie entirely or partially within its [political] borders as was London with its North American

colonies centuries ago. Neither central power could genuinely understand the shape or magnitude of the new flows of information, people
and economic activity in the regions nominally under its control." The
intended lesson is that it is counterproductive to try to arrest or deflect
trade flows, assumed to grow naturally, "in the service of nation-
defined interests" -- or traditional state policy.[5] This argument,
though perhaps overstated, is at least partially correct, and it has
important implications for the likelihood of success of officially
negotiated international trade agreements, including NAFTA.

In sum, the debate over North American free trade policy, and
NAFTA's ultimate historical significance for the United States and
also for Canada and Mexico, may finally depend on, more than
anything else, on *the interaction of powerful geoeconomic regions*
within the United States and in "neighboring" countries. These
counterpart and potentially affiliated regions may be found not only in
Canada and Mexico but also in the Caribbean, in some countries of Latin
America, and, not really so much more remotely, in Atlantic Europe and
even in the Pacific and East Asian and Southeast Asian zones.[6]
Physical distance, though still important, is not decisive.

The important foreign relations of the United States (and also of
Canada and Mexico) today are not only international -- between
traditional nation-states -- but also, especially for economic and social
purposes, increasingly *interregional*. Even the future political bearings
of the United States may be determined to some degree by the dynamics
of metropolitan-based, regionally centered transnational communication and connection. NAFTA itself was in part a product of transborder
coalition-building between and among North America's metropolitan-
based regions, irrespective of the U.S.-Canadian and the U.S.-Mexican
national boundaries. The political context and relationships of the
three countries surely have been profoundly affected thereby. The
character of that change will depend, however, on whether, in the
terms here employed, the "North American" future is to be
continentalist, hemispherist, or globalist.

It is pertinent to note that these three alternatives to the outmoded
isolationist-protectionist outlook are all geographical perspectives.
Each word suggests its own appropriate physical scale or scope. These
images of the proper sphere of a trade agreement, when applied to the
map, suggest in turn which nations should be included within it as
signatories. *Continental, hemispheric, and global* are more evocative
and compelling than the more familiar, diplomatic terms for describing
international action -- namely, *unilateral, bilateral* (or *trilateral*), and
multilateral. To be sure, these conventional terms, which are inescap-

FIGURE 9.1 The U.S. "North American" Free Trade Concept

	Unilateral	Bilateral/Trilateral	Multilateral
Continental			
Hemispheric			
Global			

ably a part of standard trade policy vocabulary, have continuing relevance. However, I believe they are often secondary rather than primary categories -- indicative rather than determinative of patterns of international agreements. In particular, the image of continentalism overpowers the idea of bilateralism or trilateralism as an organizing notion for the future of American-Canadian-Mexican relations in North America. The image of globalism, however, probably is weaker than the idea of multilateralism as a structuring concept for international economic relations.

A matrix (see Figure 9.1) exhibits the possible ways in which these three geographical images and three formal-political categories can be correlated. The focus of the present analysis, concerning the North American Free Trade Agreement and its future, will be on the central column. That is, we will be considering "bilateral/trilateral" trade accords involving the United States, Canada, and Mexico in "continental," "hemispheric," and "global" versions. The essential point to be made in connection with this diagram is the contextual variability of the U.S. "North American" trade concept. Although the agreement negotiated by the United States involved only Canada and Mexico, all geographically situated on the North American continent, NAFTA can also be thought of in hemispherist and even in globalist terms. Complementing the Canada-U.S. Free Trade Agreement (CUSFTA) that dated from January 1, 1989, the NAFTA zone of economic cooperation that came into effect among the three countries on January 1, 1994, should be seen through these several different conceptual lenses in order for it to be understood in its full complexity and evaluated more precisely.

The three perspectives are, to a considerable degree, conceptually consistent with each other. Continentalism, hemispherism, and globalism make a "nesting" set. All are, to varying degrees, outward-looking. All are more or less liberal in terms of doctrine. All are aimed basically at increasing economic growth. They also have their differences, which causes tension among them and the policies that flow from them. Specifically, they differ as to what constitutes a community, over what "North America" really is and should be -- just a trade-liberalizing area of agreement or ultimately an economic, social, and even political union? They differ also as to what is possible, over how far the net of international cooperation can effectively be cast -- among like-minded, neighboring countries only or throughout the entire heterogeneous world? They differ, too, over the proper role of state power, i.e., the function of government and diplomacy in developing international relations. Is the state only a limited facilitator of private business activity abroad or an actual manager of a country's overseas economic interests? To the extent of variance on these points, the three ideas are ideological rivals. Let us consider them in order.

Continentalism

The first concept, continentalism, implies that the United States, Canada, and Mexico, within their shared borders and mutually penetrated economies and societies, have numerous interests in common that might lead even to the formation of a common identity. Thus Americans, Canadians, and Mexicans are capable of close integration in many areas beyond trade relations. Rather than exercises in "foreign" policy, American-Canadian-Mexican relations even at the official level take on, from the continentalist perspective, almost a "domestic" character.

The progenitor of the "North American Accord" idea in recent times, former California governor Ronald Reagan, unveiled his somewhat nebulous proposal to this end in announcing his campaign for the Republican nomination for the presidency on November 13, 1979. We live on a *continent*, he said,

> whose three countries possess the assets to make it the strongest, most prosperous and self-sufficient on earth. Within the borders of this North American continent are the food, resources, technology, and undeveloped territory which, properly managed, could dramatically improve the quality of life of all of its inhabitants.
>
> It is no accident that this unmatched potential for progress and

prosperity exists in three countries with such long-standing heritages of free government. A developing closeness among Canada, Mexico, and the United States -- a North American accord -- would permit achievement of that potential in each country beyond that which I believe any of them -- strong as they are -- could accomplish in the absence of such cooperation. In fact, the key to our own future security may lie in both Mexico and Canada becoming much stronger countries than they are today.

Acknowledging the indeterminacy of his thought, Reagan continued: "No one can say at this point precisely what form future cooperation among our three countries will take." But if elected president he would "work tirelessly" with Canadian and Mexican leaders "to develop closer ties" and would invite each country "to send a special representative to our government to sit in on high-level planning sessions with us, as partners." Revealingly, he continued, "It is time we stopped thinking of our nearest neighbors as foreigners."7

An even more holistic "North American" vision was offered by then California governor, Edmund G. (Jerry) Brown, Jr. His was an ecological and ethnographical, no less than economic, perspective. Speaking to the Democratic National Convention at Madison Square Garden in New York on August 13, 1980, Brown stated:

> I have a dream that all Americans can advance together, but that we do so in a form of regional interdependence. I see a type of common market or economic community that will bring along with us our brothers and sisters who share this land of North America. Mexicans, Canadians, Native Americans -- North and South -- all are a part of our destiny and it is time that we recognize that we are a part of theirs.8

The distinctive emphasis of Governor Brown's continental model -- a "North American Community" plan to be governed by rules such as those codified by the Organization for Economic Cooperation and Development (OECD) -- was not on "securing" the continent -- the Reagan keynote -- but on "saving" it.9 By transforming our "part of the planet," as Brown liked to refer to the continent, into an ideal socio-ecological niche -- North America the Beautiful, let us call it, in contrast with Reagan's North American Bastion idea -- the citizens of the United States and their neighbors could once again elevate the imagination of the world. "Frontiers are closing," Brown had speculated in New York, "but others are opening up."

For both of these North American visionaries, the one politically conservative and the other culturally radical, the continent on which they were born and raised was the ultimate base -- the geo-psychological bedrock -- of all future American policymaking. Neither Reagan nor Brown then had the knowledge of other places or, especially, of the traditions of U.S. foreign policy and the country's commitments overseas to be disposed to any position other than putting America's interests first. Canada and Mexico were to be invited to share in the American future by them largely because those were the other countries they knew best, as governors of a state with many Canadian and Mexican residents. Theirs was not, however, an exclusive concept.

The continentalist theme that was struck in the early 1980s was repeated, usually in far more pedestrian language, throughout the later NAFTA debate. The premise of this discussion in the late 1980s and 1990s regarding the continent was threefold: that North America is primary, that it represents potential, and that it requires development. Although this version of North Americanism is not keyed on developments in other parts of the world, it cannot be considered an isolationist, "insulationist," doctrine.[10] It did not imply protectionism like that of the Hawley-Smoot Tariff (1930). Nor did continentalist thinkers generally favor banning foreign investment in the United States or prohibiting immigration from abroad. Continentalism increasingly became, essentially, a leadership strategy, if one still distinguished by a strong unilateralist tendency. Although under the free trade program of the 1980s the actual form of "North American" economic cooperation with Canada and Mexico was initially bilateral and later trilateral, the expectation implicit in the continentalist conception was that the United States would be the dominant partner.

CUSFTA and NAFTA were not only inward-looking but also outward-looking. It cannot be doubted that the U.S. justification for North America-based economic cooperation included foreign policy considerations. By the 1990s, this had become explicit. "The signal the United States wants to send to the world," said the U.S. State Department Counselor Robert Zoellick during the Bush administration, "is that we are committed to opening markets and that we will extend a hand to others who share that commitment" -- and not, he seemed to imply, to others.[11]

With the administration of Bill Clinton came a less geopolitical, more geoeconomic approach to trade policy, focused on problems at home and inclined as a result to seek ways of acting abroad that would help resolve them. The view was repeatedly expressed -- virtually a Clinton doctrine -- that the foreign and domestic spheres are insepar-able. "No issue more clearly illustrates the links between foreign and domestic policy," as the Secretary of State, Warren Christopher, commented in a Los Angeles address, "than the North American Free Trade Agreement." He added: "The European nations and Japan leave no stone unturned to compete in their regional markets, where they have a natural geographic advantage." Like the European Community and Japan, Christopher argued, "we must have a trade strategy tailored to our region -- and NAFTA is absolutely crucial to that strategy."[12]

President Clinton, though initially skeptical, appears intellectually to have accepted the geoeconomic logic of establishing a North American base. "NAFTA is essential to our long-term ability to compete with Asia and Europe," he had said when signing his administration's modifying "side agreements" to the Bush-negotiated NAFTA. "Across the globe our competitors are consolidating, creating huge trading blocks. This pact will create a free trade zone stretching from the Arctic to the tropics, the largest in the world -- a $6.5-billion market, with 370 million people. It will help our businesses to be both more efficient and to better compete with our rivals in other parts of the world. This is essential to our leadership in this hemisphere and the world."[13]

In the critical final stage of the congressional debate over NAFTA, President Clinton's argument of continent-based competitiveness took on defensive, even protectionist, overtones. The North American "rules of origin" provisions of NAFTA, in particular, were useful in this regard.[14] If Congress should reject the agreement with Canada and Mexico, and he were a foreign leader seeing the opportunity suddenly presented, Clinton said in the vernacular of Arkansas: "I would jump on this like flies on a June bug." He elaborated: "I would, if I were the Prime Minister of Japan, have the Finance Minister of my country in to see the President of Mexico on the 18th of November. That's what I would do. I'd say, 'We've got more money than they do anyway; make the deal with us.' And if I were running the economic affairs of the European Community, I would do the same thing."[15] Basically, the sentiment behind this presidential use of hyperbole suggested the North American market was to be, principally if not preclusively, for North Americans to develop.

Hemispherism

The second "North American" concept, hemispherism, places the continent even more explicitly in a foreign policy context. The hemispheric idea is virtually as old as U.S. diplomatic tradition. It dates from the Monroe Doctrine of 1823, and even earlier.[16] It is based on the notion of an antinomy between the Old World (mainly, Europe) and the New World. The distinction had ideological and moral meaning as well as political and strategic significance: the former was the home of monarchism, and the latter was to become a realm of shared republicanism -- today, democracy.

During the twentieth century, U.S. policy initiatives such as Franklin D. Roosevelt's "Good Neighbor" attitude and John F. Kennedy's "Alliance for Progress" development scheme, brought about an increased measure of Inter-American diplomatic and economic cooperation. The North Americanism of one-time Democrat Ronald Reagan, who admired the leadership styles of Roosevelt and Kennedy, was in some measure a throwback to conventional U.S. Pan-Americanism. His advocacy of statehood for Puerto Rico, also proposed by President Gerald Ford, was a more distinctively Republican idea. Reagan's 1979 proposal that "the largest countries of North America -- Canada, Mexico, and the United States -- should forge a closer alliance and become more of a power in the world," he has recalled, was intended at least indirectly, and without any handouts, to benefit the whole hemisphere. The former President explained: "Not only would it be to our mutual economic benefit -- I thought that working together, those of us in North America might be able to help the Latin American countries help themselves."[17]

In June 1990, President George Bush, extending the North American and Caribbean plans of his predecessor, announced his Enterprise for the Americas Initiative trade, investment, and debt-relief program, thus proclaiming hemispherism anew. Its most salient feature was the offer on the part of the United States to begin a "process of creating a hemisphere-wide free trade zone," linking North to Central and South America. Support for increased investment in Latin America through the Inter-American Development Bank and reduction of its indebtedness via the administration's Brady plan would strengthen the initiative. While not a fully adequate solution to the Americas' economic problems, this hemispheric scheme, intermediate in concept between a mere trading area and an integrated market, the goal of an economic entity of Pan America (plus Canada) "stretching from the port of Anchorage to the Tierra del Fuego" would constitute an impressive sphere of U.S. economic cooperation and influence.

The ideological, geographical, and historical dimensions of the Enterprise for the Americas Initiative also merit attention. President Bush said that freedom had made great gains not just in Eastern Europe but in the Americas too. Despite the one remaining exception of Cuba, "the transition to democracy is moving towards completion," and all could sense with excitement that the day was not far off when the Americas would be "fully free." The "natural wonders" of the hemisphere also received rhetorical support from him, and, by means of debt-for-nature swaps and environmental trust funds, the prospect of better-financed state protection. "From the vistas of the unspoiled Arctic to the beauties of the barrier reef off Belize to the rich rain forest of the Amazon," as President Bush urged, "we must protect this living legacy that we hold in trust." The approach in two years of the 500th anniversary of Columbus's discovery of America ("our New World") reminded him and his audience of yet another basis for hemisphere-based action. This "epic event" marked the beginning of a "shared history," that continued Columbus's voyage and "the courageous quest for the advancement of man." In sum: "Our challenge, the challenge in this new era of the Americas, is to secure this shared dream and all its fruits for all the people of the Americas -- North, Central, and South."[18]

The Clinton administration, although it did not adapt easily to using the Republican nomenclature of "Caribbean Basin Initiative" and "Enterprise for the Americas Initiative," soon recognized the hemispherist implications of the NAFTA pact with Canada and Mexico. It, too, in President Clinton's words, spoke of "a hemispheric community of democracies linked by growing economic ties and common political beliefs." Secretary of State Christopher more pragmatically used a diplomatic argument in support of NAFTA observing that the Mexican government was working with the administration "to defuse hemispheric conflicts and crises." For example, the two governments together had taken the lead in June 1993 in calling for immediate action by the Organization of American States "to stand by democracy in Guatemala." This cooperation had "made a difference" and symbolized the constructive way in which U.S.-Mexican relations were developing. Their backing the successful, negotiated end to the war in El Salvador was another case in point. Christopher predicted: "NAFTA will further solidify the productive new relationships that the United States has been seeking with Mexico and our other Latin American neighbors." He later asserted that NAFTA, by encouraging democratic governments in the Western Hemisphere that were opening up their economies to American trade and investment, would "mark a turning point in the history of our relations throughout Latin America" -- and maybe even the world as a whole. With the tentativeness and tenuousness of democratic and free-market conversion in the former Soviet Union probably in view, Christopher reflected: "In many respects, Latin America is pointing the way toward a new and better future in the post-Cold War era."[19]

Perhaps the single most remarkable, and personally expressed, private high-level appeal for passage of NAFTA on hemispherist grounds was that of David Rockefeller, former chairman of the Chase Manhattan Bank. In an article in the *Wall Street Journal*, Rockefeller began: "I can't help seeing the current debate over the North American Free Trade Agreement in the context of my own half century of work with the people of Canada and Latin America, an interest that I shared with my late brother, Nelson" -- who had begun his public career as the State Department's Inter-American Affairs Coordinator during the presidency of Franklin Roosevelt. Many of the goals the two men had hoped to see achieved in their lifetimes seemed "nearer now to realization than they have ever been," Rockefeller observed, and yet they were threatened by a rejection of NAFTA by the United States.

From the 1940s into the 1970s, Latin American and Caribbean countries pursued a course of "directed national development" based on an economic model requiring import substitution and protectionism and reflecting nationalistic thinking "often colored as Marxism." The extension of U.S. bank credit, accelerated by the need to "recycle" petrodollars from Middle Eastern oil profits, fostered high growth rates there, but at the cost of a large debt burden, as well as inflated public sectors and noncompetitive private sectors.

This lasted until the onset of the "debt crisis," when in August 1982, the Mexican government announced that it could no longer make international payments. Since then, as Rockefeller noted, "a whole new vision of economic organization has come to the fore." The free trade agreement between Canada and the United States contributed to the emergence of this view. "But a real awareness of the immense potential locked up within our own hemisphere was brought to life by leaders to the south of us." This "revolutionary" process started in Chile and continued with the decision by the Mexican government, under Presidents Miguel de la Madrid and Carlos Salinas de Gortari, to join the General Agreement on Tariffs and Trade (GATT) and to negotiate a free trade agreement with the United States, which led ultimately to NAFTA and its side agreements. Other countries in Latin America, such as Argentina and Venezuela, were moving in the direction of a market economy.

David Rockefeller and others at a "Forum of the Americas" in Washington in the spring of 1993, thus agreed unanimously to strive together to achieve "a full Western Hemisphere free trade area by the year 2000." What would have seemed "a fantasy" only a few years ago was made suddenly possible because of "a revolutionary new mood of pragmatism and enterprise" in these lands. The prospect of a hemispheric trade zone seemed especially "exciting" to Rockefeller at that time as the European Community's "Europe '92" single market plan was proving much harder to achieve in reality than in concept. "Here in the Americas," Rockefeller almost rhapsodized,

> we can contemplate the extraordinary vision of a free trading area stretching from Canada's Hudson Bay to Tierra del Fuego at the tip of South America. This 'half sphere' has a predominantly young population of more than 700 million people in a community of nations that already generates a combined gross national product of more than $7 trillion. Beyond lies an immense potential for growth .... What it comes down to is this: The changes in attitudes and policies to make this dream come true have happened. Everything is in place -- after 500 years -- to build a true 'new world' in the Western Hemisphere.[20]

The basic "NAFTA" argument of Rockefeller and other hemispherists, who were often persons who had long-term associations with Latin America and were at least somewhat familiar with its culture, was that approval of the agreement was indispensable to fulfillment of a historic "American" mission: the quasi-utopian idea of establishing a new order of things, a *novus ordo seclorum*, in the Western lands. From the perspective of the indigenous populations of the continents, of course, the *encuentro* with Columbus and his European successors (including the Anglo-American settlers of what became the United States) began a more complicated task. Yet even most Latin Americans, though recognizing the cultural difference, the North-South wealth disparity, and the asymmetry of power, seemed ready to welcome conclusion of NAFTA and the prospect of its extension to them.[21] A revolt in the Mexican state of Chiapas that was timed to coincide with the coming into effect of NAFTA was a sharp counterpoint, but probably no more than that, to the hopefulness of the overall Latin American response to the North American Free Trade Agreement.[22]

After NAFTA the purely economic arguments for proceeding with trade treaties with Central and South American countries next, rather than with major U.S. trading partners in other parts of the world, were not self-evident. "Hemispheric" reasoning, insofar as it was not simply governed by tradition or sentiment, was to some degree conditioned by events and trends elsewhere in the world, including challenging "regionalization" developments in Europe and Asia. Thus the hemispheric project will not proceed wholly autonomously.

Nonetheless, the presumption of hemispheric unity, and the expectation in Latin America that a previously stated U.S. policy -- the "Enterprise for the Americas Initiative" -- will be carried out, give the idea of somehow extending the benefits of NAFTA to other countries of the Western Hemisphere a historical momentum. In the text of the North American Free Trade Agreement itself, in the "accession" clause, there is no geographical restriction indicated. The first paragraph of Article 2204 ("Accession") states: "Any country or group of countries may accede to this Agreement subject to such terms and conditions as may be agreed between such country or countries and the [Free Trade] Commission and following approval in accordance with the applicable legal procedures of each country."[23]

At the beginning of the NAFTA talks, the trilateral negotiations were influenced by the inheritance of U.S. national policy, as formulated by the Bush administration. Neither the American nor the Canadian or Mexican governments, however, wished to seem to be "excluding" others. Therefore, while not intending to offer to open up the North American market right away to "the whole world," the three parties, on the initiative of the Mexican chief negotiator, Herminio Blanco Mendoza, agreed to state in the final text that "any country or group of countries" could accede.[24] Nonetheless, the influence of the Pan American ideal and the Enterprise of the Americas Initiative made it most likely that NAFTA would be extended southward before it was expanded in any other direction.

Already, the government of Chile had indicated its desire to conclude a free trade agreement with the United States, thereby "docking" onto NAFTA. This remains the most likely next step. Current scenarios for possible southward expansion of NAFTA are the following. First, there is the "one by one" method of accession, which would be suitable for the Chilean case. Second, there is the "cluster by cluster" approach, which would permit admission of subregional groups (the Southern Cone Common Market or Mercosur, the Andean Group, the Caribbean nations, and the Central American Common Market). Third, there is the "building-block" approach, which would entail the coordinated adoption by potential adherents of similar product standards, investment and intellectual property rules, and minimum environmental and labor standards. The complexity, both economic and political, of adding other countries, or groups of them, or of coordinating numerous national policies meant that creation of a Western

Hemisphere free trade zone, which President Clinton has accepted as his own administration's post-NAFTA objective, could require ten or fifteen years. Somewhat more hopefully, Secretary of Commerce Ron Brown has said: "Most of it could happen before the end of the century."[25]

The decision of the U.S. government to invite all of the Western Hemisphere's 35 heads of state (except Fidel Castro of Cuba) to a meeting -- a Summit of the Americas -- in Miami in December 1994 should advance this purpose. Already, as Richard Feinberg who is in charge of Inter-American affairs on the National Security Council staff has pointed out, the United States exports $80 billion in goods and services to Latin America, more than it sends to Japan. "By the year 2000," he predicted, "U.S. exports to Latin America could well exceed U.S. sales to Western Europe -- and could add one million new jobs for U.S. workers."[26] Extending the North American continental market southward, therefore, might increase the size of U.S. prosperity as well as the area of Western Hemisphere democracy.

Globalism

The very widest "North American" conceptual lens for future U.S. trade is the globalist -- or, to use the formal-legal expression, the multilateralist. Globalism is a newer term than either continentalism or hemispherism in the American political lexicon, though it may be an older idea. The image of "one world" dates from World War II.[27] The ideology itself has origins in *The Wealth of Nations* (1776) of Adam Smith and in the opposition of the Anglo-American colonials to mercantilist controls, their assertion of neutral shipping rights, and their aggressive pursuit of markets overseas.

The liberal-internationalist policies of President Woodrow Wilson committed the United States government, in principle, to the objective of universal peace through free trade. Secretary of State Cordell Hull with his Reciprocal Trade Agreements Program (1934) was a successor. The U.S. trade negotiations with Canada and Great Britain in 1937 and 1938, oriented toward expanding the Atlantic as well as the North American economy, established a broad context of policy for later trade discussions with America's hemispheric and transoceanic neighbors.

The events of World War II seemed completely to negate what was called by anti-isolationists the "myth" of continents. Analysts pointed out, for example, that Buenos Aires is physically farther away from the United States than every capital of Europe, including Moscow. In terms of economic cost-distance, cities in the United States were sometimes "closer" to cities in Europe, or even Asia, than they were to each other. In trade policy, as well as in other matters, Americans began to appreciate that they were contending in what President Franklin D. Roosevelt called, in a strategic sense, a "world-wide arena."[28]

The General Agreement on Tariffs and Trade of 1947 embodied the Wilsonian-Hullian-Rooseveltian ideology, although imperfectly, and subsequent GATT negotiating rounds have sought to realize the American goal of progressive world improvement in part through commercial liberalization. The theoretical justification for the multilateral approach to world order in international trade, as onetime GATT deputy director-general Gardner Patterson has pointed out, is the classical theory of "comparative advantage," according to which global economic efficiency is maximized if all countries specialize in the goods they can produce most cheaply. Although it rests on "heroic assumptions" about conditions in the real world, Patterson writes, "the comparative-advantage theory has served as a powerful guide to enlightened policy."[29]

This general theoretical perspective has informed the entire discussion of the North American Free Trade Agreement. "What carried the day for liberal trade policy," as Herbert Stein, a former chairman of the President's Council of Economic Advisers, observed in support of NAFTA, "was the case beyond the addition of some tenths of a percent to the national income of the U.S. It was the recognition that, in addition to serving our economic interests, liberal trade policy was an application of American principles, an expression of American concern for the well-being of others, and above all that it made a contribution to the stability of the world we live in."[30]

Stein and other multilaterally inclined economists could support NAFTA as at least a step in the right direction. In particular, most people hoped it would help to bring about the long-delayed completion of the GATT's Uruguay Round of global negotiations, in which the United States and 110 other countries were involved. To be sure, some professional economists, though not actually opposed to NAFTA, regard it as a derogation from true multilateralist principles, even if the agreement could be construed as technically GATT-consistent.[31] It could be a distraction from the diplomatic task of getting the Uruguay Round finished. Instead of President Clinton's "spending his meager political capital" on NAFTA, Yoshi Tsurumi argued, he "had best salvage the Uruguay Round Agreement to revive the multilateral and freer trading system of the world." The United States, Canada, and Mexico "would benefit more from the revived and expanded GATT than from the trade agreement, which will divert a limited amount of trade from the United States and Asia to Mexico, at the expense of American jobs."[32]

One multlilaterally oriented economist, Jagdish Bhagwati, was serving as the economic policy adviser to the GATT Director-General. As one of some 300 economists in the United States who sent a letter to President Clinton in support of NAFTA, he could be for the agreement only reluctantly.[33] He made a distinction between the "piecemeal," or geographical, approach to regionalism and "programmatic" regionalism. To him, NAFTA had to mean more than "regionalism for the Americas" (to which he believed the regionalist idea had been "confined by President Bush's men"). "If America's regionalism is not to turn into a piecemeal, world-trading-system-fragmenting force, it is necessary to give it a programmatic, world-trade-system-unifying format and agenda," Bhagwati argued.

One possible strategy for globalizing regionalism, he suggested, was for the United States to encourage, rather than discourage, Japan "to line up the Asian countries" (all the way to the Indian subcontinent) in an "AFTA" -- an Asia Free Trade Agreement -- while it proceeded to line up the South American countries behind NAFTA, on a schedule, say, of ten years. Then, Japan and the United States -- the two "hubs" -- would meet and "coagulate" into a larger free trade agreement, "finally negotiating with the EC and its associate countries to arrive at the Grand Finale of multilateral free trade for all in Geneva!"[34]

Most recent U.S. administrations, believing it necessary to "negotiate from strength," have used the strong power position of representing (through not entirely controlling) a large economy and also various bargaining devices (e.g., "Super 301" of the 1988 Trade Act) to pry open foreign markets when they have been formally closed or otherwise resistant to American exports. While not, in doctrinal terms, protectionist, neither the continental approach nor the hemispheric approach to global trade liberalization precludes leverage, exercised bloc-to-bloc, against the new European Union (EU) or the Malaysia-suggested East Asian Economic Group (EAEG) or any other such exclusive Asia-based trading combination.

"What is wrong with a dual strategy of multilateral negotiations under GATT together with a regional approach?" asked Rudiger Dornbusch in *The Economist*. "The regional approach need not cause trade wars between competing blocks. On the contrary, it may be a good way to achieve multilateral liberalisation." Multilateralism or globalism, though a correct "textbook" doctrine, "moves at the pace of the slowest. Regional integration can open up economies further and faster.

It should be given free rein." Multilateral or global progress could, and eventually would, follow. "Later may come the linking of the European and American blocks," for example.[35] Regionalism thus can be offered, as Bhagwati skeptically puts it, as "a useful *supplement*, not an alternative" to multilateralism. "'We are only walking on two legs' is the popular argument. That we may wind up walking on all fours is ignored," he adds.[36]

From either the continentalist, the hemispherist, or the globalist perspectives, the successful conclusion of a North American Free Trade Agreement was recognized as setting a precedent and exerting an exemplary effect. NAFTA also was seen as capable, along with other factors, of fostering economic justice and political freedom. Just as the European Union brought Spain, Greece, and Portugal "into the fold," stabilizing them economically and politically, so also, as Dornbusch noted, the policy of North American free trade was "designed to bring political openness to Mexico and to begin the economic and political rehabilitation that Central and South America need. Here, the Uruguay Round is simply beside the point."[37] That is, continentalism and, by extension, hemispherism were, in concept, more comprehensive approaches, allowing deeper involvement in community building than globalism-multilateralism.

Without an effective GATT, however, regionalism might fail to contribute to interregional justice -- that is, between the NAFTA partnership, the European Union, and the developing countries that constitute the majority of mankind. The GATT, as was emphasized by Lindley Clark, has been useful in "controlling the regional agreements' relations with the rest of the world."[38] The developing country producers of primary commodities could find themselves effectively excluded as regionalization in Europe and in North America proceeds. For example, in order to secure congressional approval of NAFTA, President Clinton felt obliged politically to agree to maintain tight overall restrictions on sugar imports, to the possible detriment of the Caribbean countries and sugar producers elsewhere.[39] Regional agreements "will work," as Clark contended, as long as the GATT remains the effective overseer. "Without an effective GATT, they still could work for the members of the large trade blocs," he acknowledged. However, Clark explained the consequences for the rest: "The chief sufferers would be the developing nations that belong to no big trade bloc. These countries are the ones that benefit most from GATT's efforts to open world trade for the benefit of all."[40] Globalism, in principle at least, embraces mankind.

The Winning Forces in the "Battle of Ideas"

These, then, are three master concepts through which the present North American Free Trade Agreement has emerged. The questions I now pose, with the recent fight over NAFTA approval behind us and the years of its implementation ahead, are these: Which are the factors that may determine the shifting "balance" among the concepts of continentalism, hemispherism, and globalism? And, in consequence, how will the North American Free Trade Agreement, now that it is approved, actually develop, in the near future and over a longer period?

The determinants of the outcome of President Clinton's "battle of ideas," as here redefined as being *within* the American inter-nationalist tradition (rather than mainly a struggle against isolationism) are both internal and external. The debate within Congress, and the attempts by officials of the Clinton administration and representatives of outside groups to bring influence to bear, is an intriguing subject in itself, but far too complicated a topic to examine here in detail. The surge in "deal-making" between the White House and Capitol Hill has been viewed by some participants and commentators as being the process that made final agreement on NAFTA possible -- and, indeed, determined much of its content.[41] The Clinton-negotiated NAFTA "side agreements" on labor standards, environmental safeguards, and import surge protection, in particular, have been cited as indicative of a completely process-driven method of making American trade policy, which could carry over into the GATT negotiations.[42] The White House concessions seemed to say, hold tight, because the president is always willing to bargain. Gary Hufbauer commented, "All these side agreements send a signal that the U.S. is an open bazaar."[43] In actuality, however, the compromises that resulted from the NAFTA politicking do not appear to have affected the substance of the agreement in a significant way.

Much of the outcome depended, very obviously, on the factor of leadership -- the effort that President Clinton himself made, if belatedly, during the final phase of the NAFTA battle. His appeal on November 1, to members of the United States Chamber of Commerce and other business leaders, asked to be "missionaries," showed a willing-ness to cross over from Democratic party lines to a powerful Republican constituency in order to build a winning coalition. His subsequent direct confrontation with organized labor opponents of NAFTA in television statements also was decisive. It made many wavering Democratic congressmen, who had been fearful of voting their "consciences," believe that they could do so. In any case, it would look bad (and be remembered at the White House) if they did less than the President himself was doing.

The fact that some leading opponents of NAFTA, notably House Majority Leader Richard Gephardt (D., Missouri) and Representative David Bonior (D., Michigan), also had well-thought-out, principled positions in support of the working man (Mexican as well as American and Canadian), if anything, further legitimated a pro-NAFTA vote on policy grounds. The proponents of the measure, it seemed, should have their larger rationale too. For most NAFTA supporters in Congress, approving the agreement just seemed the right thing to do socially as well as politically, as it seemed likely to be of ultimate benefit even for most Americans, as well as others, who in the short term might be adversely affected.

The external reasons for NAFTA's approval, which generally worked in favor of a widening hemispherism or even an expansive globalism, were perhaps decisive, especially on the rhetorical ("battle of ideas") level. One of the floor managers of the NAFTA bill in the House of Representatives, Bill Richardson (D., New Mexico), stated after the vote that the "framing" of the issue in terms of "our international responsibilities" was "pivotal" in determining the outcome.[44] Only a few days after the NAFTA vote the President would be in Seattle for a summit meeting of the Asia Pacific Economic Cooperation (APEC) group of nations, called and chaired by him. This event would soon be followed by the deadline of December 15, on which the administration's congressionally-granted "fast track" negotiating authority would expire, for completion of the GATT Uruguay Round.

In a speech in Seattle on November 19, President Clinton attested to the outward, internationalist, indeed globalist orientation that increasingly was his administration's trade policy, owing in part to the demonstration effect of the North American Free Trade Agreement. "Wednesday's vote for NAFTA enables me to begin this APEC meeting bolstered by a bold expression of America's intent to remain involved in the world," Clinton stated, continuing: "And the NAFTA vote, combined with this APEC conference, greatly strengthens our push for an even bigger potential breakthrough -- a new GATT agreement."[45] That achievement, too, came with the announcement on December 15, in Geneva that the Uruguay Round, which had continued for seven years, through three U.S. administrations, had ended in essential agreement -- with some difficult issues, notably trade in audiovisuals, simply being left out. The successful conclusion of the Uruguay Round following approval of NAFTA, President Clinton later stated, "cements our position of leadership in the new global economy."[46]

Such a statement, asserting world leadership, conceals the inner complexity of the American position and philosophy.   Within America's globalist policy and multilateralist program, there was a continentalist and unilateralist core.   "All of us can be proud that, at this critical moment when many nations are facing economic troubles that have caused them to turn inward, the United States has once again reached outward and has made global economic growth its cause," the president said.   At the same time, he re-emphasized the essentially domestic purpose behind his foreign posture.   "This year, we've worked hard to put the economic interest of America's broad middle class back at the center of our foreign policy as well as our domestic policy."   In summary, he stated: "Today's agreement caps a year of economic renewal for our nation."[47]

Toward a New Theory of Interregional Trade

The "nation," it is today becoming evident, is not the only, or perhaps even the most important, focus of attention for those who understand and negotiate international trade policies.   Kenichi Ohmae has gone so far as to assert:

> The nation state has become an unnatural, even dysfunctional, unit for organizing human activity and managing economic endeavor in a borderless world. It represents no genuine, shared community of economic interests; it defines no meaningful flows of economic activity. In fact, it overlooks the true linkages and synergies that exist among often disparate populations by combining important measures of human activity at the wrong level of analysis.[48]

Rather than using only the "nation" (Canada, United States, Mexico) or a broad category such as the "continent," the "hemisphere," or the "globe" as the dominant unit of analysis, the cross-cutting notion of economic "region" should also be employed.   It has long been recognized that nations, though they may meet the formal-legal definition of an integrated area, may "reflect great regional diffuseness and lack of integration."[49]   Thus, the ultimate meaning and historical significance of the North American Free Trade Agreement may depend on the interests and orientations of *parts* of the United States (and of Canada and Mexico).

Paul Krugman has pointed out that "one of the best ways to understand how the international economy works is to start by looking at what happens *inside* nations."   That is, not only a national economy but also the international economy is shaped by internal developments. These are of a pertinent kind. Krugman hypothesizes: "If we want to understand differences in national growth rates, a good place to start is by examining differences in regional growth; if we want to understand international specialization, a good place to start is with local specialization."[50] Michael Porter similarly observes: "Competitive advantage is created and sustained through a highly localized process."[51]

The factor of location can determine attitudes, as well as the actual relationships that develop from or because of the advantages that might derive from a home base. The historical and future significance of NAFTA -- whether and how it develops as a North American community -- may well depend on the outlooks of, as well as changing equilibrium among, North America's many regions. (The *Washington Post* writer Joel Garreau, in order to highlight the distinctness of these regional economies, societies, and mentalities, calls them "nations.")[52] In a number of instances -- the New England/Canadian Maritimes area, the Pacific Northwest/British Columbia area, the Northern Mexican/American Southwest area, and the South Florida/Caribbean Island area -- they are transborder, or bi-national, regions. Especially since the completion of the NAFTA, a Western Canadian/U.S. Far Western/Northern Mexican pattern of contact and exchange may be developing in a tri-national region.[53] Particularly as the United States, Canada, and Mexico -- in every case, federally structured and already therefore somewhat decentralized political systems -- are countries of extensive geographical scope, having within them concentrations of population and industry that alternate with areas of thin settlement and slight development, it is not surprising that there should be distinct, enduring, and sometimes potent differences in regional consciousness.[54] These differences have consequences for policy.

An example of particular relevance to the role of regional centers in promoting NAFTA and producing a North American economy, is that of San Antonio, Texas, at the crossroads of trade between the United States and Mexico and also Canada. More than half of all the goods exported from anywhere in the United States to Mexico pass through that city. It was there that President George Bush, Prime Minister Brian Mulroney, and President Carlos Salinas de Gortari gathered in October 1992 to watch their respective negotiators sign the North American Free Trade Agreement. The provision in the final NAFTA package approved by Congress for a "North American Development Bank," to be associated with the NAFTA secretariat, might also be

located there, if San Antonio's boosters have their way. It would like
to be, in short, the "NAFTA capital." The city has staked so much of
its future on the North American trade accord that, as a reporter noted,
its leaders like to portray it "as a kind of Hong Kong to Mexico's China
-- a city poised to take off as a banking, trading and shipping hub in a
new world of trade without barriers."[55]

Other urban-based regions, including those on the West Coast, also
see themselves as foci in the growth of trade and other exchange
between the United States and other countries, on the North American
continent and beyond it.[56] At the time of the APEC conference in
Seattle, President Clinton registered the importance of metropolitan-
regional orientations in setting the sights of the United States abroad.
"This city is the appropriate place to have this meeting," he told the
APEC Host Committee. "Not only is Washington State the most trade-
oriented state in the Union, but as I learned from the governor on the
way upstairs, 80% of your trade is tied to the Asia-Pacific region, and
90% of the imports to this port in Seattle come from Asia. Over half of
Boeing's planes, Microsoft's computer programs, and Washington's
wheat are sold abroad."[57] These go to Asia, and all over the world.

At the opposite corner of the United States, in the Southeast
(Garreau's "Dixie"), major new economic connections with Europe are
being formed. The most dramatic developments are those that have
been occurring in the "upstate" region of South Carolina -- the small
twin-city conurbation of Greenville and Spartanburg. This rapidly
growing area, which has a population of approximately 650, 000, is
already host to more than 60 European companies. In fact, the
Greenville-Spartanburg region has the highest density per capita of
European investment in the United States. France's Michelin Tire
Corporation is, other than the state government, South Carolina's
largest employer. There are also major companies from Italy and
Switzerland. The recent prize catch is the German car maker,
Bavarian Motor Works (BMW), which decided to locate its first North
American manufacturing plant on a site off Interstate 85 (known as "the
Autobahn") between the two cities. BMW's decision, though
surprising, is considered "a logical evolution of a region with an
increasingly international -- and mainly European -- economic base."[58]

How has this regional phenomenon come about? Part of the answer
is historical. As South Carolina's governor, Carroll Campbell,
explained the German move to Spartanburg County: "You have to
understand that part of the county was settled by Germans. There is a
lot of German settlement in that part of South Carolina and the western
part of North Carolina. This is a great comfort factor to BMW." These

"ties from early times," along with the mild climate, proximity to mountains, and the area's other amenities, make it "just a good bond that we have between South Carolina and Germany." There are geographically related technological factors too. The port of Charleston has become the second largest (after New York) on the U.S. eastern seaboard. This affords BMW and the other export-oriented firms in South Carolina "the ability to ship," anywhere.[59] Thus the endowments of nature, plus the manmade environment or "second nature," have conspired to create a successful "region state" economy, in Ohmae's sense.[60] It is located in North America, yes, but also linked to the world.

Comparable efforts are being made along other parts of the East Coast, whose northern half the geographer Jean Gottmann in *Megalopolis* (1961) described as historically the "economic hinge" of the continent.[61] Boston, the oldest of the Northeast seaboard cities, is making a new bid to be an Atlantic "hub."[62] Even some metropolitan regions located in the interior of the North American continent, in Canada and Mexico as well as the United States, are building "interregional" bridges abroad. The city of Chicago and its metropolitan region have long been connected with specific areas of the wider world through its commodities trade, meatpacking business, and steel industry, via the transcontinental railroad, St. Lawrence Seaway, and O'Hare International Airport. It is today a direct "gateway" to the United States from abroad, and from the U.S. heartland to dynamic industrial centers elsewhere.[63]

These connections are being made largely for reasons of economic survival. Gradually, these various North American regions, in the sense of natural economic zones, are likely to form into larger networks, in part for greater competitive resiliency. In effect, these economic regions, which may not coincide exactly with political-territorial boundaries, will probably be extended somewhat. Because of the force of geographical contiguity, which always remains a factor, these cooperative relationships probably will develop more thickly on the continent of North America than across maritime distances.

This, essentially, is the case -- an economic-competitive argument -- that has been made most convincingly for NAFTA: the need for renewal at home, first. "The North American Free Trade Agreement, from a long-term perspective, is President Clinton's most critical foreign policy decision," as Senator Bill Bradley (D., New Jersey) stated early in the NAFTA debate. "Its enactment -- or defeat -- will have a profound impact on our economy, on our relations with Mexico, and on prospects for political and social stability throughout the hemisphere." The world in general, he then went on to explain, is undergoing "a massive economic transformation." Inevitably, local "dislocations" would occur that would require strong "adjustment" measures (e.g., worker retraining, guaranteed health coverage, and pension security). "But most important," Senator Bradley advised, "we must keep our eye on the long term -- the changing nature of global competition. Economic competition in the year 2020 won't consist of scattered countries nibbling at each other, but major regions operating as economic units on the global playing field. The biggest threat to American jobs does not come from Mexico but from Europe, Japan and China."[64]

The pressures reinforcing U.S.-Canadian-Mexican cooperation are worldwide. This epitome of the case for NAFTA, incorporating as it does elements of continentalism, hemispherism, and globalism, is valid in its appreciation of the inherently outward-looking, essentially internationalist character of the U.S. "North American" trade concept. This notion is, emphatically, not a latter-day manifestation of political isolationism, or even economic protectionism. President Clinton, like Presidents Reagan and Bush before him, has made this point well and persuasively. However, NAFTA still is perceived by many, perhaps to some degree even by such forward-thinking political figures as Senator Bradley, as an expression of a presumably inherent *rivalry* in the new more pluralistic, interregional world structure that is emerging from the Cold War period. Fragmentation is assumed to mean friction -- or worse.

It can also mean new patterns of integration. Ohmae's insightful notion of the "region state" in a borderless world, though the terminology itself can be misleading, effectively suggests the point that the relationships that will develop from an increasingly integrated, regionally complex North America with regions across the Atlantic and also the Pacific can be cooperative as well as competitive. Region states are natural economic zones that form "linkages" with others, primarily within the context of the global economy rather than that of "host nations." The assumption that success in the global economy means "pitting one nation's industries against another's" is a badly dated one, Ohmae contends. He argues that the economic dynamics of the borderless world "do not flow from such contrived head-to-head confrontations, but rather from the participation of specific regions in a global nexus of information, skill, trade and investment."[65] That is, the process can be a positive-sum rather than a zero-sum game.

To the extent that a new interregionalism prevails in the world, not only within the traditional Western Hemisphere but also across the Atlantic Basin and around the Pacific Rim, the U.S. "North American" trade concept will become more broadly globalist rather than less narrowly continentalist. Hemispherism may be skipped, even as a step. "North America," in a sense, will become the world, and the "world" North America.

Notes

1. Alexander F. Watson, "NAFTA and the U.S. National Interest," address in Chicago, September 2, 1993, *US Department of State Dispatch,* Vol. 4, No. 36 (September 6, 1993), pp. 610-612.

2. "Nafta and the National Interest," *New York Times,* November 17, 1993.

3. Kenichi Ohmae, "The Rise of the Region State," *Foreign Affairs,* Vol. 72, No. 2 (Spring 1993), pp. 78-87. See also his *The Borderless World: Power and Strategy in the Interlinked Economy* (New York: Harper Business, 1990).

4. Peter Karl Kresl, *The Urban Economy and Regional Trade Liberalization* (New York: Praeger, 1992), focuses particularly on "second" cities in North America and Europe and on the strategies they are adopting in a trade-liberalizing environment. Subnational governmental units -- municipalities and states or provinces -- often are closely involved in promoting, if not actually producing, regional economic growth and interregional links. Explorations of this new theme include: Earl H. Fry, Lee H. Radebaugh, and Panayotis Soldatos, eds., *The New International Cities Era: The Global Activities of North American Municipal Governments* (Provo, Utah: David M. Kennedy Center for International Studies, Brigham Young University, 1989); Panayotis Soldatos, *Les nouvelles villes internationales: profil et planification stratégique* (Aix-en-Provence: SERDECO, 1991); and Douglas M. Brown and Earl H. Fry, eds., *States and Provinces in the International Economy* (Berkeley, California, and Kingston, Ontario: Institute of Governmental Studies Press, University of California, and Institute of Intergovernmental Relations, Queen's University, 1993).

5. Ohmae, "Rise of the Region State," p. 87.

6. For a current account of trans-Caribbean contacts, one may observe the work of Caribbean/Latin American Action (C/LAA), a Washington-based private, independent organization promoting economic development around the Caribbean Basin zone. The growing importance of subnational linkages of the United States with Europe, recognized at the top in the November 1990 U.S.-EC Transatlantic Declaration, historically analyzed in Alan K. Henrikson, "The New Atlanticism: Western Partnership for Global Leadership," *Journal of European Integration,* Vol. 16, Nos. 2-3 (Winter/Spring 1993), pp. 165-191. On transpacific trading relations and community-building, see Simon Winchester, *Pacific Rising: The Emergence of a New World Culture* (New York: Prentice Hall Press, 1991).

7. Reagan's speech announcing candidacy for the Presidency, Hilton Hotel, New York, November 13, 1979, mimeographed text obtained from Reagan campaign headquarters, quoted in Alan K. Henrikson, "A North American Community: 'From the Yukon to the Yucatan,'" in Hans Binnendijk and Mary Locke, eds., *The Diplomatic Record, 1991-1992* (Boulder: Westview Press, 1993), pp. 76-77. The Canadian and Mexican governments were somewhat alarmed by the Reagan statement, thinking they might be required to have their ambassadors or other emissaries attend U.S. Cabinet meetings. They also were worried about a possible Reagan administration effort, at a time of anxiety about the adequacy U.S. energy supplies, to win privileged access to their nations' sizable oil and gas reserves.

8. Text obtained from the Office of the Governor, Sacramento, California. Quoted in ibid., p. 77.

9. See the elaboration by Brown's associates, Mark S. Adams and Barry Steiner, "Energy and the North American Community: Canada, Mexico and the United States," *Hastings International and Comparative Law Review*, Special Edition, Vol. 3, No. 3 (Spring 1980), pp. 369-434.

10. The doctrine of "continentalism" in the 1930s, most coherently and influentially articulated by the historian Charles A. Beard, did have isolationist implications. Manfred Jonas, *Isolationism in America, 1935-41* (Ithaca, New York: Cornell University Press, 1966), pp. 75-77.

11. Robert B. Zoellick, "North American Free Trade Agreement: Extending Fast-Track Negotiating Authority," prepared statement before the Senate Foreign Relations Committee, April 11, 1991, *US Department of State Dispatch*, Vol. 2, No. 15 (April 15, 1991), pp. 254-263, quoted in Henrikson, "A North American Community," p. 67.

12. Warren Christopher, "NAFTA: In the Overriding Interest of the United States," address to the Los Angeles World Affairs Council and Town Hall of California, Los Angeles, November 2, 1993, *US Department of State Dispatch*, Vol. 4, No. 46 (November 15, 1993), pp. 785-787.

13. William J. Clinton, "NAFTA: Embracing Change," remarks at signing of the NAFTA side agreements, Washington, D.C., September 14, 1993, *US Department of State Dispatch*, Vol. 4, No. 37 (September 13, 1993), pp. 622-624.

14. Keith Bradsher, "In Twist, Protectionism is Used to Sell Trade Pact," *New York Times*, November 7, 1993.

15. Thomas L. Friedman, "Clinton Steps Up Campaign for Trade Accord," *The New York Times*, November 2, 1993. Commenting on the Clinton warning of a foreign takeover of a missed NAFTA opportunity, trade experts and businessmen in Mexico said that, on balance, the country was likely to prove more attractive to Asian and European investors with the agreement than without it. Tim Golden, "Mexican Trade Accord: Japanese Role Doubted," *New York Times*, November 4, 1993.

16. Classic accounts of U.S. hemispherism are Arthur P. Whitaker, *The Western Hemisphere Idea: Its Rise and Decline* (Ithaca, N.Y.: Cornell University Press, 1954), and Dexter Perkins, *A History of the Monroe Doctrine* (Boston: Little, Brown and Company, 1963).

17. Ronald Reagan, *An American Life* (New York: Simon and Schuster, 1990), p. 240.

18. George Bush, remarks announcing the Enterprise for the Americas Initiative, June 27, 1900, *Public Papers of the Presidents of the United States: George Bush, 1990*, Book I (Washington, DC: United States Government Printing Office, 1991), pp. 873-877.

19. Warren Christopher, "NAFTA: A Bridge to a Better Future for the United States and the Hemisphere," statement before the Senate Finance Committee, Washington, DC, September 15, 1993, *US Department of State Dispatch*, Vol. 4, No. 37 (September 13, 1993), pp. 625-626, and Christopher, "NAFTA: In the Overriding Interest of the United States," p. 786.

20. David Rockefeller, "A Hemisphere in the Balance," *Wall Street Journal*, October 1, 1993.

21. See Carlos Fuentes, "NAFTA: The Start of a New International Order," *Boston Globe*, November 24, 1993.

22. Tim Golden, "Left Behind, Mexico's Indians Fight the Future," *New York Times*, January 9, 1994; Carlos Fuentes, "Chiapas a Warning Signal for Mexico," *Boston Globe*, January 11, 1994.

23. *North American Free Trade Agreement Between the Government of Canada, the Government of the United Mexican States and the Government of the United States of America*, December 17, 1992, text (Ottawa: Minister of Supply and Services Canada, 1993), Chapter Twenty-two, Final Provisions, p. 22-1.

24. The source is a knowledgeable Canadian official. A joke was made following agreement on the nondiscriminatory accession clause that the first country to apply to join NAFTA might be Malaysia, whose leader, Datuk Seri Mahathir bin Mohamad, had been trying to establish an East Asian economic grouping from which the United States would be excluded!

25. James Brooke, "With a View of One Hemisphere, Latin America is Freeing its Own Trade," *New York Times*, December 29, 1993; Steven Greenhouse, "U.S. Plans Expanded Trade Zone: Chile is Seen as Next in Hemisphere Bloc," *New York Times*, February 4, 1994.

26. Steven Greenhouse, "Clinton Plans Meeting of Hemisphere Chiefs," *New York Times*, March 11, 1994.

27. Wendell L. Willkie, *One World* (New York: Simon and Schuster, 1943); Alan K. Henrikson, "The Map as an 'Idea': The Role of Cartographic Imagery During the Second World War," *The American Cartographer*, Vol. 2, No. 1 (April 1975), pp. 19-53; Robert A. Divine, *Second Chance: The Triumph of Internationalism in America During World War II* (New York: Atheneum, 1967), pp. 103-107.

28. Eugene R. Staley, "The Myth of the Continents," in Hans W. Weigert and Vilhjalmur Stefansson, eds., *Compass of the World* (New York: The Macmillan Company, 1944), pp. 89-108; Henrikson, "The Map as an 'Idea'," pp. 20-22, 28-31.

29. Gardner Patterson, "The GATT and the Negotiation of International Trade Rules," in Alan K. Henrikson, ed., *Negotiating World Order: The Artisanship and Architecture of Global Diplomacy* (Wilmington, Delaware: Scholarly Resources, 1986), p. 181.

30. Herbert Stein, "No Need to Be Scared of NAFTA," *Wall Street Journal*, September 28, 1993.

31. Article XXIV of the General Agreement on Trade and Tariffs allows for free trade agreements and customs unions that cover "substantially all" of the trade among the partner countries and do not raise barriers against the trade of third countries. As Gary Hufbauer and Jeffrey Schott point out, no agreement, including the 1957 Treaty of Rome which established the European Economic Community, has ever failed these two tests. Hufbauer and Schott, *NAFTA: An Assessment*, rev. ed. (Washington, DC: Institute for International Economics, 1993), pp. 111-112.

32. Yoshi Tsurumi, letter to the Editor, September 22, 1993, *New York Times*, October 3, 1993.

33. Sylvia Nasar, "A Primer: Why Economists Favor Free-Trade Agreement," *New York Times,* September 17, 1993. Signatories ranged from conservative economists such as James Buchanan and Milton Friedman to liberal theoreticians, including Paul A. Samuelson and James Tobin.

34. Jagdish Bhagwati, "Regionalism and Multilateralism: An Overview," Paper presented at conference at The World Bank, April 2-3, 1992.

35. "Dornbusch on Trade," *The Economist*, Vol. 319, No. 7705 (May 4, 1991), p. 67.

36. Bhagwati, "Regionalism and Multilateralism."

37. Dornbusch, "Dornbusch on Trade."

38. Lindley H. Clark, Jr., "Nafta Won't Work Without GATT," *Wall Street Journal*, November 10, 1993.

39. The United States has long maintained a system of quotas on sugar imports, spread among 40 countries. Under NAFTA, Mexico, even though currently a net importer of sugar, is permitted to increase its exports of sugar to the United States. Its exports of sugar above a quota are subject to a tariff, to be phased out over a period of fifteen years. Should Mexico take advantage of this expanding market opportunity (partly by substituting corn syrup for cane and beet sugar at home), the world's other sugar producers would suffer. "Indeed, Mexican exports could displace more than 25 percent of total US imports, even without a shift in Mexican consumption from cane to corn sweeteners, if the stringent US quotas on other suppliers remain intact." NAFTA might, however, accelerate reform of U.S. sugar-quota policy, especially if coupled with GATT Uruguay Round proposals to convert sugar quotas to tariff equivalents. "Indeed, the US-Mexico farm pact seems to have been drafted with the GATT talks in mind. The big sugar quota expansion for Mexico only begins in year 7, giving ample time for the Uruguay Round reforms to be substantially implemented." Hufbauer and Schott, *NAFTA: An Assessment*, pp. 51, 56.

40. Clark, "Nafta Won't Work Without GATT."

41. These articles are descriptive: Clifford Krauss, "In Finagling on Trade Pact, Legislators' Barter is Votes," *New York Times*, October 5, 1993; Michael Wines, "A 'Bazaar; Method of Dealing for Votes," *New York Times*, November 11, 1993; B. Drummond Ayres, Jr., "Perot Asserts President is Using Pork Barrel to Pass Trade Accord," *New York Times*, November 15, 1993; Keith Bradsher,

"Clinton's Shopping List for Votes Has Ring of Grocery Buyer's List," *New York Times,* November 17, 1993.

42. "NAFTA Supplemental Agreements," August 13, 1933, *US_Department of State Dispatch,* Vol. 4, No. 34 (August 23, 1993), pp. 589-596. The agreements created a Commission on Labor Cooperation, a Commission on Environmental Cooperation, and an "Early Warning System" to monitor import surges.

43. Bob Davis and Jackie Calmes, "House Approves Nafta, Providing President with Crucial Victory," *Wall Street Journal,* November 15, 1993.

44. Bill Richardson, news conference following NAFTA vote, C-Span, November 17, 1993.

45. William J. Clinton, "The APEC Role in Creating Jobs, Opportunities, and Security," address to the Seattle Host Committee, Seattle, Washington, November 19, 1993, *US Department of State Dispatch,* Vol. 4, No. 48 (November 29, 1993), pp. 813-818.

46. William J. Clinton, "GATT Negotiations Concluded," opening statement at news conference, Washington, DC, December 15, 1993, *US Department of State Dispatch,* Vol. 4, No. 51 (December 20, 1993), p. 873.

47. Ibid.

48. Ohmae, "Rise of the Region State," p. 78.

49. Richard N. Cooper, *The Economics of Interdependence: Economic Policy in the Atlantic Community* (New York: McGraw-Hill Book Company, 1968), p. 9.

50. Paul Krugman, *Geography and Trade* (Cambridge, Massachusetts: The MIT Press, 1991), p. 3.

51. Michael E. Porter, *The Competitive Advantage of Nations* (New York: The Free Press, 1990), p. 19. A key concept for Porter is the notion of "home base," which he defines as the location of many of the most productive jobs, core technologies, and most advanced skills. Although he associates the home base with the "nation," these are analytically distinct. The actual base, or geographic location, of employment, technology, and skill may well be regional--that is, internal to a nation, or in some cases transnational.

52. Joel Garreau, *The Nine Nations of North America* (Boston: Houghton Mifflin Company, 1981).

53. See, for example, the interregional analysis, "Western Canada-Mexico Trade ... Realizing Strategic Opportunities," given in the Canada West Foundation's publication, *Western Canada Economic Destiny* (March 1993).

54. Of the three countries, Canada is the one with the strongest forces of regional identification and action. For an early analysis, see Mildred A. Schwartz, *Politics and Territory: The Sociology of Regional Persistence in Canada* (Montreal: McGill-Queen's University Press, 1974).

55. San Howe Verhovek, "San Antonio's Wild About Free Trade," *New York Times,* November 15, 1993; Scott Pendleton, "San Antonio," *Christian Science Monitor,* February 16, 1994.

56. On many of the connections between American west-coast states and Asian regions, see "A Flirtation with the Pacific," *The Economist,* Vol. 320, No. 7724 (September 14, 1991), pp. 25-26, and James O. Goldsborough, "California's Foreign Policy," *Foreign Affairs,* Vol. 72, No. 2 (Spring 1993), pp. 88-96.

57. Clinton, "The APEC Role in Creating Jobs, Opportunities, and Security."

58. Matthew Davis, "Europe Loves Dixie: BMW's Move Into South Carolina Highlights Region's Eurosuccess," *Europe: Magazine of the European Community,* No. 320 (October 1992), pp. 30-31, 34-36.

59. "Interview: South Carolina Governor Carroll Campbell," ibid., pp. 32-33.

60. The concept of "second nature" is developed, with reference particularly to the role of railroads in regional growth, by William Cronon, *Nature's Metropolis: Chicago and the Great West* (New York: W. W. Norton, 1991).

61. Jean Gottmann, *Megalopolis: The Urbanized Northeastern Seaboard of the United States* (Cambridge, Massachusetts: The M.I.T. Press, 1961), chap. 3, "The Continent's Economic Hinge."

62. Massachusetts Governor William Weld imaginatively considers Boston "the capital of the Atlantic Rim" ("The Hub of the Rim," *Boston Globe,* February 3, 1993). Regarding plans being made to hold a conference in Boston in November 1994 to reassert the importance of the New England region in the circum-Atlantic sphere, see James H. Barron, "Building an Atlantic Rim Network and Planning for the First International Congress on the Atlantic Rim," draft proposal, rev. October 1993. On the larger foreign-policy context of this and other such American-European interregional linkages, see Henrikson, "The New Atlanticism."

63. On the genesis of Chicago's larger role, see Cronon, *Nature's Metropolis.* The Canadian counterpart is Toronto ("gateway to the United States"). The Province of Ontario, at an "interregional conference" held in Toronto in June 1990, signed a formal Declaration of Partnership with The Four Motors for Europe (Baden-Württemberg, Rhônes-Alpes, Lombardia, and Catalunya), regions described as the "technological and industrial heartlands" of their respective countries. "Ontario's Partnership with The Four Motors for Europe," Ontario Ministry of Industry, Trade and Technology, 1992.

64. Bill Bradley, "Nafta Opens More Than a Trade Door," *Wall Street Journal,* September 16, 1993.

65. Ohmae, "Rise of the Region State," pp. 80, 86. Ohmae's critical allusion is to Lester C. Thurow, *Head to Head: The Coming Economic Battle Among Japan, Europe and America* (New York: William Morrow and Company, 1992).

10

Bringing Values "Back In": Value Change and North American Integration

Neil Nevitte

Introduction

The North American Free Trade Agreement (NAFTA) represents an historic policy shift, one that raises a variety of theoretical and practical questions many of which are familiar to students of the Western European experience: Why do countries pursue greater economic integration? What explains the timing of these policy shifts? And, can the countries work together effectively within the new frameworks? The economic reasons for why countries pursue such agreements as NAFTA are multiple: Free trade agreements are a strategic response to the realities of globalization and to the emergence of vigorous new trading blocs; they help countries reap the joint benefits of comparative advantages and the economies of scale that come from controlled access to large markets. From the North American perspective, NAFTA has also been interpreted as the logical extension of evolving patterns of closer commercial cooperation.[1] From that standpoint the puzzling question is not why NAFTA was signed but why such an agreement was not formalized decades ago.

The economic case for free trade is powerful and economic interests undoubtedly are vital to the dynamics of continental integration. But economists were among the first to recognize that economic explanations, taken alone and viewed narrowly, fail to provide a convincing account for why, and when, countries take such decisive steps towards integration.[2] In the 1970's, more comprehensive explanations emerged. These focused on the importance of such factors as leadership, levels of institutional coordination, and styles of decision-making. They brought politics "back in."[3]   More recently others have restored the state to the integration equation by highlighting the connection between the state and society, interest groups, and the interdependence of international and domestic decisionmaking.[4] This chapter aims to extend the above perspectives further still by bringing values "back in" to the analysis of integration.

In general, public values have occupied a marginal place in explanations of the dynamics of integration. Even so, two kinds of explanations for why values might matter can be detected in the existing literature. The most forceful contemporary account is supplied by Putnam[5] who argues that international negotiations, such as those leading up to NAFTA, can be thought of as "two-level games":

> At the national level, domestic groups pursue their interests by pressuring governments to adopt favorable policies, and politicians seek power by constructing coalitions among these groups. At the international level, national governments seek to maximize their own ability to satisfy domestic pressures, while minimizing the adverse consequences of foreign developments. Neither of the two games can be ignored by central decision-makers, so long as their countries remain interdependent yet sovereign.[6]

In a nutshell, Putnam makes the case that public values count for two reasons. First, those sitting at negotiating tables trying to strike trade deals like NAFTA do not have independent policy preferences.[7] And second, for such agreements to "fly," negotiators must satisfy both the hard bargainers sitting on the other side of the negotiating table as well as the relevant domestic constituencies that each represents. Domestic constituencies have to be satisfied because publics are positioned to ratify these agreements.   The mechanisms for ratification, Putnam points out,[8] can be either formal or informal and in each case they may well differ depending upon the institutional rules of the game and opportunities. Presumably, too, those who count as the "relevant" domestic constituencies may also differ depending upon a variety of factors such as how open or closed governing regimes might be.

The second explanation for why public values may matter to integration is a more general one and it comes from a much earlier set of speculations about integration. The main task of this chapter is to revisit those earlier theoretical perspectives, focusing upon the contributions of Karl Deutsch. It begins by generating a simple model that captures the essential chain of reasoning underpinning Deutsch's theory. Then, the empirical section of the essay employs a unique body of survey evidence -- the Canadian, American and Mexican segments of the World Values Surveys -- to examine the plausibility of the Deutschian perspective. These surveys, first undertaken in 1981 and replicated in 1990, provide matched cross-time and cross-national data on public values. The data were collected during the "run up" to NAFTA. The key finding is that the essential elements of the Deutsch model, which was generated on the basis of Western European case study evidence, holds up in the North American setting. The final section of the analysis draws on some elements of the 1990 Canadian, American and Mexican surveys that were developed with a specific eye to NAFTA. Responses to a variety of open-ended questions as well as experimental scenarios, or "vignettes," provides support for Putnam's contention, namely, that attitudes to North American political integration are sensitive to the domestic policy preferences of each of the three North American publics.

Deutsch's Theory

Forty-five years ago a number of scholars concerned with the prospects of securing a lasting peace in Western Europe joined forces to explore a common question: how to achieve greater cross-national integration through strategic institution building. From those coordinated efforts, informed by comparative evidence from a variety of European case studies, there emerged a variety of theoretical perspectives about the dynamics of integration. Haas,[9] for example, developed a functionalist interpretation which held that economic integration has an inherent tendency to "spill over" into political integration, an idea that appealed to the founders of the European Community. As it turned out, the process of integration in the European setting was much less automatic than functionalists supposed. Determined opposition by Charles de Gaulle blocked most early attempts to forge an expanded Community and such obstacles as recalcitrant publics in the smaller European partner states stalled the process later on. In the long run though, the European experience does suggest that economic forces are difficult to disentangle from political ones. Successful economic integration did lead to regular intergovernmental consultations and eventually to a Europe with a common currency unit, the beginnings of a common foreign policy, and a wide range of coordinated domestic policies.

The most comprehensive account of the place occupied by values in the dynamics of regional integration springs from, and builds upon, the early work of Karl Deutsch.[10] Deutsch's[11] social learning perspective involves a four step chain of reasoning. He begins by arguing that high volumes of transactions between peoples (communications flows, trade, and the movement of peoples) encourages greater similarities in the main values of publics in adjacent states. Second, similarities in main values, in turn, are conducive to greater trust between peoples. Trust is the expectation that another's behavior will be predictable and friendly.[12] Third, he suggests that higher levels of trust encourage greater cooperation and economic integration. And economic integration, Deutsch concludes, is conducive to greater political integration. The essential logic of the Deutsch line of reasoning might be schematically represented as in Figure 10.1.

Deutsch's account of the dynamics of regional integration is plausible and influential; the essential elements of that perspective are still reflected in contemporary versions of integration theory.[13] Further, some of the basic links between key elements of the Deutsch model have been empirically tested in a number of settings. It has been shown, for example, that interpersonal trust plays an important role in economic and political cooperation.[14] Systematic empirical research about trust between nationalities is more scarce, but the general finding

FIGURE 10.1   Values and the Dynamics of Integration

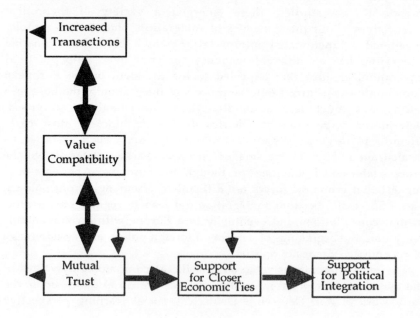

is that cross-national trust is a stable attribute[15] though there are important exceptions (France and Germany, 1945-1988). The weight of the accumulated evidence seems to work in ways that are consistent with expectations contained within the Deutsch model. Even so, Deutsch's perspective remains speculative. The kinds of data that might have enabled him to launch a direct test of the central propositions of his theory were simply not available at the time the theory was first developed and, since then, no attempt has been made to mount such a test. The central questions addressed by this analysis are: Do public values matter in the way Deutsch supposed they do? And, more generally, does his theory, which was informed by the European experience, hold up when it is applied to the North American setting?

The North American context is a promising test site for examining the Deutsch model for a combination of reasons. First, the signing of NAFTA provides *prima facie* evidence that greater economic integration among the three countries has taken place. Second, we can also show that Deutsch's key precondition, increased volume in cross-border transactions, is plainly satisfied. The volume of Canada-U.S. two way border crossings (the movement of peoples) rose from 72 million visits in 1980, to 94 million visits in 1989.[16] Trade in goods and services also increased sharply in the decade immediately prior to the signing of the Canada-U.S. Free Trade Agreement (CUSFTA).[17] The very same trends are mirrored in U.S.-Mexican cross-border transactions over the same period. Finally, Deutsch himself claims that the dynamics of integration work in the same ways in different places. Thus, evaluating Deutsch's model in the North American setting amounts to a test of the generalizability of his speculations.

Directions of North American Value Change

The case has been made that the North American setting satisfies a basic precondition of the Deutsch model. That is, volumes of cross-border transactions (Canada-U.S.; Mexico-U.S.) increased during the decade leading up to NAFTA. According to Deutsch's perspective (Figure 10.1) the next critical issue has to do with "value compatibility." Put in its simplest form, the central issue here is whether or not the "main values" of North Americans were more alike by the time the three countries were preparing to sign NAFTA than they were a decade before. Relatedly, there is the question of whether the trajectories of value change were consistent with each other. That is, for example, whether all publics were becoming more secular or not.

What do the directly comparable cross-time data show?

Table 10.1 summarizes the key relevant findings of a large body of evidence that has been examined in great detail elsewhere.[18] It reports the changes that have taken place across thirteen value domains each of which represents clusters of values determined by factor analysis. The right hand column of the table reports the key finding, namely, that the overall pattern of value change is clearly one of convergence. In 9 out of 13 value domains considered, Canadian, American and Mexican values were more alike in 1990 than they were in 1981. More particularly, the directions or trajectories of value change were also remarkably similar in all three countries during the course of the decade. For example, publics in all three countries became less "sexually restrictive" between 1981 and 1990. In all three countries publics increasingly exemplified the value of "autonomy" rather than "obedience for children." Confidence in institutions dropped. Publics became more willing to participate in unconventional forms of political participation, and so on.

TABLE 10.1   Changes Predicted from 1981 Data and Changes
              Observed, 1981-1990

Variable and Countries (1)	Direction of Change (2)	Consistent Correlations (3)	Responses Shift? (4)	Changes (5)
A. Sexual restrictiveness				
U.S.	falling	Yes	Yes	Converging
Canada	falling	Yes	Yes	
Mexico	falling	Yes	Yes	
B. Emphasize independence, imagination over obedience, good manners for children				
U.S.	rising	Yes	Yes	Converging
Canada	rising	Yes	Yes	
Mexico	rising	Yes	Yes	
C. Favor greater respect for authority				
U.S.	falling	Yes	Yes	Converging
Canada	falling	Yes	Yes	
Mexico	falling	Yes	Yes	
D. Religious outlook				
U.S.	falling	Yes	Yes	Diverging
Canada	falling	Yes	Yes	
Mexico	falling	Yes	Yes	

(Continues)

TABLE 10.1 (Continued)

Variable and Countries (1)	Direction of Change (2)	Consistent Correlations (3)	Responses Shift? (4)	Changes (5)
E. Church attendance				
U.S.	falling	Yes	(Yes)	Converging
Canada	falling	Yes	Yes	
Mexico	falling	Yes	Yes	
F. Civil permissiveness				
U.S.	rising	No	-	Diverging
Canada	rising	Yes	Yes	
Mexico	rising	No	-	
G. Emphasis on family duty				
U.S.	rising	Yes	No	Converging
Canada	rising	Yes	No	
Mexico	falling	Yes	No	
H. Confidence in gov't institutions				
U.S.	falling	Yes	Yes	Converging
Canada	falling	Yes	Yes	
Mexico	falling	(Yes)	Yes	
I. Confidence in non-gov't institutions				
U.S.	falling	Yes	Yes	Diverging
Canada	falling	Yes	Yes	
Mexico	rising	Yes	(No)	
J. National pride				
U.S.	falling	Yes	Yes	Diverging
Canada	falling	Yes	Yes	
Mexico	falling	Yes	Yes	
K. Unconventional political participation				
U.S.	rising	Yes	Yes	Converging
Canada	rising	Yes	Yes	
Mexico	rising	Yes	Yes	
L. Support for employee participation in business				
U.S.	rising	Yes	Yes	Converging
Canada	rising	Yes	Yes	
Mexico	falling	No	-	

(Continues)

TABLE 10.1 (Continued)

Variable and Countries (1)	Direction of Change (2)	Consistent Correlations (3)	Responses Shift? (4)	Changes (5)
M. Following instructions at work				
U.S.	falling	Yes	Yes	Converging
Canada	falling	Yes	Yes	
Mexico	rising	No	-	

Total number of cases which generate predictions: 35

Correct predictions: 31 (89%)

Incorrect predictions: 4 (11%)

Column 1 = Variable and Country
Column 2 = Direction of change; rising, falling or stable?
Column 3 = Does this variable show consistent correlations with both age
    and value type (i.e. old; young = Materialist: Postmaterialist?)
Column 4 = Do the responses to this variable shift in the predicted
    direction from 1981 to 1990?
Column 5 = Trajectories of changes; converging, diverging or parallel?

() Indicates weak relationship
- Indicates no prediction

Source: 1981 and 1990 World Values Surveys

The consistency of these findings is striking and it raises the question of whether or not there is a systematic explanation for the shifts. The left and center columns of Table 10.1 indicate that nearly all of the North American value changes explored are entirely consistent with the expectations coming from a general theory of value change-postmaterialism.[19] Moreover, there are clear age-related variations in values. These variations are intriguing because they suggest sharp generational differences in each of the three North American publics. Thus, when we ask whether the directions of value change between 1981 and 1990 can be predicted on the basis of postmaterialist orientations and generational change, the answer is "yes" nearly 90 percent of the time.[20]

Not surprisingly, there are some "wrinkles" to these general findings. For instance, when it comes to "religious outlooks" publics in all three countries moved down the same value trajectory between 1981 and 1990; they all became more "secular." But Canadians and Mexicans became more secular at a faster rate than their American counterparts with the net effect being value divergence. Then again, orientations towards "civil permissiveness" -- the cluster of values having to do with "law and order" -- changed hardly at all and the net effect, once again, was divergence. Attitudes towards authority in the workplace conform to a different pattern. As Figure 10.2 shows, they moved along very different trajectories. Between 1981 and 1990, Canadian and American publics became less deferential in the workplace; they became less likely to want to "follow instructions at work." On this dimension, Mexicans moved in the opposite direction. They became more deferential and the net effect of these changes in this instance is value convergence.

FIGURE 10.2   Attitudes Toward Authority at Work, 1981 vs. 1990
(Percentage saying "should follow instructions")

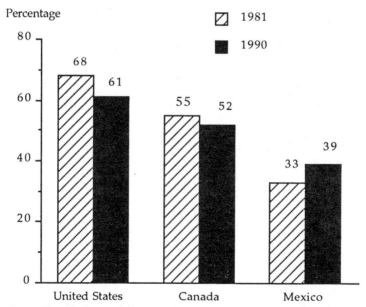

Question: "People have different ideas about following instructions at work, some say that one should follow the instructions of one's superiors even when one does not fully agree with them; others say one should follow one's superior's instructions only when one is convinced that they are right. With which one of those two opinions do you agree?"

Source: 1981 and 1990 World Values Surveys

FIGURE 10.3 Percentage Belonging to Given Geographical Units, 1981 vs. 1990

A. UNITED STATES

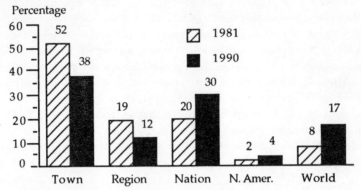

B. CANADA

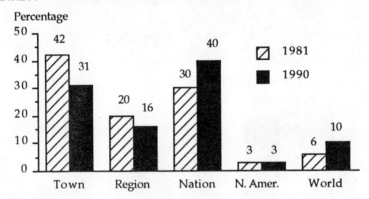

C. MEXICO

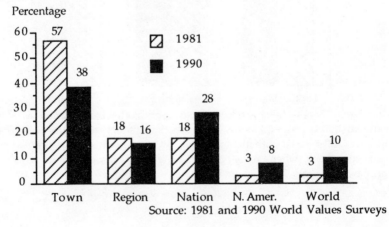

Source: 1981 and 1990 World Values Surveys

In some cases the findings cannot be neatly sorted into the "convergence" or "divergence" outcomes. One intriguing and particularly relevant example of this is illustrated in Figure 10.3. In 1981 and 1990, all three publics were asked: "Which of these geographical groups would you say you belong to first of all?" Then they were presented with the following alternatives:

-Locality or town where you live
-State/province/region where you live
-Your country as a whole
-North America
-The world as a whole

The question is intended to tap how parochial or cosmopolitan publics are. Interpreted that way, the trend is clear. Publics in all three countries became less parochial and more cosmopolitan in the decade preceding NAFTA. Notice too, though, that the proportion of each public declaring an attachment to "the nation" did not decline; in every case it increased.

Despite these "wrinkles" and the occasional conceptual awkwardness of some categorizations, the general pattern of North American value change is clear. In the vast majority of cases, publics in Canada, the United States and Mexico were all moving along very similar value trajectories and overall, the net effects of these value changes are consistent with the expectations coming from Deutsch's line of speculation.

The Linkages in the Deutsch Model

There is no simple strategy for connecting multiple indicators of value change with such structural variables as shifts in cross-border transactions or even with single indicators about feelings of mutual trust. Nor are there any cross-time data available that allow direct comparisons of how levels of mutual trust between the three North American publics may have changed during the course of the 1990s. But we do know that, compared to publics in other advanced industrial states, the levels of mutual trust between Canadians and Americans is relatively high.[21] Our data show that nearly two-thirds of Americans (64%) said they "trust Canadians" while only four percent reported not trusting Canadians very much or not at all. Similarly, more than half of Canadian respondents (55%) said they trust Americans, fifteen percent did not trust Americans. Trust of Mexicans is higher among

American respondents (52%) than their Canadian counterparts (37%). But American trust of Mexicans is not reciprocated; only twenty percent of Mexicans reported that they trusted Americans and more than half of the Mexican sample (52%) said they did not trust Americans. Absolute levels of trust are undoubtedly important but from the Deutschian perspective, they are not the critical issue. According to Deutsch, the central question is whether higher levels of trust vary systematically with support for closer economic ties and that question can be explored with our data. The 1990 surveys asked respondents in all three countries whether their own country should have closer, or more distant, economic ties with the other NAFTA countries. Here, the expectation coming from Deutsch's theory is clear: respondents with higher levels of trust for other nationalities should be more likely than their non-trusting counterparts to support "closer economic ties." On this point, data shown in Figure 10.4 are unequivocal.

In every country and for every set of relationships higher levels of mutual trust always correspond to greater support for closer economic ties. All of the relationships are robust and none is weaker than gamma = .39.

Support for closer economic ties is one thing, support for political integration is quite another. 1990 surveys asked respondents a variety of questions about political integration including one question that tapped attitudes to what, arguably, is the most radical and unambiguous option: "All things considered, do you think that we should do away with the border between ... Canada and the United States (Canadians)/the United States and Canada (Americans)/ Mexico and the United States (Mexicans) ...?"

The idea that Canadians, or Mexicans, would seriously entertain the idea of "doing away with" the borders between their own country and the United States is a radical one, not least of all because it flies in the face of longstanding policy efforts aimed at resisting the economic, political and socio-cultural influences of the United States. From this historical standpoint it would be surprising if more than a handful of Canadians or Mexicans would support such an alternative. The basic finding is striking: nearly one in four Canadians (24%) and just less than half (46%) of Americans respond that they would favor "doing away with" the Canada-U.S. border. Remarkably, too, one quarter of Mexicans responded that they favored "doing away with" the border between Mexico and the United States.

Not surprisingly, support for "doing away with borders" is connected to a variety of factors.[22] Of more concern to an evaluation of Deutsch's theory, though, is the question how support for political integration is

FIGURE 10.4   Support for Closer Economic Ties with a Given
                Nation by Trust in That Nationality

                (Percentage in favor of "much closer" or
                "somewhat closer" economic ties)

Attitudes of United States Public:

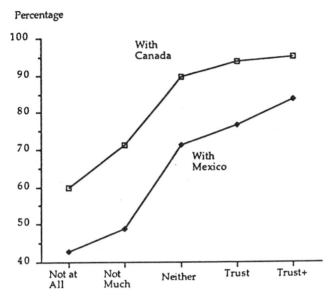

Attitudes of Canadian Public:

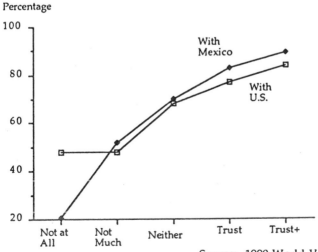

Source: 1990 World Values Survey

(Continues)

FIGURE 10.4 (Continued)

Attitudes of Mexican Public:

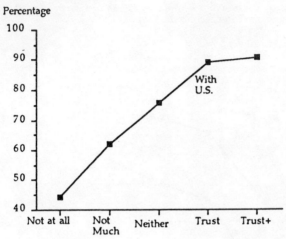

Source: 1990 World Values Survey

FIGURE 10.5 Support for Political Integration by Support
for Closer Economic Ties

A. United States (% for abolishing border with Canada)

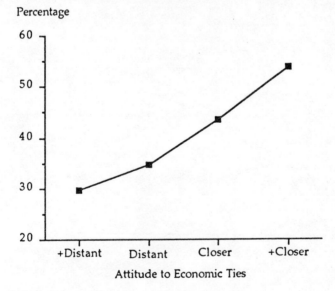

(Continues)

FIGURE 10.5 (Continued)

B. Canada (% for abolishing border with U.S.)

Percentage

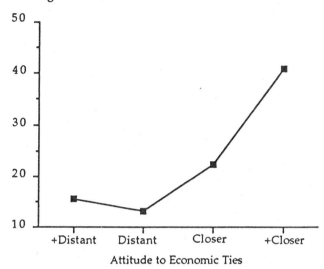

Attitude to Economic Ties

C. Mexico (% for abolishing border with U.S.)

Percentage

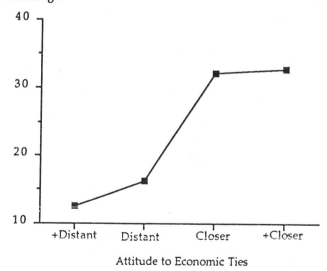

Attitude to Economic Ties

Source: 1990 World Values Survey

related to support for closer economic ties. Are the supporters of "closer economic ties" also "political integrationists," that is, are they more likely to support "doing away with borders?" Once again, the evidence provides support for Deutsch's line of speculation. As Figure 10.5 shows, support for closer economic ties is related to support for doing away with borders. The relationship is consistent in all three countries and, as before, the relationships are reasonably strong.

When we step back from the details of each particular set of linkages to evaluate the broader pattern of findings, the weight of the evidence provides some more support for the Deutsch perspective on integration. Cross-border transactions increased during the period preceding NAFTA. Significant changes in the values of three North American publics took place between 1981 and 1990. And in most, but not all, instances North American values seem to have converged. As Deutsch would predict, levels of mutual trust are indeed related to support for closer economic ties. Furthermore, support for political integration is significantly and positively related to support for closer economic ties. Figure 10.6 provides further grist for Deutsch's theory. Notice that the direct relationship between mutual trust and support for political integration turns out to be quite weak. This implies that mutual trust does indeed work through support for closer economic ties to encourage support for greater political integration. In more technical terms, re-specifying Deutsch's model by taking links out of his chain of reasoning has the effect of producing much weaker results.

FIGURE 10.6   The Deutsch Model of Integration

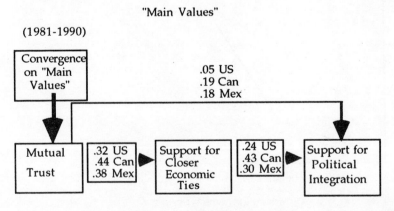

Source: World Values Surveys: Canada, U.S., Mexico

Do Domestic Policy Preferences Make a Difference?

The preceding assessment of support for political integration relies exclusively upon responses to a single "bottom line" question: "All things considered, do you think that we should do away with the border ...?" The sentiments tapped by that question certainly go far beyond the kind of arrangement that governments envisioned when they negotiated NAFTA. But how robust is support for political integration? And, is there any evidence for Putnam's claim that public support for expanding trade environments is contingent upon domestic policy preferences?

In addition to the common "bottom line" question about integration, the 1990 Canadian, American and Mexican surveys tapped attitudes towards political integration using other strategies. One set of open-ended questions probed what people thought the advantages and disadvantages might be if Canada and the United States (or the United States and Canada-Americans; Mexico and the United States-Mexicans) were to form "one country." The responses to this battery reflect the tension between anticipated economic gains and potential socio-cultural kinds of trade-offs. One-third of Americans, for example, cite economic advantages to "forming one country" with Canada and another third see socio-cultural problems coming from such a union. In the Canadian case, 44% see economic advantages while 60% oppose "forming one country" for socio-cultural reasons. The figures for Mexico are about the same. Moreover, 32% of Americans, 42% of Canadians and 32% of Mexicans see "no advantages" to any political union. If we take these responses to indicate genuine outer limits of opinion, the striking implication is that some 68% of Americans and Mexicans, and about 59% of Canadians could conceivably be moved to support political union under the "right" circumstances. Is it possible, then, to shed some light on the mix of conditions that might move publics to support political integration?

All three of the 1990 surveys presented the three publics with seven equivalent "scenarios" and each of these scenarios, or "vignettes," spelled out a possible policy consequence of political union. Respondents were asked whether they would support Canada and the United States (the United States and Canada-Americans; Mexico and the United States-Mexicans) forming one country if it meant:

(1) that you would enjoy a higher standard of living?
(2) losing Canada's/Mexico's cultural identity (Canada and Mexico)/having a large French speaking minority (U.S.)?
(3) that we would deal more effectively with environmental

issues like acid rain and pollution?

(4)   Canada would form 12 new states in the U.S.?/Mexico would form 32 new states?

(5)   a better quality of life?

(6)   having a government funded (rather than private) health care system (U.S.)/having a privately funded rather than a government funded health care system (Canada)?

(7)   slightly higher taxes and more government services (U.S.)/slightly lower taxes and fewer government services (Canada and Mexico)?

Figure 10.7 reports the impact of responses to each of these scenarios against two benchmarks. It indicates the extent to which the policy scenarios move support from the "bottom line" position in each country (i.e., support for doing away with borders). It also indicates which of the scenarios could produce a majority support for political union. Overall, the evidence suggests just how fluid public attitudes to political union are. Notice that a majority of Canadians[23] appear to support political union with the United States under two conditions: (1) if it meant a better quality of life; and (2) if it meant that we could deal more effectively with environmental issues. The "better quality of life" scenario is difficult to interpret for obvious reasons; it taps an imagined "best of all possible worlds" outcome and in that sense it is intended only to signal an upper limit. The environmental scenario, though, is relatively concrete. The promise of a "higher standard of living" boosts Canadian support for political union with the United States but that scenario is not sufficiently attractive to produce a majority in favor of forming one country. All other scenarios depress support for political union.

In the case of the United States, the scenarios produce majorities for political union in five of the seven vignettes. Significantly, the promise of government funded health care boosts support for political union. The prospects of getting twelve new states also boosts support for political union. At the same time, Americans are less enthusiastic about the ideas of adopting a francophone minority.

Mexican responses also indicate fluidity. The quality of life and environmental scenarios produce majority support for political union with the United States, as in the Canadian case. For understandable reasons, the promise of a "higher standard of living" has a very substantial impact on Mexican support for political union. But, as in Canada, the potential loss of cultural identity depresses support for

FIGURE 10.7   Moving Public Opinion -- Scenarios

A. Canada with U.S.

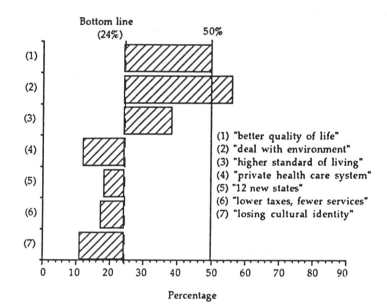

Percentage

B. U.S. with Canada

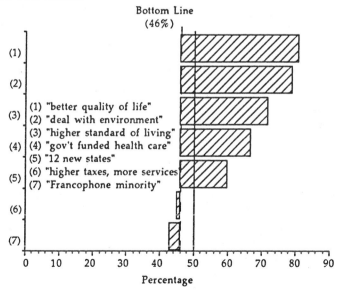

Percentage

(Continues)

FIGURE 10.7 (Continued)

C. Mexico with U.S.

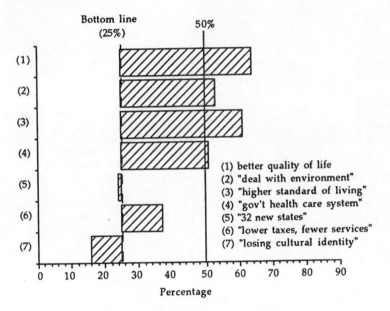

Source: 1990 World Values Survey (Canada, U.S. and Mexico)

political union with the United States. Together, these data indicate that domestic policy preferences do have a significant impact on support for integration. Moreover, they suggest that opposition to political integration may be far less robust than has previously been supposed.

Conclusion

We began with the observation that explanations for why countries pursue trade agreements, like NAFTA, pay little attention to values. The aim of this chapter has been to evaluate whether values, or more particularly public values, should become part of those explanations by empirically exploring two lines of argument which suggest that values matter to the dynamics of integration One line, presented by Putnam, argues that public values count because they constrain negotiators by bringing domestic policy preferences to the bargaining table. The other, supplied by Deutsch, brings together a more comprehensive set of economic, cultural and political considerations, many of which have featured prominently in public debates about the wisdom of NAFTA.

It is useful, by way of conclusion, to place the central findings of this chapter in perspective and the first general point is a cautionary one. Overall, there does seem to be empirical support for Deutsch's predictions. All of the findings are quite consistent with the expectations derived from Deutsch's theoretical perspective. Moreover, the data from which the evidence comes is clearly well-tuned for examining the connections between elements that are central to Deutsch's theory. Even so, the evidence falls far short of a "proof" that Deutsch was right. Instead, the preceding analysis should more properly be considered as a broad gauged plausibility test. Certainly, the findings are intriguing because they are entirely consistent with Deutsch's logic. They suggest, more generally, that Deutsch's theory may well be generalizable to non-European settings.

The evidence is suggestive in another respect. Showing that the "main values" of North American publics have become more alike raises intriguing issues about why this is so. One popular explanation for North American value change is that Canadian, and Mexican societies are exposed to American cultural exports and thus value change can be explained in terms of the "Americanization" of these societies. The corollary of this argument is that American values "lead" and those of Mexicans and Canadians "lag." The evidence, however, provides no support for either the "Americanization" or "cultural lag" explanations of value change. Instead, the data suggest that all three North American societies are subject to broader patterns of value change, patterns that are evident in all advanced industrial states.

The third general point is that there is sufficient evidence here to make the case that values ought to be brought "back in" to analyses of the dynamics of integration. This is for two reasons: first, not only are the data consistent with Deutsch's theory; but they also indicate that the policy preferences of publics are not independent of support for political integration. Arguably, the policy preferences of publics matter only when publics have the opportunity to express their preferences or to directly "sign off" on trade agreements. The Danes exercised that opportunity with the Maastricht referendum. In 1988, Canadians had the opportunity to say "yes" or "no" to free trade with the United States. The argument, here, is not that value convergence "drives" integration; it is that value convergence, or divergence, may "gear" the process.

The most controversial findings to come from the data, likely, are those that relate to public support for "doing away with" borders. The findings are striking because they are so counter-intuitive to the histories of the Canadian and Mexican nation-building projects. This analysis does not advocate "doing away with borders" nor does it argue, as some have, that opening economies is a slippery slope towards political integration. Providing a precise interpretation to the finding that one in four Canadians (and Mexicans) are prepared to contemplate political integration is a treacherous business. One implication might be that state boundaries carry little relevance for domestic publics. In his insightful chapter, Denis Stairs suggests that Canadians are becoming "continentalists" because they have no choice. The data presented in this chapter suggest that Canadians (and Mexicans) have qualms about the cultural implications of expanding trade environments. At the same time, they also show that they may be far less reluctant continentalists than is sometimes supposed.

Notes

The data upon which this research is based comes from a larger project which is supported by the Donner Canadian Foundation for its financial support. The conclusion reached here are those of the author only.

1. Murray G. Smith, "The Free Trade Agreement in Context: A Canadian Perspective" in Jeffrey Schott and Murray G. Smith (eds.), *The Canada-U.S. Free Trade Agreement: The Global Impact* (Washington, D.C., and Ottawa: The Institute for International Economics and the Institute for Research on Public Policy, 1988), pp. 37-64.

2. Harry Johnson, "An Economic Theory of Protectionism, Tariff Bargaining and the Formation of Customs Unions," *Journal of Political Economy*, Vol. 73, No. 3 (June 1965), pp. 256-283 and Helen V. Milner and David B. Yoffie, "Between Free Trade and Interest on Attitudes Toward Foreign Countries," *Public Opinion Quarterly*, Vol. 42, No. 1 (Spring, 1979), pp. 68-78.

3. Joseph S. Nye, Jr., "Comparative Regional Integration: Concept and Measurement," *International Organization*, Vol. 22, No. 4, (Autumn 1968), pp. 855-880; Donald J. Puchala, "The Pattern of Contemporary Regional Integration," *International Studies Quarterly*, 12, 1968, pp. 38-64; Leon Lindberg and Stuart Scheingold, *Europe's Would-Be Polity: Patterns of Change in the European Community* (Englewood Cliffs: Prentice Hall, 1970).

4. Peter Gourevitch, *Politics in Hard Times: Comparative Responses to International Economic Crises* (Ithaca: Cornell University Press, 1986); Joseph S. Nye, Jr., "Neorealism and Neoliberalism," *World Politics*, Vol. 40, No. 2 (January 1988), pp. 238-239; Helen V. Milner, 1988, *Resisting Protectionism: Global Industries and the Politics of International Trade* (Princeton, N.J.: Princeton University Press, 1988); Ronald Rogowski, *Commerce and Coalitions: How Trade*

Affects Domestic Political Alignments (Princeton: Princeton University Press, 1989).

5. Robert D. Putnam, "Diplomacy and Domestic Politics: the Logic of Two-Level Games," *International Organization*, Vol. 42, No. 3 (Summer 1988), pp. 427-460.

6. Ibid., p. 436.

7. Ibid.

8. Ibid., pp. 436-40.

9. Ernst Haas, *The Uniting of Europe* (Stanford: Stanford University Press, 1958).

10. Karl W. Deutsch, *Nationalism and Social Communication* (Cambridge: MIT Press, 1952) ; Karl W. Deutsch, et. al., *Political Community and the North Atlantic Area* (Princeton: Princeton University Press, 1957); Karl W. Deutsch, *Political Community and the North Atlantic Area* (Garden City: Doubleday, 1968).

11. Karl W. Deutsch, *Nationalism and Social Communication*.

12. Dean G. Pruitt, "Definition of the Situation as a Determinant of International Action," in Herbert C. Kelman, ed., *International Behavior: A Social-Psychological Analysis* (New York: Holt, Rinehart and Winston, 1965).

13. Lindberg and Scheingold, *Europe's Would-Be Polity*, Robert O. Keohane and Joseph Nye, *Power and Interdependence*, (Boston: Little, Brown and Company, 1977); William Diebold, ed., *Bilateralism, Multilateralism and Canada in U.S. Trade Policy* (Washington: Council on Foreign Relations, 1988). Typically, the focus on the role of values, though, has been limited to elites. Schmitter, for example, suspects that "the more complementary elites come to acquire similar expectations and attitudes towards the integrative process, the easier it will be to form transnational associations and to accept regional identities." Philippe Schmitter, "A Revised Theory of Regional Integration," in Leon Lindberg and Stuart Scheingold, eds., *Regional Integration: Theory and Research* (Cambridge: Harvard University Press, 1971), p. 253.

14. Laurence Wylie, *Village in the Vaucluse* (Cambridge: Harvard University Press, 1957); Edward Banfield, *The Moral Basis of a Backward Society* (Chicago: Free Press, 1958); Gabriel Almond and Sidney Verba, *The Civic Culture* (Princeton: Princeton University Press, 1963); Niklas Luhmann, *Power and Trust* (Chichester and New York: Wiley, 1979); Paul Abramson, *Political Attitudes in America* (San Francisco: W.H. Freeman, 1983).

15. Karl W. Deutsch, *Nationalism and Social Communication*; William Buchanan and Hodley Cantril, *How Nations See Each Other* (Urbana: University of Illinois Press, 1953); Deutsch, *Political Community and the North Atlantic Area*; Richard L. Merrit and Donald J. Puchala, *Western European Perspectives on International Affairs* (New York: Praeger, 1968); Miroslav Nincic and Bruce Russett, "The Effect of Similarity and Interest on Attitudes Toward Foreign Countries," *Public Opinion Quarterly*, Vol. 43, No. 1 (Spring 1979), pp. 68-78. Nincic and Russett, 1979).

16. Statistics Canada, *Canada 1991: An International Business Comparison* (Ottawa: Canada Communication Group, 1991).

17. Smith and Schott, *The Canada-U.S. Free Trade Agreement*.

18. Ronald Inglehart, Miguel Basanez and Neil Nevitte, *Convergencia en Norte America: Comercio, Politica y Cultura* (Mexico: Siglo xxi, 1994).

19. Inglehart relates the rise of postmaterialism to the kinds of structural shifts that are characteristic of late industrialism and he comprehensively demonstrates the host of ways in which postmaterialist orientations are connected to the content and dynamics of social and political behaviors in a wide variety of settings (Ronald Inglehart, "The Silent Revolution in Europe: Intergenerational Change in Post-Industrial Societies," *American Political Science Review*, Vol. 65, No. 4 (December 1971), pp. 991-1017; Ronald Ingelhart, The Silent Revolution (Princeton, N.J.: Princeton University Press, 1977); Ronald Inglehart, "Postmaterialism in an Environment of Insecurity," *American Political Science Review*, Vol. 75, No. 4 (December 1981), pp. 991-1017; Ronald Inglehart, "Cultural Change in Advanced Industrial Societies: Postmaterialist Values and Their Consequences," *International Review of Sociology*, Vol. 3 (1988), pp. 77-100; Ronald Inglehart, *Cultural Shift in Advanced Industrial Society* (Princeton: Princeton University Press, 1990) Central to Inglehart's theory are the combined effects of two hypotheses. First, the scarcity hypothesis holds that an individual's priorities reflect the socio-economic environment. "One places the greatest subjective value," Inglehart notes, "on those things that are in relatively short supply." Second, the socialization hypothesis draws attention to the importance of formative experiences in shaping durable value orientations. "The relationship between socio-economic environment and value priorities," Inglehart cautions, "is not one of immediate adjustment; a substantial time lag is involved for, to a large extent, one's basic values reflect the conditions that prevailed during one's pre-adult years," Inglehart, "Cultural Change in Advanced Industrial Societies," p. 881. Armed with these twin perspectives and informed by Maslow's conceptualization of a needs hierarchy (Abraham Maslow, *Motivation and Personality* (New York: Harper, 1954), Inglehart demonstrates that those segments of the population with direct experience of the great traumas of the 20th century, the second world war and the Great Depression, give relatively high priority to "materialist goals" -- economic security and "safety needs" (Inglehart, "The Silent Revolution in Europe," *Cultural Shift in Advanced Industrial Society*). Alternatively, those born since 1945, without direct experience of these traumas and "drawn largely from the younger segments of the modern middle class" have very different formative experiences. They have, he notes, "been socialized during an unprecedently long period of unprecedently high affluence. For them, economic security may be taken for granted as the supply of water or air we breathe once could" (Inglehart, "The Silent Revolution in Europe," p. 991). In effect, those with these postmaterialist orientations have moved up the needs hierarchy: they are no longer preoccupied with material security and instead give priority to aesthetic and intellectual needs and to the need for belonging.

20. Another intriguing finding is the discovery that there is little evidence from these data for the "lead and lag" thesis of Canadian value change; there is nothing in the data indicating that American values lead Canadian ones. In other words, there is no support for the idea that when it comes to values, the United States shows Canada the picture of its own future. For a statement of this thesis see I.L.

Horowitz, "The Hemispheric Connection," *Queen's Quarterly*, Vol. 80, No. 3 (Autumn 1973).

21. Ronald Inglehart, *Culture Shift in Advanced Industrial Society.*

22. For instance, one in three Quebecois support doing away with the Canada-U.S. border compared to one in five in the rest of Canada. More detailed analysis also shows that such factors as patriotism, partisanship and where respondents are located in their domestic economies also come into play. (For a more detailed analysis of these aspects see Inglehart, Nevitte and Basanez, *Convergencia en Norte America.*)

23. The very same analysis of value change was replicated for two groups within Canada -- francophone and anglophone. In that analysis, there is value convergence on 8 out of 13 value domains. Anglophone Canadians appear to have political and economic values that are more similar to American orientations. Anglophones and francophone Canadians are closer on social values.

11

Trilateralism and North American
Defense Relations:
Some Preliminary Thoughts

Joseph T. Jockel

Groucho Marx is reputed to have claimed that "politics is the art of looking for trouble, finding it everywhere, diagnosing it incorrectly and applying the wrong remedies." Academic analysts may be suspect of suffering from the same professional deformation. At first glance, introducing "trilateralism" into a consideration of North American defense relations appears to be precisely the wrong remedy applied to a problem that really does not exist.

After all, it is overwhelmingly economics that has been driving North American integration. No urgency exists in the defense interests of either Canada, the United States or Mexico that would parallel the economic urgency that has led to the negotiation and ratification of the North American Free Trade Agreement (NAFTA) and which would lead their national governments or legislatures to tie them militarily more closely together. On the contrary, with the Cold War over and with the Soviet Union gone, the defense efforts of both Canada and the U.S. are being cut back heavily. As a result, longstanding Canada-U.S. military ties are in the process of loosening, faster, in fact, than many people in either country realize.

Moreover, the differences, with deep roots in history and geography, in existing levels of bilateral military cooperation among the three North American countries, are great. They are seemingly so great that it would appear futile to think of them in trilateral terms. Canada and Mexico have had scarcely any military relationship at all. A recent exception is to be found in the participation by peacekeeping forces from both countries in the United Nations' Observer Mission in El Salvador (ONUSAL). This was Mexico's first venture in international peacekeeping.

It is startling to an observer used to Canada-U.S. defense relations that there is almost no military relationship between the U.S. and Mexico apart from the Joint Mexico-U.S. Defense Commission, a residue of the Second World War that has hardly been used since then. Only between Canada and the U.S. can there be said to be defense cooperation of any true extent, and there, of course, it has been of legendary, and to some Canadians painful, intensity.

Nonetheless, the disappearance of the Soviet Union has begun fundamentally to transform the Canada-U.S. defense relationship. At the same time, the "normalization" of relations between Mexico and the United States precipitated primarily by the recent, historic changes in Mexico's approach to the U.S., may open the door to some new, useful, but quite limited forms of military cooperation between the three countries.

At the center of any such trilateral cooperation, of course, will be the U.S. with its huge defense establishment. Strikingly, as the post-Soviet threat diminishes, the security interests of the U.S. on its northern border will more closely resemble those on its southern border with Mexico. And while great care must be taken to not push the point too far, Canada's military relationship with the United States will resemble more than it has in the past the Mexico-U.S. military relationship.

It is important to emphasize at the outset a point that will be developed in greater detail below. Because of enduring Mexican concerns, any conceivable military trilateralism as well as Mexico-U.S. and Mexico-Canada military cooperation could not entail, at least in the short run, classical international security cooperation: coordinating the ability of the military to use force or threatening to use force against other countries. Nor is it likely to involve Mexican collaboration in the architecture of western hemispheric cooperation. Rather, it is in a very limited realm of the "non-military" uses of the military in support of civilian authorities, that Canada, Mexico and the U.S. should explore some new joint approaches.

The (Now) Historic Canada-U.S. Defense Relationship

The Canada-U.S. defense relationship is entering a period of sweeping change. That relationship was created in response to two shared, long-standing security interests which antedate the Cold War.

The first of these interests was to prevent any power from establishing hegemony in Europe. While sentiment may have played a prime role in Canada's going to Britain's aid in both 1914 and 1939, preventing a German victory was fundamentally in Canada's interest. It was also in the interest of the U.S., as Americans somewhat belatedly recognized in 1917 and 1941.

In 1945, the Soviet Union succeeded the shattered Germany as the potential hegemon in Europe. Canada and the United States joined in the creation of the North Atlantic Treaty Organization (NATO), among other responses. Canada generally supported the U.S. as it sought to confront the Soviet Union, and its hostile, expansionist ideology across the globe, although Ottawa from time to time during the Cold War doubted the wisdom of specific applications of Washington's containment policy. As Melvin Conant, an astute observer of the Canada-U.S. relationship, put it "Canadians often think that their neighbor to the south exhibits wild swings of emotional attachments in its relations with other countries; that it is impatient, is prone to making sweeping judgments, and generally lacks sophistication and subtlety in its approach to the Soviet bloc and the cold war."[1]

Beyond its fundamental security interest, Canada's acceptance of military obligations in Europe was strengthened by its enduring desire to retain ties to that continent as a counterweight to the U.S., especially as Canadian-American economic and cultural links intensified. These obligations were seen for over forty years to include the deployment of Canadian forces in Europe. As well, membership in NATO was Canada's guaranteed entry to the big leagues of East-West security negotiations.

But whatever the motivations, Canada and the U.S. accepted almost from the very beginning of the Cold War that they had retained a common security region, that of the North Atlantic treaty area binding Western Europe and North America. The alliance's formal structures brought Canadian diplomats and politicians together with American and European counterparts, while military personnel were engaged in specific, functional cooperation at sea and in Europe.

After 1949, the fact that the two countries were in a common security area and a collective defense organization, which included Europe, often made it easier for Canada to deal with the second security interest it shared with the U.S. This was to defend against, or deter, an attack on North America. The purely bilateral, that is, Canada-U.S., arrangements for continental defense were never part of the

NATO multinational command structure, but if Canadians squinted hard they sometimes seemed to be. And it was always indisputably true, as Canadian governments liked to point out, that whether or not their bilateral defense arrangements fell under the aegis of the North Atlantic Treaty *Organization*, Canada and the U.S. were part of the North Atlantic Treaty *area*. So it could also be asserted that anything Canada and the U.S. did together militarily contributed to the security of the NATO area. And it was undoubtedly true that the Western Europeans, who depended upon the U.S. strategic nuclear deterrent, benefited from the protection Canadian air defense efforts afforded that deterrent.

Bilateral arrangements date back earlier than NATO and the Cold War, to the Second World War. In the summer of 1940, with the Low Countries and most of France occupied by Nazi Germany, and with Britain apparently on the verge of being invaded and perhaps subdued, it was the realization in Washington and Ottawa that a real and direct threat to North America could materialize that led to the creation of the intimate Canada-U.S. defense relationship. That August, in the small St. Lawrence River town of Ogdensburg, New York, President Franklin Delano Roosevelt and Prime Minister William Lyon Mackenzie King established, on an urgent basis, the Canada-U.S. Permanent Joint Board on Defense (PJBD).

The PJBD was briefly useful in bringing together two defense establishments that had scarcely had contact with one another. The Board still meets, although for years it has been of little more value than its Mexican counterpart. For once the armed forces of the two countries were authorized in 1940 to deal directly with one another, they swiftly established a pattern that continued into the Cold War and remains, for the moment at least, a hallmark of the bilateral defense relationship: intense functional cooperation, which soon rendered the formal sessions of the PJBD superfluous.

This point cannot be emphasized enough. Units of the two armed forces that have shared functional defense responsibilities have maintained very close transboundary ties. Such closeness has not extended to other parts of the Canadian and U.S. armed forces. For example, there have been few ties between the Canadian Armed Forces on the one hand, and the U.S. Marines on the other, there being no Canadian military units with tasks which they would today undertake in cooperation with the Marines.[2] The same could be said for the Canadian Armed Forces and the commands of the U.S. Air Force and U.S. Navy that have been responsible for strategic nuclear weapons, Canadians having no direct role to play in the deployment or potential use of those weapons.

Functional closeness with Canada has suited the interests of the U.S. particularly well. The U.S. has taken Canada on as a partner in those areas where the Canadian Armed Forces have been able to make contributions to joint security. Moreover bilateral cooperation has helped to ensure that access to Canadian waters, airspace and territory, where necessary for military purposes, would be made available. But the American government has never accepted the notion that functional closeness with the Canadian military entitles the Canadian government to special influence over U.S. decision-making. The Diefenbaker government learned this unhappy lesson in the 1962 Cuban missile crisis, when the Kennedy administration acted without consulting Ottawa, even though the 1958 exchange of diplomatic notes formalizing the North American Air Defense Command's (NORAD) creation had included, at Ottawa's insistence, pledges of consultation in the event of an emergency affecting continental defense.

Functional closeness to the U.S. has also often served Canada's interests, although, as will be discussed below, there have also been considerable drawbacks. Cooperating with the Americans has saved Canada money, inasmuch as the costs of facilities and operations necessary in Canada could be shared with the U.S. Canada has also gained access to American defense technology and planning. Finally, close functional cooperation at the very least has provided Ottawa with a framework for dealing with Washington. This was especially true of NORAD. As the distinguished Canadian diplomat and scholar John Holmes put it, "NORAD, which seems a step in the continentalization of North American defense, can be regarded from another angle as a means of preserving a Canadian role and an appropriate degree of sovereignty in a situation in which, if there were no rules, the Americans would simply take over the defense of the continent."[3]

At the end of the Second World War it seemed unlikely to the Canadian and United States defense establishments that any hostile power would soon acquire the capability to threaten North America. But the Soviet Union rapidly developed long-range aircraft that could reach the North American continent, as well as the nuclear weapons that could be carried in them. As a result, both Canada and the U.S. increased their air defense efforts beginning in the late 1940s and then accelerating in the early 1950s. As a look at the map showed, an air attack on the U.S. would be made chiefly through Canada. The Canadian air defense system was thus important to the U.S. Eager to drive the point home, Brooke Claxton, Minister of National Defense at the time, emphasized time and again that "Every cent we spend on this in Canada helps the United States."⁴

The Canadian and U.S. efforts were gradually intertwined, to the point in the mid 1950s where there were common plans, shared radar lines and ground intercept environments, and the delegated authority for fighter aircraft of one country to cross the international boundary in an emergency to destroy hostile aircraft. Within such a context it only made military sense to place all Canadian and U.S. air defense efforts under a single command. This occurred in 1957, with the creation of NORAD at Colorado Spring, Colorado, with a U.S. commander and a Canadian deputy. NORAD was given operation control over both the Canadian and U.S. air defense systems.

Similar -- and to this day far less chronicled -- developments occurred at sea. The anti-submarine forces of the U.S. Navy and Royal Canadian Navy established extremely close working relations for both tactical and strategic anti-submarine warfare. There were, however, two differences with respect to air defense. First, naval cooperation occurred under both NATO and bilateral auspices, but NORAD was strictly a Canada-U.S. entity. Second, whereas NORAD had standing, peacetime operational control over all U.S. and Canadian air defense efforts in North America, Canadian naval forces were supposed to remain strictly under national control unless specifically instructed by higher Canadian authority to place themselves under U.S. or NATO command.

The prime drawbacks of functional closeness for Canada were two-fold. First, Canadian decision-makers worried that they might lose control over the Canadian Armed Forces to the U.S., especially with respect to air defense forces under NORAD. As the Cuban missile crisis also indicated, there was substantial justification for such concern, although it was the Canadian navy, not the air force, which more fully drifted out of political control during the crisis.

Second, there were the fears that Canada would lose control over its territory, waters, and airspace. These concerns dated from the Second World War, when the U.S. "army of occupation" in northwestern Canada inadvertently threatened to overwhelm local control. In the late nineteen fifties, with American personnel manning radar stations in both northern and southern Canada, and with U.S. fighter aircraft routinely undertaking patrols in Canadian skies, these concerns returned. In later decades Canadians worried that sovereignty over their northern waters could be threatened by the passage of U.S. vessels, eventually including nuclear-powered submarines.

During much of the Cold War many Canadians also fretted about the relationship between their country's role in NORAD and U.S. nuclear strategy. Canadians were periodically surprised to learn that U.S. strategy included threatening the Soviet Union with a strategic nuclear attack if it invaded Western Europe. In other words, the purpose of the strategic nuclear weapons the Canadian air force was helping to defend was not simply to deter a nuclear attack on North America.

The shift in the Soviet threat from bombers to missiles, which occurred essentially in the 1960s, coupled with the United States decision to forego, at least temporarily, a ballistic missile defense, began the decline in the importance to the U.S. of Canadian territory and airspace, and of the Canadian Armed Forces. Significantly, no system to detect a ballistic missile attack on North America was ever located in Canada or operated by the Canadian Armed Forces. With no system in place to defend against missiles, it made little sense to maintain the vast North American air defense system at the levels reached by the beginning of the 1960s.

Yet the Canadian air force and U.S. aerospace defense forces remained close. This was due to inertia. The Americans were used to working with Canadians at Colorado Springs. It was also due to bureaucratic politics within the U.S. defense establishment. The United States air force several times relied on NORAD's bi-national status to frustrate the plans of the U.S. Navy to downgrade it. Finally, while the bulk of the threat to the continent had shifted to missiles, a vestigial air defense was still necessary, in order to make sure that the back door remained closed. Indeed, for a while in the mid-1980s, with the advent of the advanced cruise missile (both air-launched and sea-launched) North American air defense made a brief comeback. A renewed air defense effort seemed to make all the more sense at a time when President Ronald Reagan's Strategic Defense Initiative (SDI) was launched to investigate and potentially to develop a ballistic missile defense system.

All this meant that Canada remained important to the defense of the U.S. In 1989, the two countries signed an agreement to modernize the continent's air defenses which included the transformation of the old, American built and operated Distant Early Warning (DEW) Line, which had been constructed in the high Canadian and Alaskan Arctic in the early 1950s, into a North Warning System. The new North Warning System was to be operated by Canadians, the culmination of the "Canadianization" of air defense in Canada which had been underway since the late fifties and which had accelerated as the air defense system had shrunk. The American part of the 1985 package included the construction of four great Over the Horizon-Backscatter

(OTH-B) radars, one in Alaska, one looking outward on the U.S. east coast, one on the west coast, and one looking southward.

In summary, the Canada-U.S. defense relationship, prompted by the twin security concerns of preventing hegemony in Eurasia and providing for defense at home, had several key features: a common security region incorporated in a broader alliance with other countries, intense functional closeness between certain elements of the armed forces of both countries, and a desire on the part of both countries to limit the extent of the closeness.

The Eroding Canada-U.S. Defense Relationship

The disappearance of the Soviet Union undercut both of the historic motivations for the Canada-U.S. defense relationship. As the *Economist* recently put it, today there is "nobody who can cause military trouble for the democracies on a global scale. No power now exists whose soldiers might imaginably occupy Western Europe, whose nuclear warheads could devastate America, whose navy reaches into all the world's oceans, whose guns and money support local friends on every continent."[5] Even if Russia, after a substantial period, should re-emerge as a hostile power with expansionist ambitions, it could not threaten to dominate Europe in the way the old Soviet Union once did. In other words, for the first time since Canada took responsibility for its external relations, there is no potential hegemon in Europe.[6]

In the absence of such a potential hegemon, the shared perception of a common, North Atlantic security region is rapidly waning, especially on this side of the ocean. Whether it will disappear altogether, along with NATO itself, is not at all clear. Canada, for its part, is out of the business of keeping troops in Western Europe, although it still earmarks forces that could be deployed to Europe in the event of an emergency. Canada's declining involvement in European security seems motivated as well by what appears to be a growing recognition that Europe can no longer serve as a "counterweight" to the U.S., especially not an economic counterweight.

To be sure, Americans and Canadians may continue to share a new, multilateral approach to security that is geographically much broader than the North Atlantic Treaty area should the armed forces of both countries continue to participate in peacekeeping and peace enforcement operations, usually under the auspices of the United Nations. Canada, of course, has a record in international peacekeeping unmatched by that of any other country. (Canadians, however, are usually surprised to hear that the U.S. record in peacekeeping is slightly older than

Canada's.) But the end of the Cold War has deprived Canada of its special status as the West's peacekeeper. A host of countries, East and West, including the U.S., Germany, Japan and republics of the former Soviet Union, have been equipping their forces with blue helmets or berets.

There is little reason to believe that such multilateral operations can recreate the very strong sense of common purpose that NATO often imparted to the armed forces of its participating countries, among them, Americans and Canadians. Peacekeeping operations are frequently short-lived and often rely on small numbers of personnel, unlike the old very long-standing national contributions to NATO. Moreover, peacekeeping has become much more difficult as it moves from dealing with international conflict to intrastate problems, Somalia and Yugoslavia being painful examples of the emerging form. As this transition occurs, even the longstanding Canadian commitment to peacekeeping may come under substantial questioning at home. Certainly the U.S. experience in Somalia has helped to dampen earlier enthusiasm for a rapid expansion of American peacekeeping activities.

Some day Canada may, once again, join in a U.S.-led multinational peace enforcement coalition, as it did in the Persian Gulf War. But the ability of the Canadian Armed Forces to contribute effective combat forces overseas is eroding as a result of cutbacks in the defense budget. In the face of the country's serious fiscal problems, further reductions are all but inevitable. The new Liberal government elected in October 1993 has ordered a review of defense policy which may well result in a further lessening of Canada's ability to contribute forces to combat operations overseas.

With the disappearance of the Soviet Union, the threat to North America is also rapidly declining. To be sure, as long as nuclear weapons remain in the hands of the successor states to the Soviet Union, a danger still exists. But the chances that those weapons actually would be used have declined to the lowest point in years. Several third world states may acquire nuclear weapons, but these threats will probably be marginal. Nonetheless, the U.S. may still decide that meeting them will require the deployment of a limited ballistic missile defense system. There is little reason, however, to believe that such a system would necessitate the use of Canadian territory. Nor is there any reason to believe that a system of global warning of missile attack, which the U.S. is also considering, would require Canadian territory or cooperation.

Accordingly, the North American aerospace defense system is being scaled back, especially its only active defense efforts -- those providing limited air defense. No one at NORAD headquarters is yet quite prepared to turn off all the air defense radars, sell them off for surplus, and go home. But the OTH-B systems are in fact being turned off most of the time, mothballed, or not being built. The U.S. Congress has also balked at providing the funding to continue the American share of completing the North Warning System in Canada. At the same time, NORAD's air defense aircraft are standing down from 24 hour a day, seven day a week alert status, and the fighter inventory, already limited, is being further reduced. The Chairman of the U.S. Joint Chiefs of Staff observed of the cuts, "Now that the threat has largely disappeared, we simply no longer need such a large, dedicated continental air defense force."[7] As the need to defend North America against nuclear attack wanes, what air defense forces the U.S. and Canada decide to leave in place will find themselves devoting an increasing amount of time to such matters as narcotics control.

The next step in all probability will involve major changes in command arrangements, especially as Colorado Springs shifts its focus from defending and warning of attack on North America towards providing global warning of missile attacks. The NORAD agreement may very well not be renewed when it comes up for renewal in 1996. Because Canada contributes nothing directly to the detection of a missile attack, it is far from certain that the U.S. will want to retain Canada as a major partner at Colorado Springs -- or that Canada will want to retain NORAD. As Maj. General Jean E. Boyle, Associate Assistant Deputy Minister of National Defence recently explained, "The Americans are looking at NORAD doing global warning. We would have to return to Parliament to expand the NORAD mission." As for the Americans, Boyle said that "the issue on the American agenda would be: is it imperative for them to have Canada on board or are we a liability in their rethinking of how they want to do things."[8]

In other words, the functional military closeness that has been the hallmark of Canada-U.S. defense relations is also waning as the threat to the continent declines. The same process, although less chronicled, is also underway with respect to naval cooperation. The two navies have cooperated most closely in strategic anti-submarine warfare and in preparing to keep the sea access to NATO Europe open in the event of a war. With the former Soviet navy rusting away in port, both of these tasks have become all but superfluous.

Towards Limited Trilateralism?[9]

Mexico has never shared the two security interests that led to the creation of the Canada-U.S. defense relationship and then sustained it for decades. Unlike the United States and Canada, it has not in this century seen its security as being deeply and directly linked to developments in Europe, although it did formally join the nations united against Nazi Germany in the Second World War, motivated by opposition to fascism. It can be convincingly argued that Mexico's lack of interest in European security affairs was made possible because the U.S. helped shield Mexico from aggression arising outside the hemisphere. But to Mexicans, the U.S. itself has been the historic aggressor and always a looming power to be coped with.

Mexico and the U.S. do share what could be called a "natural" security region, that is, Central America and the Caribbean. But here the two countries have rarely seen eye to eye. On the contrary, in the period before World War II Mexico was at the forefront of the countries that were critical of U.S. policy in Central America and the Caribbean. The Mexican government was particularly anxious to obtain guarantees of non-intervention from Washington as the condition for favorable hemispheric relations. After the war (during which Mexico guardedly cooperated with the United States), Mexico City returned to its posture of attempting, on principle, to obstruct U.S. designs for western hemispheric security. While Mexico's participation in ONUSAL undoubtedly represented a new level of participation in hemispheric security affairs, Mexico City can still be expected to shy away from any direct military intervention in the hemisphere and to be wary of U.S. initiatives.

The physical defense of the North American continent did not draw Mexico toward the United States and Canada during the Cold War. Put most directly, if somewhat obviously, the Soviet Union was on the other side of Canada, not Mexico. The North American air defense system was oriented northward, not southward, with the special exception of monitoring Cuba. Consequently, the U.S. and Canada never really needed to open the possibility of close defense relations with Mexico.

That was most fortunate, for Mexico's historic grievances against the United States make Canada's traditional sovereignty concerns vis à vis the U.S. pale by comparison and would have made significant military

cooperation extremely difficult to establish and maintain. Nonetheless, Mexico today is in the midst of far-reaching domestic change,
coupled with a rethinking of its overall relationship with the U.S.,
the new centerpiece being the North American Free Trade Agreement.

As defending the continent from nuclear attack fades from the U.S.
security agenda, it is tempting to suggest that the moment has come to
try to incorporate Mexico and the Mexican armed forces into the
vestigial remains of the North American air defense system, that will
now increasingly serve border control and sovereignty protection
purposes. NORAD, according to this line of thinking, could be swept
away and replaced by new trilateral arrangements.

But such a sweeping approach would be unrealistic. Mexico will
remain for the foreseeable future uncomfortable with any close, direct
military cooperation that operationally extends across the
international boundary. The Canadian air force will probably want to
retain what it can of its privileged relationship with the U.S. and
would not welcome the arrival of the Mexicans. And the U.S. defense
establishment cannot yet expect to be comfortable with the thought of
taking the Mexican armed forces as a privileged partner.

Nevertheless, it is surely in the interests of the United States and
Canada to gently encourage the historic Mexican opening to the north in
the direction of greater functional cooperation where possible.
Cooperation with Mexico in such areas as drug control can also serve
U.S. and Canadian interests. It may, therefore, be useful to explore
areas of trilateral cooperation in which the military can be used for
traditionally non-military purposes, especially in support of civilian
agencies. Because of historic worries, Mexicans may prove to be more
comfortable in a broader context involving Canadians, as well as
Americans. Low key discussions between Canadians and Mexicans
concerning peacekeeping experiences are already occurring under a
number of auspices.

In all probability, one non-military use of the military which might
suggest itself to the U.S. as an area of cooperation with Mexico can be
ruled out, at least for the moment. This is immigration control. The
issue is still much too sensitive in Mexico, for obvious reasons. A short
list of areas for Canada, Mexico and the U.S. to explore could include:

1. Sovereignty protection and the drug trade. Mexico, it should be
   underlined, would resist the outright militarization of anti-drug
   efforts, in particular any proposals for direct military
   intervention across borders to help stem the drug trade. But
   military *support* of civilian law enforcement agencies within

each country may be another matter. The prospects for greater technical cooperation between North American militaries in this area, including the training of Mexican soldiers in the U.S. and Canada for drug-related missions, should probably be explored.

2. Environmental protection. There has been growing interest in all three countries in the role of the military in environmental disasters. Consultative arrangements, joint explorations of techniques and technologies and perhaps some joint training may prove useful.

3. Rescue and disaster relief. Joint plans and procedures for military support could probably be developed in this area, as well as training for such activity.

Notes

1. Melvin Conant, *The Long Polar Watch: Canada and the Defense of North America* (New York: Harper and Brothers, 1962), p. 67.

2. In the early 1980s both the Canadian Armed Forces and U.S. Marines were solidifying their ability to reinforce Norway. Had this persisted it probably would have lead to a much closer relationship.

3. John Holmes, *The Shaping of Peace: Canada and the Search for World Order, 1943-1957*, vol. 2 (Toronto: University of Toronto Press, 1982), p. 291.

4. Brooke Claxton, address (Ottawa, June 23, 1951). Claxton papers, vol. 189, National Archives of Canada.

5. "Defense in the 21st century: meet your unbrave new world," in "A Survey of Defense in the 21st Century: Breaking Free," *Economist* (September 5, 1992), p. 3.

6. For an exploration of this theme, see Joseph T. Jockel and Joel J. Sokolsky, "Dandurand revisited: Rethinking Canada's Defence Policy in an Unstable World," *International Journal*, Vol. 48, No. 2 (Spring 1993), pp. 380-401.

7. United States, Chairman of the Joint Chiefs of Staff, *Roles, Missions and Functions of the Armed Forces of the United States*, Washington: February 1993, III-12, III-13.

8. Quoted in Sharon Hobson, "Extending NORAD's Reach," *Jane's Defence Weekly*, (September 25, 1992), p. 22.

9. This section draws on "Intensifying North American Relationships: Implications for Defense," Report prepared by the Center for Strategic and International Studies Americas Program for the U.S. Department of Defense, International Security Affairs, Inter-American Region, December 1992.

PART FOUR

The European Union: Lessons and Impact

12

Managing Economic Convergence in the European Union

Gretchen M. MacMillan

The European Union (EU), unlike the economic area created by the North American Free Trade Agreement (NAFTA), has been self-consciously supranational since the establishment of the European Coal and Steel Community (ECSC) in 1951.[1] Forty years later, the management of the customs union and internal market has resulted in a degree of institutional and economic integration that extends to issues traditionally associated with sovereign states. At the same time, the conduct of policy and management of conflict in the European Union can be characterized as intergovernmental, and it is through complex and often time-consuming processes that member states of the EU approach issues of integration and harmonization of policies to promote the free movement of goods, services, labor and capital.[2] While the Union has and is experiencing enormous difficulties, it is the most successful example of trade integration among industrialized and democratic states. Whether it provides a model for economic integration and lessons for North America is another matter.

The purpose of the EU and its progenitors has been more ambitious than that of NAFTA. The goal of the political leaders who established the ECSC and later the European Economic Community (EEC) was for a greater degree of economic integration than free trade. This chapter will concentrate on the problems and conflicts related to the move towards Economic and Monetary Union (EMU) which precipitated the latest changes in the founding Treaties and the adoption of a new name: the European Union.[3] Initially it examines the mechanisms by which the member states and the Union manage convergence and harmonization of policies. The management of conflict in the EU through cooperation among the member state governments (intergovernmentalism) has ensured their domination of the process, often at the expense of the Commission's power and authority, even while they have been the catalyst for increased integration and convergence. After reviewing the progress made towards economic integration, the chapter will conclude with an examination of some of the weaknesses of the intergovernmental process and their possible impact on the future of the Union. It will also consider the relevance of the European experience for North America.

Economic integration among and between sovereign states can involve several stages. The first step is the establishment of a free trade area. Tariffs and quotas that exist on trade between the countries involved are removed. The second stage is the creation of a customs union, in which the countries remove internal barriers to trade while establishing a common external barrier against other countries. The establishment of a common internal market is the third stage. This includes the free movement of all the factors involved in the production and distribution of goods, labor, capital and services. A further step is taken when a monetary union is created and states establish a common currency or a system of irrevocably fixed exchange rates. At this stage some national economic policies of the member states may need to be harmonized. Finally total economic integration is achieved when the economic polices of the member states are integrated.[4] While the North American states are at the first stage, the attempt to establish a free trade area, the European Union states have reached the stage of attempting to create an economic and monetary union. They have already established a customs union (1968) and an internal free market (1992). More significantly, unlike NAFTA or the earlier Canada-U.S. Free Trade Agreement (CUSFTA), the member states of the EU established as early as the ECSC the concept of supranational institutions that are supreme in their areas of competency.

While convergence in the EU usually refers to the mechanisms needed to establish the foundations for EMU and a common currency, it can also mean any process by which operations, policies, management and/or effects are drawn together and directed to the achievement of a common goal. In the context of the EU, convergence can be used to describe the means used by the twelve member states[5] to create a set of institutions and policy procedures that provide the foundations of a customs union, a common internal market with free movement of labor, capital, goods and services and increased political and legal union, even while they maintain a major control over the process.

Intergovernmentalism and Supranational Organization

The EU's   decision-making process operates within a framework of interlocking institutions and agencies that at most levels is more like the decision-making process in a federal state than it is in an international organization. Intergovernmentalism then, as applied to the EU, can be used to describe a decision-making process that involves state-to-state relationships as in international affairs as well as between a central government and sub-governments or between sub-governments as in a federal state.[6]

Decision-making in the Union is therefore more interconnected than in free trade agreements but also more complex than it is in federal states.[7] The institutional framework as well as the policy process includes both Union institutions and national governments. The Union's institutions under the Treaties are assigned responsibility for selected areas of economic policy among the member states. They therefore possess a degree of autonomy and sovereignty not true of other international trade and economic organizations, and certainly not of NAFTA, which is why the term supranational rather than international is usually applied to the EU.[8]

The Union, as is true of federal systems, possesses two distinct levels of government, each with defined constitutional authority operating within the same territory. In certain delineated areas under the constitution/Treaties, the laws of the central institutions are supreme over those of the component units. However, the member states have assumed key roles in policy and decision-making in the EU through the use of their veto power in the Council of Ministers. Furthermore, while legally the role of initiating policy lies with the Commission, politically this power has been exercised by both the Council of Ministers and the Commission. This has allowed the member states to hold onto their sovereignty and to protect their national interests.

In some ways the Union might be described as a supranational "state." While the EU clearly lacks a major state characteristic in that it has no coercive forces at its disposal (these remain in the hands of the member states), it does possess other characteristics associated with a state -- it has its own tax base, its laws take precedence over member state laws and its institutions are supreme in their areas of competency. It is this supremacy of EU law over member state law, upheld through the European Court of Justice (ECJ) through the power of judicial review and recognized by the highest courts of the member states, that provides the basis of "federalism" for the Union.[9]

It is important to emphasize that the center of political authority and the management of conflict and convergence remain and are clearly driven by agreements among the member states. Even the move to closer political and economic union codified in the Single European Act (SEA) of 1985 and the 1991 Treaty on European Union (the TEU, popularly known as the Maastricht Treaty) were initiated and controlled by the member states' political elites.[10] The rough passage of the TEU is a reminder that those elites often ignored or underestimated the reactions of ordinary citizens who often felt excluded by the creators of the new Europe.

A major reason for the lack of accord between the political elites and the larger societies of the member states has been the lack of democratic accountability of the Union institutions, as well as the complex and often arcane issues dealt with by those institutions. The Union possesses an executive (Commission), a bicameral legislature (Council of Ministers and European Parliament) and a judiciary (European Court of Justice). However, the distribution of power and authority among these bodies means that in actuality the member states through the Council of Ministers have emerged as a co-executive with the European Commission and have maintained a substantial influence over the composition and activities of the central institutions.[11]

The ultimate ability of the member states to control the policy and integration process has been through the European Council.[12] In spite of or maybe even because of the complexity of the EU's process of decision-making the member states found that they needed to create a further supranational executive body to facilitate agreements. The European Council, created by the member states outside the framework of the Treaties, is composed of the heads of government and state.[13] Its influence is based on the political authority of its members which head the governments of the member states. (The closest analogy to the European Council is probably the first ministers conferences in Canada, which consist of the prime minister and the 10 provincial premiers.)

While the European Council lacks any executive or legislative role in the Union, it has, paradoxically, become the engine of increased integration and federalism. It has played the most important role in each stage of further political and economic integration of the member states. Its existence and its control of the major aspects of state power -- foreign policy and defense -- ensures that however convergence develops in the future the member states will continue to be the effective engine of change at the center. Furthermore, the member states' control of the agenda through the European Council is enhanced by its linkage to a Treaty institution: the presidency of the European

Union which rotates through the twelve states.

While the Council of Ministers allows the member states to control much of the policy process at the Union level, it does not necessarily mean that all member states are equal or that there are not major areas of disagreement among them. The increased use of weighted voting in the Council of Ministers, especially in the implementation of the internal market, also has made the process of negotiation and compromise among and between the member states much more important.[14] At the same time, while there are some issues on which unanimity is required, most decisions are derived by building consensus. Moreover, from the number of votes in the weighted voting procedure, to the difference in the number of Commissioners, to the number of seats in the Parliament, some member states are more equal than others. For example, the Franco-German axis has been central to the existence of the Union from the agreement to create the ECSC through to the Treaty on European Union.[15] Conventional wisdom indicates that if the two central states agree on an issue then it will be part of the agenda.

Policy differences among the member states are influenced by their geographical location and the importance of the Union to their economy, including such issues as support for their agricultural sector or support from the social and economic cohesion funds. Italy, Belgium, the Netherlands and Luxembourg, along with France and Germany, are probably the most self-consciously integrationist in orientation. Among the outer-six, Ireland is the most supportive of further integration, but Spain and Portugal have also been more reticent than the other three outer-six states, Greece, Denmark and the United Kingdom, in opposing further integration. Another major source of difference centers on those poorer states that have become more financially dependent on the Union, including Spain, Portugal, Greece and Ireland.[16]

As indicated above, the control and domination sought by the member states is related to policy issues that reflect domestic as opposed to foreign policy. The Treaty of Rome, the Single European Act, and the Treaty on European Union have all assigned powers to the Community and now to the Union.[17] While the degree to which the policies are actually carried out at the supranational level varies from issue to issue there is no doubt that on some policy topics such as agriculture, all decisions are now made at the center even if the member states maintain their dominance through the Council of Ministers. Yet it is important to keep this in perspective. In many areas the powers of the Commission are greater on paper than they are in reality and pressures by the member states at the center contribute to the practical limits placed on the ability of the Union to make policy.

Pressures that have to be taken into account at the supranational level include not only the views and positions of individual member state's political leadership, national cabinet, legislature and civil service, and interest groups, but also those of the Union leadership and institutions. In summary, to carry out many of the tasks associated with economic and domestic policy, European political leaders have to share these traditional tasks of the state with each other and with the Union. This has certainly been true of the developments towards closer economic integration.

Economic Integration

The role of intergovernmentalism in the management of policy convergence, as indicated above, operates at two levels: one within the framework of the Union's institutions; the other outside of it. Intergovernmental agreements outside the Union institutions often include issues more clearly associated with the powers and authority of traditional nation states such as the Western European Union (defense), the Schengen Agreements (immigration and police forces) and the Exchange Rate Mechanism (currency regulation). At the same time, as will be demonstrated in the following discussion, the lines between what is within and what is outside the Treaties has become increasingly blurred. Certainly the move towards increased economic integration has proceeded within and outside the Treaty framework.

The Treaty of Rome outlined an agreement to remove both tariff and non-tariff barriers among the signatory states to ensure the free movement of goods, services, labor and capital. The removal of tariff barriers went further than in NAFTA. It also created a customs union so that there was a common tariff barrier against all third parties. While the original six states managed to eliminate the tariff barriers between themselves by 1968, the removal of non-tariff barriers and the creation of a free internal market among the member states would take longer and be much more difficult to achieve. Although some non-tariff barriers still existed, the internal market came into affect January 1, 1993.

The creation of the internal market was possible to some extent because the member states had taken some further steps towards closer integration by establishing a fixed exchange rate mechanism among their currencies. This led to discussions about the possibility of establishing an Economic and Monetary Union with a common currency. The argument in support of EMU is relatively straight forward.[18] A customs union and an internal market, to be effective (according to this argument), require a comparatively level playing field of interest rates, rates of inflation and currency values. This is best achieved by the creation of a single body that will be able to do this legally and legitimately -- such as the central government and a central bank in a federal unit. However, for national, historical, cultural and linguistic reasons, the twelve sovereign states of the EU have not and are not likely to seriously entertain the idea of an United States of Europe. At the same time, the move towards completion of the internal market in 1992 created a situation in which many member state leaders felt that a resolution of the differences in interest rates and inflation rates would require either irrevocably fixed exchange rates or a common currency.

The idea of creating an Economic and Monetary Union has existed since the 1960s. At the Hague Summit in December 1969, the leaders agreed to the establishment of an Economic and Monetary Union by 1980. In 1971, they even drew up a plan for its creation. This did not happen, primarily because of the changes in the world monetary system that followed the collapse of the Bretton Woods system. As a result of the volatility of exchange rates, countries had to find a new basis for their currencies. An early example of the then Community's attempt to stabilize exchange rates while maintaining flexibility against the dollar was the setting up of the "currency snake" in 1972. This proved unsuccessful, primarily because the system lacked a mechanism for maintaining a balance between and among the currencies in the snake.

Further and more successful attempts were made in the late 1970s, with the establishment of the European Monetary System (EMS) and the Exchange Rate Mechanism (ERM) in 1979. Initially eight of the nine states (the United Kingdom being the exception) participated. They agreed to maintain their exchange rate mechanisms within certain fluctuating margins. After some initial difficulties they settled on fixed though adjustable bands of exchange for participating currencies, with all of them pegged against the deutschmark. The ERM remained outside the Treaty system because of concern over what a rigid system inside the Treaties might involve and because not all member states wished to join. It did, however, provide a strong basis for establishing strong monetary policies within the member states.

The earlier plan of establishing EMU by 1980 had long since been abandoned, for the member states lacked the political will to carry through all the changes needed to create a common currency or fixed exchange rates. Furthermore, they had not managed to complete the framework of the internal market, and until that was accomplished, the creation of an economic and monetary union was impractical. At the same time, however, they made agreements among themselves to move forward in other areas. These included the creation of the ECU, a currency unit, which would become the medium of exchange between the Community and the member states and is traded on the foreign exchange markets.

The members states also set up a system of regular meetings of finance ministers, government representatives and national bank officials to consult and exchange information on macroeconomic policy. They mandated the Council of Ministers (Ecofin), made up of member states' finance ministers, to attempt to establish macroeconomic policies. Ecofin was, of course, a Community institution and its use for coordinating policies that were outside the Treaties indicated the fluidity of intergovernmental relations. Policies were discussed therefore at all levels both within and outside the Treaty system. While this resulted in exchanges of information at all levels of the economic policy process it did not result in any concrete changes.

The arguments at the time the ERM was established have continued to be important as the member states have sought mechanisms to further economic convergence. There were genuine differences among the member states over the value of economic union versus financial harmonization and over which should come first. Furthermore, the implications for what Economic and Monetary Union would mean differed from state to state. For some states the possibility of pooling key macroeconomic and financial policies or even handing them over to central institutions raised important questions of sovereignty.

The issue of economic and monetary policy became more cogent for most of the member states and the Commission as a result of the adoption of the SEA. In April 1989, Jacques Delors, President of the Commission, submitted a report to the European Council that had been commissioned the previous June at the Hanover European Council under the German Presidency.[19]

The "Delors Report" outlined a three stage progression to EMU. Stage 1 called for the completion of the internal market. Member states would improve coordination of their economic policies, all EC currencies would be brought into the ERM, the committee of central bank governors would advise the national governments and Ecofin on national policies, and preparations would begin to set up a treaty on monetary union.

In Stage 2 a European System of Central Banks (ESCB) -- also known as the Eurofed -- with a federal structure would be established. The ESCB would take over the functions of the existing EC monetary institutions.

In Stage 3 member states would move to permanent fixed exchange rates and the eventual creation of a single EC currency. All monetary policy authority would be transferred to the ESCB.[20]

The driving force behind the furtherance of integration has been the European Council and the presidency of the Community. Against the backdrop of the momentous changes in Eastern Europe, the collapse of the Berlin Wall and the disintegration of the Soviet Union, they worked out a timetable to implement the Delors Report and arrangements that would bring them closer to Economic and Monetary Union.

At the Madrid Council meeting in June 1989, the leaders agreed that Stage 1 of the Delors plan would begin in July 1990.[21] At the Strasbourg Council in December 1989, they agreed to establish, at the Rome Council in December 1990, the Intergovernmental Conference (IGC) on Economic and Monetary Union.[22] At the first Rome Council in October 1990, it was agreed to move to Stage 2 of the Delors Report on January 1, 1994. The Eurofed would be established along with monetary union but without fixed parities. Stage 3 of a common currency was to be completed no less than three years later. If the member states could agree on a mechanism at the IGC, Economic and Monetary Union could be achieved by the end of the century. The process, which was spelled out in the Maastricht Treaty, signed in December 1991, was very elaborate and required convergence among the member states on interest rates, currency fluctuations and inflation rates that even then would have been difficult for most of them to achieve.

The means by which the member states would decide if they were ready to move to a common currency were hammered out between the states in IGC on EMU leading up to the Treaty on European Union.[23]

The central component of the EMU was to be the Exchange Rate Mechanism. By April 1992, all of the currencies except the Greek drachma were included in the ERM. The system, to be successful, was dependent on the German Bundesbank and the international money markets. The difficulties encountered in securing approval of the Maastricht Treaty in Denmark and France made the markets anxious about the possibility of the EC implementing EMU. Between October 1992 and August 1993, the markets' reaction led to the Italian lira and the British pound being forced out of the ERM, and to the devaluation of the Spanish peseta, the Portuguese escudo and the Irish punt.

It was not only the markets' judgment that led to the ERM's problems. The soaring costs of German unification played a major role as well. The Bundesbank whose mandate was to control costs in the German economy maintained high interest rates to check inflation. This had affected the other currencies in the ERM and accusations were leveled at Germany during the attack on the British and Italian currency and later when the Irish punt was devalued. The maintenance of high German interest rates and the market's judgment led to the devaluation of the French franc in August 1993. This was followed by the widening of the old bands in the ERM , with the exception of the Dutch guilder against the deutschmark.

The collapse of the Exchange Rate Mechanism -- or at least the expansion of the bands of the ERM -- was due to the markets' reactions to the Community's move towards Economic and Monetary Union and also to the policy agenda of the member states whose domestic needs were difficult to mesh with the idea of an overall Community ideal. The decision of the Bundesbank to keep interest rates high met German economic requirements but had negative effects on other member states, whose economic needs required lower interest rates. The damage in the end was not just to the ERM but also to the ideal of achieving EMU by the end of the decade.

The attempt to create a common currency and common economic and monetary policies remains in disarray. This does not necessarily mean that the Union will not try again. The experience, however, indicates that political elites find themselves in difficulty when they attempt to move forward on idealistic, grand designs. The more successful policies are often those that involve incremental convergence in policy-making rather than grand designs. Furthermore, in spite of the difficulties confronting the member states and societies of the Union, there are strong indications that at least some of the inner six are willing to move forward on EMU. Difficulties remain in convincing the international money markets and the national societies of the Union states that further economic union and integration is viable and desirable.

Conclusion

The development and integration of the EU to this point has largely been the work of the major political elites in the member states. Actors in the EU institutions have also played important roles in this process. However, these institutions lack legitimacy within member states' societies. The EU itself has no political community. It has been dependent for its existence upon agreement among state actors. If it is to become even a supranational state, it will require its own political community. In theory, the Treaty on European Union provides the framework for such a development, but can it overcome the objections of both the member states and their own political communities in turning this into reality? Can a European nationality be created on top of, or instead of, the regional identities already in place? Is it necessary to do so? The answer is at this point not likely.24

The present EU, however, has achieved, in relation to a trade agreement like NAFTA, a remarkable degree of economic and political integration. While the major policy-makers under NAFTA will be the governments of the three states, there are major differences between its mechanisms and those of the EU for the making of policy. It is here that the mechanisms of convergence are clearly to be seen in the EU. The member states must work through the Union to provide a legal basis for their negotiations. While it might be in the member states' interests to indicate the "powers of Brussels" to impose rules on the member states, both the Commission and the member states share in the decision-making process as regards common policies. For the Union it is not a question of sending the issue to a arbitration board. If the Commission feels member states are dragging their heals in implementing policies, they can resort to the European Court of Justice and sometimes to the national courts which increasingly take their directions from the decisions of the ECJ.

The degree of integration and convergence of policy-making and harmonization of laws in the European Union is therefore much more extensive than anything that has been imagined in NAFTA. There is little doubt that the Maastricht Agreement reflected the vision of the inevitability of an United States of Europe. The crises since the "No" result in the first Danish referendum on the Maastricht Treaty through the lukewarm French "Yes" vote and the unenthusiastic approval of the British Parliament all indicated the limitations of these grand designs among the peoples of Europe. Even more damaging to the grand design theories were the series of crises that buffeted and effectively limited the ability of the Exchange Rate Mechanism to act as means of convergence in the move to EMU.

For some it might seem that these crises indicate a much more haphazard situation than one might previously have expected. Yet, it can be argued that they are reflected in how the EU has advanced throughout most of its history. Successful development of the EU has always been more like the movements of a crab than that of an eagle.

At the same time the difficulties confronting the Union in relation to EMU should not blind us to the degree of integration that has already occurred in Europe. Much of this has been top-down and has been driven by the European institutions, that is, integration is more legally based than societal based. Some of these issues were addressed in the Maastricht Treaty with its provisions for the creation of a common

European citizenship. But citizenship like issues of legitimacy, sovereignty and identity go to the root of what makes a nation and a nation-state. In large part it is because these issues have not been dealt with from the grass roots upward that there was such local opposition to the Maastricht Treaty.

Is the EU a model that the states of North America might wish to consider as a blueprint for the future? My answer is basically no. This is not because of the current difficulties confronting the Union but because the system which works more often than it does not is much more integrationist and supranationalist than North Americans want or expect either at the elite level or the mass level. While there have always been individuals whose vision included the United States of Europe, most members of the European political elites, who initiated the integration process in the 1950s, had narrower economic and political goals. However, the route taken by EU member states indicates that incremental centralization at both the economic and political level is difficult to avoid once the journey has been undertaken. In the end the incremental nature of the EU process is perhaps the most important lesson that the NAFTA states can learn from the European experience.

Notes

1. As a result of the final ratification and implementation of the Treaty on European Union (otherwise known as the Maastricht Agreement) in October 1993, the European Community has now become known as the European Union (EU).

2. For background on the theoretical questions of integration see B. Laffan, *Integration and Co-operation in Europe* (London: Routledge, 1992), pp. 1-21; see also S. Bulmer, "Domestic Politics and European Community Policy Making," *Journal of Common Market Studies*, Vol. 12 (1982-83), pp. 349-363;   G.M. MacMillan, "The European Community: Is it a Supranational State in the Making?" in S. Randall and R. Gibbins, eds., *Federalism in the Post-Cold War Era: The Gorbachev symposium on the Future of Federalism* (Calgary: University of Calgary Press), forthcoming.

3. The constitutional documents of the EU include the Treaty of Paris, 1951, which created the European Coal and Steel Community (ECSC); the Treaty of Rome, 1957, which created the European Economic Community (EEC) and the European Atomic Energy Community (Euratom); the Treaty establishing a Single Council and a Single Commission of the European Communities, 1965 (The Merger Treaty); The Treaty amending Certain Budgetary Provisions of the Treaty, 1970; Treaty amending Certain Financial Provisions of the Treaties, 1975; The Single European Act, 1985; Treaty on European Union, 1991 (Maastricht Agreement).

4. See Laffin, *Integration and Co-operation in Europe*, p. 5.

5. The member-states of the Community are France, Germany, Italy, Belgium, the Netherlands, Belgium (the original signatories to the Treaties of Paris (1951) and Rome (1957); the United Kingdom, Ireland, Denmark (1973); Greece (1981); and Spain and Portugal (1986).

6. For intergovernmentalism see Bulmer, "Domestic Politics and European Policy Making"; S. Bulmer, "The Council of Ministers and the European Council: Two-Faced Institutions in a Federal Order," in G.M. MacMillan, ed., *The European Community, Canada and 1992* (Calgary: University of Calgary Faculty of Social Sciences, 1994), pp.15-36.

7. See W. Wallace, "Less than a Federation, More than a Regime," in H. Wallace, W. Wallace and C. Webb, eds., *Policy-Making in the European Community* (Chichester: John Wiley and Sons Ltd., 1983), pp. 403-436.

8. For supranationalism see MacMillan, "The European Community: Is it a Supranational State in the Making?" see N. Nugent, *The Government and Politics of the European Community*, 2nd ed. (London: Macmillan, 1991) for a sustained examination of the Community as a supranational organization.

9. For the courts see A-M. Burley and W. Mattli, "Europe before the Court: a political theory of legal integration," *International Organization*, Vol. 47 (1993), pp. 41-76.

10. For an analysis of the Single European Act see A. Moravcsik, "Negotiating the Single European Act," in Robert O. Keohane and Stanley Hoffman, *The New European Community: Decisionmaking and Institutional Change*, eds. (Boulder: Westview Press, 1991), pp. 41-84; for the Maastricht Agreement see W. Sandholtz, "Choosing Union: Monetary Politics and Maastricht," *International Organization*, Vol. 47 (1993), pp. 1-39. Both articles emphasize the role of domestic politics and intergovernmentalism in the decision-making process leading up to these two agreements.

11. For the overview of the Community see R.O. Keohane and S. Hoffman, ed., *The New European Community: Decisionmaking and Institutional Change*; W. Nicol and T.C. Salmon, *Understanding the European Communities* (London: Philip Allen, 1991); and Nugent, *Government and Politics of the European Community*.

12. For The European Council see S. Bulmer and W. Wessels, *The European Council* (London: Macmillan, 1987); Bulmer, "The Council of Ministers and the European Council"; W. Wessels, "The EC Council: The Community's Decision Making Centre," in Keohane and Hoffman, *The New European Community*, pp. 133-154.

13. Outside the Treaties refers to those decision-making processes and institutions of the EU agreed to and set up under the several agreements made among the member states from the Treaty of Paris in 1951 to the Treaty on European Union in 1991. Decisions made under these arrangements are not subject to the Union's elaborate law-making process nor justiciable before the IJC.

14. Under the weighted voting mechanism each state is assigned a number of votes which are cast en bloc. There are a total of 76 votes and 54 are required for a motion to pass the Council. It is structured in such a way that large states cannot defeat the small states or small states the large states.

15. For the Franco-German relationship in the Community see H. Simonian,

The Privileged Partnership: Franco-German Relations in the European Community (Oxford: Clarendon Press, 1985).

16. For the other member states see Laffan, *Integration and Co-operation in Europe*, pp. 195-201. For Britain see S. George, *An Awkward Partner: Britain in the European Community* (Oxford: Oxford University Press, 1990).

17. These include free movement of persons, services, goods and capital; agriculture; transportation; common rules on competition, fiscality, approximation of legislation; economic policy; social policy; education, vocational training; the European Investment Bank (1957); economic and social cohesion; research and technological development; the environment (1985); economic and monetary policy; culture; consumer protection; trans-European networks; industry (1991).

18. For a discussion of the background to EMU see Laffan, *Integration and Cooperation in Europe*, pp. 75-120; Sandholtz, "Choosing Union."

19. See N. Thygessen, "The Delors Report and European Economic and Monetary Union," *International Affairs, Vol. 65* (1989), pp. 637-652.

20. Sandholtz, "Monetary Policies and Maastricht," p. 15.

21. It is important to note that all the changes agreed to at the Council meetings between Madrid in June 1989, and Maastricht in December 1991, when the final argument was signed, were opposed by the British, who did agree to sign the Treaty.

22. The changes in Europe leading to the collapse of the Soviet Empire led the leaders to create the second Intergovernmental Conference on Political Union to run in tandem with the first IGC on EMU. Both were included in the Treaty on European Union signed at Maastricht in December 1991.

23. These included five criteria states would have to meet: (1) a rate of inflation in the consumer price index no more than one and one-half percentage points higher than the average of the three states with the best performance in price stability; (2) interest rates on long-term government bonds no more than two percentage points higher than the average of the three countries with the lowest rates; (3) a central government budget deficit no more than 3 percent of gross domestic product (GDP); (4) a public debt of no more than 60 percent of GDP; (5) a national currency that has remained within the narrow (2.25 percent) fluctuation margins of the ERM for the previous two years and has not been devalued against any other member state currency over the same period.

24. I deal with some of these issues in more detail in "The European Community: Is it a Supranational State in the Making?"

13

The Impact of European Economic Integration on North America: Adjustment Versus Radical Change

Evan H. Potter

Introduction

The metamorphosis of Europe since 1989 presents policy challenges both subtle and long term for Canada, the United States, and Mexico as participants in the North American Free Trade Agreement (NAFTA). Europe is being redefined and its place in the global system reset. The completion of the Single European Market (SEM) in 1992, the quick absorption of a united Germany, the creation of Economic and Monetary Union (EMU) by the end of the decade, the achievement of political union, and the establishment of a pan-European economic zone[1], are all indicative of the speed and breadth of the changes that have swept across Europe.

The European Community (EC), known as the European Union (EU) since the ratification of the Maastricht Treaty in 1993, has either created, or is directly affected by, the above events and processes.[2] More subtle, perhaps, is the EU's growing influence outside of Europe through its independent voice in international organizations, most notably in the United Nations, the Group of Seven (G7), the General Agreement on Tariffs and Trade (GATT), the Quadrilateral Group, and as a dialogue partner with numerous groupings of states.[3] For these reasons, the European Union has become the dominant European institution and force in Europe today.

Rather than try to examine the impact of European integration on North American interests in political, security and economic terms, this chapter's much more modest ambition is to examine post-Cold War era transatlantic economic relations in the final stages of the GATT Uruguay Round. It is an open question whether the types of market access challenges posed by the creation of a pan-European market will create an incentive for greater North American integration. Indeed, without the unifying pressure of East-West polarization, the member states of the EU may increasingly feel it unnecessary to maintain a common front with North America on international security or trade issues, leading to the unraveling of the traditional transatlantic political-security nexus. This may in turn create a fertile environment for the politicization of transatlantic trade relations, and thus the very real possibility of bloc-to-bloc antagonism -- a situation in which, for example, the smaller members of the North American community, Canada and Mexico -- could get side-swiped in a pattern of EU-U.S. conflict.

Understanding, however, that economic, security and political relations cannot be analyzed in isolation, the first section of this essay discusses why post-1989 transatlanticism has rendered the traditional security alliances of the Cold War less effective sources of North American leverage in Europe. In order to put North America's current approach to its relations with Western Europe in historical perspective, the second section explores the vicissitudes of Canadian, American and Mexican policy responses to European integration. The third section describes the specific changes in EU trade policy brought about by the movement to create the Single European Market and examines their impact on North American-EU economic relations. The final section explores the types of trade and economic frameworks that may characterize EU-North American relations in the coming years.

North American Leverage and the Reconfiguration of Transatlanticism

The evolution of the EU into other spheres of competence as its founders had envisaged, that is, beyond the completion of a customs union, through the 1985 White Paper, the Single European Act (SEA) in 1986 and the creation of the European Union on November 1, 1993, raises fundamental questions about the approach of the three NAFTA signatories towards the EU. For Canada and the United States, the underlying problem in their approaches to the EU has always been that of leverage. The new political and institutional context of the post-Cold War and post-Maastricht EU make this problem even more acute.

In the years following the Treaty of Rome in 1958, as the European Community anchored West Germany within the Western alliance and acted as a bulwark against Soviet expansion, Canada and the United States as members of the North Atlantic Treaty Organization (NATO), were able to use their security roles in Europe as subtle but effective levers in their bilateral relations with Community institutions (primarily the Commission and the Council of Ministers). Since EC jurisdiction at the time was reserved only for the member states' external trade policy, Canadian and U.S. commitments to European security were linked to their respective, overwhelmingly economic, diplomacy with Brussels. This lever never approximated direct linkage, however. Issues in transatlantic relations were never resolved in a tit-for-tat manner. Indeed, given the broad distribution of power within the transatlantic community, it has always been difficult to predict the outcomes of specific disputes or tensions and to disentangle the links on the fluctuating agenda of political, security and economic concerns.

In the transformed arena of the 1990s, however, issues of partnership and leverage have even more salience. The removal of major structural features such as the Cold War and the difficulties encountered in completing the Uruguay Round, have created a situation in which the broad, traditional expectations and images of Europe held by North American decision-makers are no longer sustainable. Although the focus of this paper is on transatlantic economic rather than security links, it must be recognized that in the 1990s, the concept of linkage is now more important because notions of economic partnership and security alliance can no longer be consigned to separate boxes.

An Historical Overview of North American Responses to the Process of European Integration

1960s and 1970s: Partial Partners

During much of the 1960s, rapid economic growth in Europe combined with successful tariff cuts of the Kennedy Round, meant that there were few barriers to the access of Canadian exports and investment (apart from agriculture) in the EU market.[4] By the late 1960s, however, confrontations between Canadian and EC negotiators at GATT over the Community's Common Agriculture Policy (CAP), highlighted Canada's inability to ensure adequate trade access through multilateral channels, and suggested that there was perhaps a need for a more direct bilateral link to the Community. With these bilateral problems coinciding with a recurrence of Canadian fears of "excessive" dependence on the United States and the election in 1968 of a more nationalist Liberal government headed by Prime Minister Pierre Trudeau, the stage was set for relations with Europe to become a key foreign policy priority for Ottawa.

On the U.S. side, by the early 1960s, Washington had begun to lose its influence over EC integration. Roy Ginsberg characterizes the U.S.-EC relationship between 1963 and 1970 as one that "gyrated between insensitivity and hostility" as both sides tried to adjust to their changing relative positions in the world.[5] During this period, bilateral relations were marred by the Community's granting of tariff reductions on certain imports from close trade partners in the Mediterranean and Africa; the notorious chicken war of 1963-64 caused by the CAP which had a devastating effect on U.S. market share of the EC poultry market; the EC's toughness in its negotiations with United States during the Kennedy Round; and by EC member states' silence over, or condemnation of, American involvement in Vietnam.[6] The Nixon administration broke with traditional American support for EC bodies, preferring instead bilateral ties with member state governments.

By 1972, just as closer EC-Canadian relations came to be identified with the "Third Option,"[7] the United States was becoming increasingly disillusioned with the impact of European integration on its interests. Secretary of State Henry Kissinger's ill-fated "Year of Europe" initiative brought this to a head; the Europeans viewed the attempt by the United States to redirect the development of EC foreign policy back to an Atlantic-based center as "patronizing and clumsy."[8] So while EC-U.S. relations stagnated even further in the 1970s (*e.g.*, the foreign policy differences between the two sides over the Yom Kippur War) and are characterized by Ginsberg as moving between unilateral neglect and bilateral cooperation[9], there was a steady institutionalization of Canadian-EC relations: diplomatic missions were opened in Ottawa and Brussels; and "high-levels" (as semi-annual meetings between senior Canadian and EC officials came to be known) were established. The EC, increasingly intent on exercising its own diplomatic role, was receptive to Ottawa's overtures on formalizing and intensifying bilateral ties. It saw Canada, particularly during the period of Organization of Petroleum Exporting Countries (OPEC) induced economic crises in the early 1970s, as an alternate source of abundant raw materials (in particular uranium).

This process of formalizing bilateral relations reached its peak with the signing of the Canada-EC Framework Agreement for Commercial and Economic Cooperation in 1976 to promote increased trade and investment.

Although Canada took considerable pride in its status as the first "industrialized" nation to sign a framework agreement with the Community, Mexico had signed its own framework agreement with Brussels a year earlier. Similar to the Canadian agreement, the Mexican accord granted mutual most favored nation status and created a joint committee to oversee bilateral trade. The Community had always valued highly its relations with Mexico because of that country's position in Latin America and because of the leading role it played in the North-South dialogue. But, apart from the framework agreement, Mexican-EC relations were not substantially institutionalized or formalized until 1985 when there was an exchange of high-level political visits centered on the mutual desire to contribute to peace initiatives in Central America, and in 1989 when the European Commission opened a mission in Mexico City.

Ironically, by the mid to late 1970s, just as Canada was enhancing its institutional links with the Community, a combination of factors ensured that the constituency for the EC in Canada -- federal officials, politicians, and business people -- underwent severe attrition. For example, the lack of market access provisions in the Canada-EC framework agreement ensured at best an indifferent, and at worst a suspicious, Canadian business audience. When the increase in trade that was augured by the agreement did not materialize, due in part to the onset of "Eurosclerosis" in the EC itself, this fed perceptions both at the political and business levels that the framework was of little practical use.

The 1980s: Mutual Benign Neglect

Nearly two decades of economic nationalism in Canada ended in 1984 with the election of Prime Minister Brian Mulroney's Progressive Conservative government. The government quickly became convinced that Canada's future economic prosperity lay in integration with the United States. This conviction led to the conclusion of the Canada-U.S. Free Trade Agreement (CUSFTA) in 1989. It is ironic that paralleling the apparent indifference to the strengthening of transatlantic economic mechanisms during this period, was the belief that Canada's security interests were more than ever anchored in Europe and thus by extension in the transatlantic security institutions of NATO and the

Conference on Security and Cooperation in Europe (CSCE). In the words of one observer, the government's European policy "disclosed a curious tension between the reaffirmation of Canada's commitment to NATO and the military contribution to defence on the one hand, and, with the exception of current trade irritants, the relative indifference to developments in the EC on the other."[10]

The improvement in U.S.-EC relations that had occurred after President Jimmy Carter came to power in 1977 was replaced by renewed economic antagonisms and heightened foreign policy differences after the Reagan administration took office in 1981. During the early 1980s, the U.S. and the EC were on the brink of trade wars, the biggest problem areas being steel and agriculture. The accession of Spain and Portugal to the EC in 1986, at significant cost to U.S. farm exports, exacerbated bilateral tensions and began the politicization of trade relations that was reflected in trade disputes played out in the Uruguay Round. Differing, often opposing, positions on East-West (e.g., U.S. opposition to European sales of high-technology to the Soviet Union and its allies) and North-South relations (e.g., U.S. opposition to EC support -- in its traditional foreign policy backyard -- for the Contadora peace process) affected the way the EC and the U.S. chose to trade with one another and with others.[11] The politicization of EC-U.S. relations was problematic from an institutional viewpoint since, unlike the Canadian and Mexican cases, there existed no bilateral organizational mechanisms to coordinate their policies: NATO's purview is regional and -- except for the moribund Article 2 -- rules out economic affairs; the EC -- with the exception of the then inactive West European Union -- excludes military issues. EC-U.S. disputes in the 1980s often fell between the two. In sum, by the end of the 1980s the growing fissures in the EC-U.S. alliance -- especially as the common threat from the East dissipated -- highlighted the fundamental change the relationship had undergone since the early 1970s. The institutional and policy-making frameworks of transatlantic relations were anachronistic and had to be reformed.

1989-1991: Radical Changes in Transatlantic Relations

The tangled economic, political, military and social events in Europe in 1989 forced a cautious reassessment of the respective approaches of the United States and Canada towards Europe.

Speeches by President George Bush and his Secretary of State, James Baker, provided the necessary impetus to reverse North America's "benign neglect" of its relations with the EC. In May 1989, Bush called for a "European partnership in world leadership"; Baker took this a step further, noting that as the EC moved toward its goal of a common internal market, embarked on institutional reform and assumed increasing responsibility in certain foreign policy areas, the United States' relationship with the Community would have to evolve as well. He called on the U.S. and the Community to achieve "a significantly strengthened set of institutional and consultative links ... whether in treaty or some other form."[12] Thereafter, the United States and the EC embarked on a series of exploratory meetings to put some flesh on the calls of Bush and Baker for closer transatlantic links.

Although the notion of a 13th (American) seat at the European table, as proposed by then U.S. Secretary of Commerce Robert Mosbacher, was quickly dismissed by the Europeans, the evident rapprochement in EC-U.S. relations -- given their history of acrimony -- was certainly not lost on senior Canadian cabinet ministers. It raised the specter of Canadian marginalization in Europe -- the avoidance of which had always been and continues to be the leitmotif of Canada's transatlantic strategy.

Adjusting to Change

With growing criticism leveled at Canada for lagging behind in its policy approach to the dramatic changes in East-West relations, Prime Minister Mulroney's trip to the Soviet Union in November 1989, added stimulus to the comprehensive policy review that was underway on Canada's relations with Europe. This was reflected in a series of important addresses by Mulroney and his Secretary of State for External Affairs, Joe Clark, in the first half of 1990.[13]

Canadian and American thinking on the changing nature of transatlanticism received further impetus when, in the aftermath of the fall of the Berlin Wall, Hans Dietrich Genscher (then German foreign minister and vice-chancellor), responded to Baker's proposal, by calling for a new architecture to bind Europe more sec ·ely to Canada and the United States in a speech to the Canadian Parliament.[14] Following Genscher's address, discussions among Mulroney, Clark, and their American and European counterparts ensured that Canada's relations with Western and Eastern Europe and, in particular, the EC had -- after 16 years -- again gained priority in the Canadian cabinet.

By the summer of 1990, with the Canada-U.S. free trade pact completed, senior Canadian officials began to seriously look at the economic ramifications of the new Europe for Canada's interests. Derek

Burney, then Canada's ambassador to the United States, believed that there was a causal linkage between the management of transatlantic trade and economic relations and the prospects for security and stability. He felt that the failure to agree on trade and economic matters could undermine prospects for security.

The most significant outcome of the Canadian policy discussions was the conclusion that the existing framework agreement and the GATT would not ensure Canadian access to the new European market. There was concern on the Canadian side that any EC-U.S. agreement would create a privileged position for the United States while diminishing Canada's already small place in Europe. Washington's willingness to negotiate a trade pact with Mexico in 1990 confirmed Canadian officials' perception that the United States preferred to deal bilaterally, and thus suggested a high probability that the Americans would also strike a bilateral deal -- trade or otherwise -- with the Community, leaving Canada in a vulnerable position. Canadian officials (primarily at the Department of External Affairs and International Trade) concluded that Canada had two broad options: a Canada-EC free trade agreement; or a North Atlantic free trade association, with the latter arrangement being preferred because it would permit Canada to achieve influence not available through existing arrangements or, indeed, through a separate bilateral agreement. The second option was also favored because it would impose substantial obligations on the Community (as well as on Canada and other participants) in areas currently within the exclusive competence of the EC which were the principal instruments for European integration.[15]

The "necessity" of Canada's engagement in the new Europe was made public in a speech delivered by Clark in May 1990, in which he called for an examination of the desirability of a formalized open, trading arrangement between Canada and the EC, perhaps including the U.S. and other members of the Organization for Economic Cooperation and Development (OECD), after the conclusion of the Uruguay Round.[16] This marked the first time that Canada attempted to apply the multilateral security model (e.g., NATO) to its trade relations with the Community. The proposed economic and trade agreement was to focus on issues of access (as CUSFTA did), rather than just cooperation as did the existing Canada-EC framework agreement.

The Formulation of Parallel Declarations

In the absence of any real interest evinced by the EC or the United States (which had been steadily formalizing its bilateral political -- as opposed to economic -- links with the Community), a transatlantic free trade deal in practical terms was a non-starter.[17] The Bush administration argued that Canadian participation in a proposed trilateral declaration would dilute the effectiveness of its preferred bilateral declaration with the Community, not to mention whetting Mexico's appetite for inclusion. But the Canadian side persevered, asking for and receiving support from some EC member states (particularly the UK and Germany) as well as from sympathetic officials within the Commission. The spin put on the transatlantic dialogue by Canadian politicians and officials was that to exclude Canada was tantamount to betrayal by its closest allies since the very term "transatlanticism" had always included Canada.[18] The intensive lobbying paid off. In the end, after much consultation and drafting the European Community-Canada Transatlantic Declaration (TAD) was issued on November 22, 1990, and followed a day later by the EC-U.S. declaration.[19]

In assessing the significance of the TADs, it must be noted that both were "issued" rather than signed, indicating that the North American and European parties were not legally bound to adhere to each declaration's terms. This in the first instance gave both documents more symbolic than substantive qualities.[20] As well, when compared to the signing of the Charter of Paris on November 21, 1990, by the 34 participating states of the CSCE, which formally declared the end of the Cold War, the institutionalization of bilateral political and economic relations through the TADs appears to be a fairly modest achievement.[21]

The key element of both TADs was the establishment of a new transatlantic institutional framework. The declarations reaffirmed the need for the full use of the mechanisms established under, in Canada's case, the framework agreement and of the already existing political contacts, such as the annual meetings between the External Affairs minister and the EC Commissioner for External Relations and Trade Policy under the accord's Joint Cooperation Committee. In the U.S. case, the TAD formalized the increased political and bureaucratic contacts that had developed since the latter half of the 1980s. But most importantly, under the TADs meetings would now take place "regularly" between the Canadian prime minister and the president of the European Council and the president of the Commission; the meetings are "annual" in the U.S. declaration between the president and the president of the European Council and the Commission. In addition, both declarations called for increased European Community-North American cooperation on transnational issues such as terrorism, drug trafficking, and the environment. Although clearly a "political" document, the Canadian TAD did make reference to encouraging bilateral investment, something not found in the U.S. declaration. In sum, the TADs appeared to be an attempt to fill the legitimation vacuum that is dogging post-Cold War transatlantic relations.

Sources of Changing Transatlantic Trade Relations

A number of structural changes in the world economy continue to affect the framework of North American-EU economic relations. Canada and Mexico as smaller economies will continue to feel the effects of problems in U.S.-EU economic relations in multilateral trade talks, although both countries will benefit from the successful completion of the Uruguay Round. The positions of Canada and Mexico must be seen in terms of the more deep-seated structural features of transatlantic economic relations, such as the relative increase in the economic muscle of the EU compared to the U.S., the loss of Canada's "Atlanticist" influence, and continued growth in economic interdependence without commensurate progress in policy convergence between North America and the Community.

The EU's population of 340 million is more than 12 times larger than Canada's, almost 100 million larger than that of the United States, and more than 200 million larger than Japan's. Until the ratification of NAFTA, the EU represented the largest trading area in the world, with a total gross domestic product (GDP) in excess of U.S. $6 trillion in 1991 -- roughly equal to the Canadian and U.S. GDP combined and below the total North American GDP, including Mexico, of about U.S. $7 trillion. However, if we include the GDPs of all the European Free Trade Association (EFTA) member states to create the European Economic Area (EEA) and then extend this area through Central and Eastern Europe (including the former Soviet republic of Ukraine), the GDP of this pan-European market continues to exceed that of North America.

Another indicator of the European Union's economic stature is that exports originating in the EU account for almost 25 per cent of the

Union's GDP and 41 per cent of total world exports, including exports to other EU countries.[22] It should be noted, however, that omitting trade among the member states, the EU accounts for 16 per cent of world exports. In fact, excluding intra-EU trade, the Union's share of world trade decreased slightly between 1985 and 1990 as a result of the growing importance of the newly industrializing Pacific Rim economies.[23] In contrast, Canada's exports make up less than 4 per cent, of total world exports, while U.S. exports account for about 15 per cent.

The most significant feature of these trends is not only that the EU's total trade is surpassing that of the North American 'bloc' but the degree to which it is internalizing multilateralism. This is reflected in the fact that although its share of world trade has increased much of this, as we noted, is due to intra-EU trade, that is, total exports including intra-EU trade have risen by 5 per cent (from 36 per cent to 41 per cent) since 1980.[24]

Direct investment in the European Union has also steadily increased since 1985, reaching U.S. $72.2 billion in 1990, compared to U.S. $12.2 billion in 1985. In fact, for the first time since the end of the 1970s, the EU had larger direct investment flows in 1990 than the United States. In addition, the EU includes four of the G7 states and some of the world's most dynamic companies. If EU membership expands to include other Western and Eastern European countries, raising its population to twice that of the United States and increasing its output to about a third more than that of the U. S., it is easy to see how the Union may become North America's (and specifically the United States's) chief rival in the 1990s.[25]

The EU's External Trade Policy:
Integration with EFTA and Eastern Europe

The EU's external trade is conducted through a hierarchy of preferential trading agreements built around a network of about 50 bilateral agreements, introducing strong elements of discrimination into the multilateral trading system. Its most important preferential ties are with other states in Europe, usually described as the first and second concentric circles of influence.

EFTA represents the first concentric circle of third countries and is the EU's largest single trading partner, accounting for more than one-fifth of trade outside the Union. The EEA, ratified by all EFTA countries in 1993, will significantly expand the size and importance of the Single European Market. It is easy to see why many observers view the EEA as but a short step before some EFTA states receive full membership in the EU.[26] The second concentric circle is made up of those Central and East European countries having "association" agreements with the Union; meanwhile, the Mediterranean countries of Malta, Cyprus and Turkey have also requested EU membership.

As the above countries obtain preferential access to the EU market, they are also accepting the *acquis communautaire* (i.e., the established EU norms) and thus being effectively integrated into the Union's sphere of influence. This will occur even without full membership. Although the use of EU legislation and regulations by EFTA and East European countries does not constitute "a conscious effort on the part of the EU to supplant multilateralism," nevertheless such an "expansive regionalism" has a similar effect.[27]

North American-EU Economic Diplomacy

Since the European Community was primarily concerned with its member states' external trade until the ratification of the Maastricht Treaty, it is not surprising that it is on the economic side that North America's links to the EC were largely reflected in more than three decades of diplomacy.

The European Union and the United States are the world's largest trading actors, together accounting for more than one third of world trade. Bilaterally, the EC and the U.S. have consistently been each other's largest trading partner, with two-way trade between them at about $200 billion (the EC accounts for 23 per cent of American exports and the U.S. for 18 per cent of EC exports). Most significantly, in comparison to the composition of EU-Canadian and EU-Mexican trade, manufactures account for 81 per cent of U.S. visible exports to the EU, and agricultural products 10 per cent; in the other direction 89 per cent of EU exports are manufactures and only 5 per cent are agricultural exports. Thus, there is a high degree of economic interdependence between the two major trading partners.

Although the European Union is the second largest source of trade and investment for Canada and Mexico, the United States is by far their most important economic partner. Trade with the EU accounts for only about 10 per cent and 12 per cent of Canada's and Mexico's respective total world merchandise trade. The major components of both countries' export mixes are raw materials, pulp and paper exports for Canada, and petroleum exports for Mexico. As well, both countries have experienced a steady erosion in their trading relationships with the EU over the last ten years. For example, in 1982, the United States was the destination of 68.3 per cent of Canada's merchandise exports and the source of 69.1 per cent of Canada's imports; by 1992 Canada's exports to the United States totalled 77 per cent while its imports from the United States were 63.7 per cent. In the same time period, Canadian exports to Asian markets stayed level in percentage terms, hovering just below 10 per cent. If exports and imports are combined, the figures show that total trade with the U.S. and with Asia rose over the decade while trade with Europe as a whole (i.e., with the EU, EFTA, and Eastern Europe including Russia and the Ukraine) was flat, accounting for approximately 11 per cent (down from approximately 14 per cent in 1980).[28] In Mexico's case, total trade with the EU has been dropping steadily since 1989. The implementation of NAFTA will lead to even more dependence on the North American market which will mean that in the years to come the United States will be responsible for more than its current 73 per cent of Mexico's total world trade.

An enormous amount of cross-investment, more than $50 billion, also buttresses Canadian ties with the EU. By the end of 1991, some $19.9 billion (or 20 per cent) of total Canadian foreign direct investment (FDI) abroad was in the EU, with 61 per cent or $12.2 billion of it located in the UK. The bulk of this investment is directed toward the manufacturing sector. The investment flows are two-way, of course. While the European companies are preparing themselves for a more open internal market, many EU firms have turned to Canada in recent years, partly in response to the Canada-U.S. free trade pact. The Community's FDI into Canada during the period 1983 to 1990 rose from $13.4 billion (17.3 per cent of total inward investment stock) to an estimated $32 billion (23 per cent of total inward investment stock). This made the EU the second largest source of FDI stock in Canada after the United States. The EU has now replaced the United States as the leading foreign investor (in terms of annual inflows, not total capital stock) in Canada.

The substantial growth of FDI flows has also greatly increased the economic linkages between the European Union and the United States. In 1991, EU investors owned more than half of the FDI stocks in the U.S., while of two-fifths of American-owned FDI stocks were located in the EU. At historical prices, these investments together are worth more than U.S. $420 billion.[29]

In summary, Canada's and Mexico's economic relationship with the EU can be characterized as one of "asymmetrical vulnerability interdependence." It is "asymmetrical" because the cost of altering the relationship is much higher for Ottawa and Mexico City than it is for Brussels, since trade with Canada and Mexico each represents only 1 per cent of the EU's world trade. This is not to belittle Western Europe's still sizeable economic stake in Canada and Mexico. Nevertheless, from a market access standpoint any changes in regulations in Europe will put Canada and Mexico in more "vulnerable" positions than the United States.

Could the Single Market Lead to Greater Protectionism?

Since approving the Single European Act in 1986, the EU's twelve member states have progressed steadily toward enacting the 282 directives to create a fully integrated market which will allow the free movement of persons, services, goods and capital. The total potential gain form the single market -- by eliminating technical barriers through harmonization of standards or mutual recognition, by opening government procurement, by creating a single market in services, and by allowing the free circulation of salaried workers -- has been estimated by the EU at 200 billion European currency units (ECUs), or almost $300 billion dollars Canadian.[30] The Commission has estimated that the medium term impact of the SEM on the Union's GDP will amount to a cumulative 4 to 7 per cent gain during a five-year period.

As the above discussion shows, the implementation of the single European market will have trade creating effects. But the continuing process of increasing trade liberalization among members will also have trade diverting effects. One measure of this, as already mentioned, is the "regional bias ratio," that is, the ratio of intra-regional trade to the share of world trade, in which the EU's regional bias rose from 1.28 in 1980 to 1.77 in 1989.[31] This constitutes a more important increase in regional bias than in other regions including North America or East Asia.

Trade diversion is due to the common commercial policy which protects all European Union members with respect to imports from the rest of the world, as well as to the multiplicity of non-tariff barriers, regulations and administrative practices. The free market philosophy of the SEM implies that a single EU market will be open equally to third country and EU companies. However, Europe's refusal to compromise with the United States, Canada and other agricultural exporters over farm subsidies in the Uruguay Round, the export restraints on Japanese automobiles, and calls for the protection of Europe's electronics industry, highlight fears that the EU could implement discriminatory measures toward other countries' trade and investment. The concerns usually focus on five potential threats: anti-dumping measures (used primarily against Japanese exports), rules of origin, reciprocity (particularly in the financial services sector), technical standards and certification, foreign investment rules, and industrial policy.

Unfortunately, in recent years the debate over bilateral economic relations between North America and the European Union has focused primarily on the external implications of the 1992 program and whether this represents a move towards a "regional" bloc or even a "fortress Europe". There has been less discussion of bilateral relations in terms of market access issues in the EU and North America and how this relates to the multilateral trading system. In many areas of the "new" trade policy (i.e., non-tariff barriers), the Uruguay Round agenda and the EU internal agenda overlap, which may permit a smaller country such as Canada -- given its strong commitment to a multilateral trading system -- to blunt the more damaging elements of the European trade policy agenda in the future.

The process of European economic integration has brought a number of trends to light which will affect third country market access. First, the creation of the Single European Market is reducing or removing regulatory barriers, but in so doing it is throwing the structural impediments that exist in Europe into sharper focus. Second, as the Union assumes greater responsibilities, especially where policies of the member states impinge upon its external economic relations, this process will have spill-over effects in the rest of Europe. Third, the EU's readiness to intervene in order to create a genuine internal market, and thus to pursue more intrusive policies to remove structural impediments to access within the Union, has involved the exercise of supranational powers in competition policy and the introduction of common procedures in areas such as purchasing practices and common standards. Moreover, the exigencies of increased integration have necessitated EU intervention in new territories and the reinforcement of some other common policies. Thus the integration process has an effect on "flanking" issues such as social policy, science and technology, transport policy and environmental policy. For these reasons, integration can also be seen as a process of re-regulation at the European-level. The question is how the above processes, feeding through into EU policies, will condition North American policy responses and whether this means a "fortress" or "partner" Europe?

The Single European Market presents both risks and opportunities for North American firms. The harmonization and elimination of technical barriers in the SEM, for example, will benefit North American suppliers since they will be permitted to meet a single European standard. Of course, there are still uncertainties. For example, the Canadian forest industry, with annual sales in the EU of more than $3 billion, is monitoring closely the European Committee for Standardization on which all of Canada's major Scandinavian competitors are represented. The EU policy on testing and certification is another major concern for North American producers. They fear having to undergo much more costly and time consuming approval procedures than EU-based competitors. Local content requirements are another source of concern. For example, in the proposed EU directive on competitive bidding procedures in four important sectors (traditionally known as the excluded sectors) -- water, energy, transport, and telecommunications -- bidders having more than 50 per cent European "content" would be given a 3 per cent price preference over bids with less than the required content. This would present a significant market barrier for Canadian firms without manufacturing facilities in the EU.

About 60 per cent of European Union imports originate from preferential sources, Canada and the United States (Mexico benefits from the Union's generalized system of preferences, [GSPs]) being among the relatively few countries that deal with the EU only on a most favored nation basis.[32] In general, EU tariffs are relatively low. The main Canadian exports to the Union, a range of raw materials, are subject to very low or zero tariffs. Included are wood (e.g., $1.6 billion in wood pulp entered EU without tariffs or quotas in 1990), hides and skin, unwrought copper, nickel and tin. By contrast, semi-finished and finished products based on these raw materials are dutiable at more than 5 per cent. In certain sectors, such as metals and tobacco, there is a considerable degree of tariff escalation. Thus except for some limited items, Canadian exports do not face very high tariffs. But the fact that tariffs do not represent significant barriers to existing trade does not necessarily mean that they do not still have an influence on the nature and volume of Canadian exports. In fact, since Europe imposes low or zero tariffs on primary, unprocessed products and increases its tariffs as the degree of processing of a particular product increases, Canada faces particular barriers to the upgrading of its natural resource exports.

The new EU competition, government procurement and standardization policies will have a greater impact on value-added goods than on the raw materials and semi-manufactures that Canada has traditionally exported to Europe, but if Canada increases the value-added proportion of its export mix these will be slapped with higher duties. Thus Canada is caught in a catch-22 with regard to diversifying its export base away from the traditional weighting in raw and semi-finished materials. Nonetheless, Canada will have no choice but to upgrade because with the increasing competition from EFTA states, particularly in resource exports, there is the danger that in the medium to long term that it will become only a residual supplier to the European market.[33] Mexico, although also heavily dependent on its resource exports to the EU, has an advantage over Canada in that it has access to the EU's GSPs.

New Transatlantic Mechanisms

While United States' influence relative to the European Union faded in the 1970s and 1980s, the former was still able to shape the agenda and the outcome of multilateral trade talks. But since 1987, the development of a distinctive European approach to accommodating intra-EU systemic differences has meant that the U.S. will be less able to shape the multilateral system in its own image in the future. The difference in 1993, the first year of the SEM, is that the EU has now developed a new approach to market liberalization, one that is of direct relevance to the kinds of barriers to market access that will be the focus of multilateral trade policy in the later 1990s.

The changing international configuration of economic power will decisively influence any meaningful North American initiative to improve transatlantic relations. This is because the management of transatlantic trade and economic issues will prove critical to prospects for North American security as economic security becomes a paramount national interest. Bearing this in mind, a number of frameworks can be considered for the future of North American-EU relations.

Frameworks for North American-EU Economic Relations

North America has seven options for its relations with the EU in the 1990s:

1. An improved framework agreement
2. A traditional EU-EFTA-style link/An EEA-type link
3. A Canada-EU free trade agreement/U.S.-EU free trade agreement
4. A transatlantic free trade agreement
5. Bilateral sectoral and issue agreements

The first choice, the status quo, is no longer appropriate for the management of transatlantic relations. The Mexican and Canadian framework agreements have had very limited impacts on trade and investment flows; it is unlikely that restructuring them will have a large effect on bilateral economic relations.[34] This chapter's historical overview of North American-EU relations has also demonstrated the low probability of a bilateral EU-U.S. or EU-Canada transatlantic trade accord. There are therefore three realistic options: (1) an EFTA or EEA-style trade agreement; (2) a transatlantic free trade area; or (3) bilateral sectoral agreements.

EFTA- or EEA-Style Arrangements

For Canada and the United States, the GATT is the primary mechanism which governs the terms of access to the EU and Canadian and American markets, provides dispute settlement procedures, and serves as forum for Canada and the United States in multilateral trade negotiations (as noted, Mexico, as a developing country, benefits from the EU's GSPs). But the GATT applies to trade in industrial products only (although a General Agreement on Trade in Services is being negotiated). Also, the GATT has not prevented the erection of preferential barriers to North American goods by virtue of the EU's network of bilateral trade agreements with non-member European countries, former colonies, and other "dialogue partners."

Virtually every nation that has entered into a cooperation agreement with the European Union has found it insufficient for the overall management of its relationship with the EU. Many of these countries have seen their cooperation agreements as temporary "second-best" solutions, or as steps to achieving full member status. For instance, the EU has traditionally concluded agreements with individual EFTA countries on a bilateral basis (primarily tariff-free treatment for most industrial goods). Although the preferential agreements with the EFTA countries excluded trade in agricultural goods, those association agreements with some Central and East European states (e.g., Hungary) did provide preferences on their agricultural exports.

In looking at these preferential agreements, a number of considerations must be taken into account. For example, what sector-specific or issue-specific arrangements has the EU been prepared to negotiate with particular countries? In the case of Sweden, cooperation goes beyond the EU-EFTA free trade agreement. Formal agreements on the exchange of information on transport, environment, consumerism, and fishing, have become important. There are also informal meetings on industrial policy, development aid, and economic policy. Indeed, it is precisely these types of broad-based regular meetings and agreements that are envisaged by Canadian officials under the umbrella of the

TAD.

If Canada, the United States and Mexico were to emulate a traditional EFTA-style link it would be restricted to free trade in industrial goods through the abolition of tariffs and quotas. It would not include trade policy issues including procurement, subsidies and trade in services -- precisely those issue areas that will greatly affect, for example, value-added Canadian exports. Additionally, in the financial services area, the lack of mutual recognition regarding rules governing trade in bank supervision and securities has been a major obstacle to bilateral trade in the EFTA-EU case.

Furthermore, would it be in North America's interest to pursue this track if EFTA members now consider these arrangements to be inadequate? EFTA's motivation to renegotiate the agreements arises not so much from shortcomings in the agreements themselves as from the success of the single market initiative, the creation of which has presented the EFTA states with a lack of immunity from EU trade remedy law.

An EEA-type agreement would rectify the lack of breadth of the existing EFTA-EU agreements, since, as we have already noted, it would entail the free movement of goods (except agriculture), services, capital and persons on the basis of the relevant *acquis communautaires*. It would entail extending to North America, or harmonizing, EU policies in fields as diverse as competition policy, government procurement, social programs, research and development, and consumer protection. However, a major question arises as to whether the expanded harmonization of trade policies envisaged by the EEA could be extended to North America, since this would undermine the preferential nature of the EU's agreements with EFTA, not to mention the preferential rights of the NAFTA signatories.

Transatlantic Free Trade

In light of this chapter's discussions of North American options, the lack of confidence in structures outside the GATT, such as the framework agreements by which to deal with an emerging global superpower, and the continuing acrimony in post-Cold War EU-U.S. relations, has led to renewed speculation about the utility of a free trade agreement with the Union. Indeed, the new "third option" for Canada's relations with the Europe of the 1990s could be an Atlantic free trade association that would embrace Canada, the United States, Mexico, the EU and potentially the EFTA countries.[35] In its broadest conception, it could also be extended to an OECD member such as Japan.

Its objective would be, under the overall umbrella of the TAD, to act as the new economic architecture for North American interests in Europe, and to protect European interests against the risk of a protectionist bloc in North America.

A North American-EU free trade scenario could be modeled on the Canada-U.S. Free Trade Agreement or it could go beyond an EEA-style accord. It would involve the elimination of tariff and non-tariff barriers to trade and services, including those arising from product standards, restrictive rules of origin, and government procurement restrictions (agriculture could also be considered, although it would be a very sensitive area for all parties). It would expand conditions for investment and services liberalization through national treatment, building on the Uruguay Round's General Agreement on Trade in Services, CUSFTA, or the OECD's National Treatment Instrument; it would facilitate conditions for fair competition within the free trade area, and establish effective procedures for the joint administration of the agreement and the resolution of disputes modeled on CUSFTA and NAFTA. Finally it would lay the foundations for further bilateral and multilateral cooperation to expand and enhance the benefits of the agreement.[36] A permanent secretariat would be charged with institutional management and servicing the dispute settlement mechanism.

A transatlantic free trade agreement would enable Canada and, to a lesser extent, Mexico, to achieve influence not available to them in Europe through current arrangements or indeed a separate bilateral agreement. It would give North America a seat at the European table -- one that is looking increasingly precarious as NATO and the Conference for Security and Cooperation in Europe search for new roles. Of course, in weaving itself and the U.S. into the European preferential trading system, Canada and Mexico would still be faced with the perennial dilemma that the EU and the United States would dominate such an arrangement and that Canadian interests in EU eyes would not be seen as distinct from American interests.

During a fact-finding trip to Europe in the summer of 1992, a Canadian parliamentary sub-committee raised the possibility of a free trade agreement with European contacts. The answer was "yes, but please not now."[37] This was not surprising since the EU was preoccupied with a host of internal matters including the implementation of the single market, ratification of Maastricht, the question of enlargement, and the Uruguay Round negotiations.

But there are other reasons why Canada is not likely to generate the momentum necessary (the United States has never seriously pursued a bilateral transatlantic free trade deal with the EU) for the negotiation of a true, GATT-consistent, free trade agreement with the Union. Even countries with much closer ties with EU countries have had to settle for partial coverage, with preferential access but not barrier-free. The EFTA countries have come the closest under the EEA, but the Union has been careful to reserve substantial discretionary powers in managing these relationships. Moreover, as mentioned, in EU eyes, countries such as Canada, the United States and Mexico, are always likely to rank in an outer, or third concentric ring, behind the EFTA countries and the Central and European nations. On specific trade policy issues such as government procurement, resources, and liquor boards, where sub-national governments are involved, it would be particularly difficult to guarantee the EU reciprocity without also admitting Canadian provinces as well as U.S. and Mexican states to the negotiating table. This is not to mention the difficulty in administering two free trade agreements with differing provisions on such matters as rules of origin, dispute settlement, procedures, and contingency measures.

In addition, in comparison to the SEM, CUSFTA is a modest initiative, that is, it removes tariffs between Canada and the United States over a 10 year period, something the EU abolished 20 years ago. There is thus the question of the lessons of European economic integration for North American integration: the EU's "single banking license" versus the fact that all financial institutions in the United States and Canada must comply with host country regulations; the principle of mutual recognition on standards and norms between member states and pan-European standards in matters of health, safety, and the environment versus the fact that mutual recognition of standards is not a formal part of CUSFTA; competition in the realm of public procurement and the transparency of tendering procedures versus the fact that the CUSFTA does not cover provincial, state, and local governments and thus opens up only a small segment of the U.S. and Canadian procurement markets. Finally, a successful monetary union, now slated for the end of the decade, means a single European currency and central European bank, neither of which is being contemplated by Canada, the United States and Mexico.[38]

The side agreements on environment and labor under NAFTA bring Canada, the United States and Mexico a step closer to broadening the integration process, as are steps to removing Canada's deleterious inter-provincial trade barriers which the Canadian Manufacturers Association in 1991 estimated cost the Canadian economy approximately $6.5 billion a year. But it is unlikely that the Europeans would contemplate (in the near to long terms) a comprehensive transatlantic agreement either individually or multilaterally with Canada, the United States, and Mexico given the lack of parity in the EU and North American levels of integration.

Clearly, as it devotes more and more of its attention to a pan-European preferential trading area, there is a developing tendency for the EU to shape the international system rather than for it to be a passive taker. For this reason there are those who believe the Union will inevitably lock horns with the United States as the other shaper, leaving Canada and Mexico in the vulnerable positions of being side-swiped as the two giants grapple.[39] A trade war would be ironic at a time in the history of U.S.-EU relations when there is increased contact at the political level. Taking the view that a confrontational approach to the EU is not in the interest of the United States, the Carnegie Study Group on U.S.-EU Relations, in July 1993, issued a call for joint action. Its report, *Atlantic Frontiers*, calls for the building of a single market, based on broader and improved contacts over a range of new areas, including better coordinated microeconomic, environmental, and monetary policies. The aim of the report is to expand and deepen the constituencies that support Atlantic ties.[40]

Rise of Sector and Issue-Specific Agreements

In the end, the vital question for the smaller North American partners is: how much are the Canadian and Mexican markets worth to the EU? As we have already seen, with the trend toward increasing intra-EU trade, the Canadian market is steadily losing its significance. Niche markets, that is, those in which Canada has a comparative advantage, and where the EU will look to Canada, will be primarily in the telecommunications and power transmission sectors. With a bilateral free trade arrangement, or even a trilateral one, not a viable option, there is a larger problem of how well the GATT is likely to serve as a regulatory framework for Canada-EU, U.S.-EU, and Mexico-EU commercial relations in the post-Uruguay Round setting?

There is also the problem of how Canada and Mexico can ensure equal terms of access for their still resource-heavy export mix to the European Union? It is the non-tariff barriers such as phyto-sanitary controls and environmental limitations that are and will remain significant hurdles for Canadian suppliers.[41] The EU has given little ground on Canada's access concerns in these areas in the past.

For these reasons, in the Canadian case, in addition to the GATT, a network of bilateral sectoral and issue agreements are likely to be the foundation of Canada-EU economic relations in the coming years. For instance, the European Council has given the Commission the mandate to start negotiating a science & technology agreement with Canada. The Standards Council of Canada and the European Organization for Testing and Certification (EOTC) are working on a Mutual Recognition Agreement (MRA) for products in non-regulated sectors. For regulated products, the Commission has given Canada notice that it is ready to negotiate.[42] An MRA on national testing and certification procedures will enable Canadian laboratories to certify the Euroworthiness of Canadian exports in a number of specific categories of products and would level the playing field for Canadian business in these categories. There will be a requirement for reciprocity, meaning that the EOTC should also be able to test and certify European conformity to Canadian standards. In other issue and sectoral areas, Canada and the EU have negotiated a memorandum of understanding (MOU) on competition policy that is now awaiting ratification before going into effect. There is a Canada-EU customs cooperation agreement. A Canada-EU fisheries agreement is also awaiting ratification. Finally, in March 1993, Canada signed on as a partner of BC-NET (Mexico had previously been given access), the Community's partnering network that allows small and medium sized EC firms to source strategic partnerships which, according to Ottawa, is the best way for Canadian firms to reap the maximum benefits from European integration.

On the issue of investment, the larger EU market has many U.S. major multinationals but relatively few major Canadian and Mexican corporations established on a scale that will enable the latter two to take advantage of the single market. A provision for national treatment of investments could help to (1) ease the way for smaller Canadian, Mexican and American firms to form alliances in Europe, and (2) increase two-way flows of investment at all levels. Thus bilateral Canada-EU/U.S.-EU/Mexico-EU agreements to accord national treatment to investments could still be of considerable interest to all parties.

Conclusion

The challenge for North American decision-makers in the 1990s is to realize that the existing transatlantic trade mechanisms such as the 1975 Mexico-EU framework agreement, 1976 Canada-EC framework agreement, Mexico's GSP, GATT, and the 1990 EU-Canada and EU-U.S. Transatlantic Declarations, are necessary but not sufficient conditions to maintain, much less to increase, North American market access to the EU. At the same time, in the absence of a Soviet-type security threat, the North American stake in the transatlantic security alliance is much weaker and leaves the Europeans much less willing to accept political imperatives in the face of North American demands for increased market access. The chapter concludes that although a transatlantic free trade agreement is a non-starter as a new framework within which to conduct bilateral commercial relations, in the coming years the North American states can expect that their GATT rights (especially in the case of Canada and the United States) will be supplemented by an increase in sectoral and issue-specific MRAs and MOUs. Mexico may also enjoy these types of bilateral agreements in addition to the benefits it derives from its status as a developing country.

North Americans should not gloat over or take comfort in the stumbles of the European idea. The vital interests of Canada, the U.S., and Mexico are at stake since an economically viable, non-protectionist Europe will continue to be in their individual and collective interests. That being said, putting the European integration process into historical perspective -- it has always progressed gradually, and rhetorically it has always been ahead of reality (witness the crisis in the Exchange Rate Mechanism in late 1992, and the close results in ratifying the Maastricht Treaty in France, the UK and Denmark) -- it is likely that the creation of a pan-European market will create increased incentives for the process of North American economic integration.

Notes

1. This comprises the European Economic Area -- the European Union and the European Free Trade Association (Austria, Finland, Iceland, Liechtenstein, Norway, Sweden, and Switzerland) and the EU's "association" agreements with a number of Central and East European countries).

2. The Maastricht Treaty broadens and enhances the powers of the Community institutions (Parliament, Commission, Council of Ministers, European Court of Justice) and, in addition to economic and trade policy, the EU will have more influence and legislative power in the formulation of common social and foreign and security policies.

3. It is important to note that the G-7 summits are made up of no less than four EU Member States (Germany, France, UK, Italy) plus the President of the Commission to represent the interests of the smaller Community members. The Quadrilateral Group includes the EU, U.S., Canada and Japan. The EU is also a dialogue partner of the following groups of countries: ACP states (69), Andean Pact, Arab League, ASEAN, Contadora, Central America, Council of Europe, EFTA, Front Line states, G8, GCC, Mediterranean states and SELA. See Table 5-1 in Christopher Hill, "The Foreign Policy of the European Community," in Roy C.

Macredis, ed., *Foreign Policy in World Politics*, 8th ed. (Englewood Cliffs, New Jersey: Prentice- Hall Inc., 1992), p. 127.

4. Charles Pentland, "Europe 1992 and the Canadian Response," in Fen Osler Hampson and Christopher J. Maule, eds., *Canada Among Nations 1990-1991*, (Ottawa: Carleton University Press, 1991), p. 126.

5. Roy H. Ginsberg, "US-EC Relations," in Juliet Lodge, ed., *The European Community and the Challenge of the Future* (London: Pinter Publishers, 1989), p. 265.

6. Ibid., p. 266.

7. The Third Option was the Liberal government's conceptual framework for formally rejecting closer integration with the United States in favor of diversified trade ties. It was prompted by the United States's refusal to grant Canada an exemption from a 10 per cent surcharge on dutiable imports imposed by President Nixon in 1971.

8. Roy H. Ginsberg, "US-EC Relations," p. 268.

9. Ibid., p. 266.

10. Paul Buteux in *The Financial Post*, May 2, 1988.

11. Ginsberg, "US-EC Relations," p. 273.

12. Reprinted in *Europa-Archiv*, Vol. 45, No. 4 (1990), pp. D77-84.

13. For example, in a speech at McGill University on February 5, 1990, Clark *did* mention the increased trade opportunities for Canada in Europe in light of the single market, but not surprisingly he focused on Canadian responses to the collapse of communism in Eastern Europe. In addressing his cabinet colleagues two days later Clark stressed that if Canada did not seek to intensify its links to Europe through its three pillars -- NATO, the CSCE, and the EC (in that order) -- it would increasingly be marginalized in Europe.

14. Europe, as a formidable political and economic actor, had been encouraged by German Foreign Minister Genscher's proposal to Joe Clark for an EEC-North American Declaration "which would confirm shared principles and interests in openness and enhanced co-operation." See text of speech by Joe Clark, "Canada and the New Europe," External Affairs and International Trade Canada *Statements and Speeches*, May 26, 1990, p. 7.

15. Evan Potter, "Canadian Foreign Policy-making and the European Community-Canada Transatlantic Declaration," *Policy Planning Staff Papers* (Ottawa: External Affairs and International Trade Canada, April 1992), p. 14.

16. See text of Joe Clark's speech, "Canada and the New Europe," and Canada, House of Commons *Debates*, May 31, 1990, p. 12091.

17. Potter, *Canadian Foreign Policy-making*, p. 17.

18. Ibid., p. 24.

19. Government of Canada, *News Release*, "Canada-European Community Agree on Transatlantic Declaration," November 22, 1990, and "Declaration on EC-US Relations," in *European Political Cooperation Press Release*, November 23, 1990.

20. Signing would have required ratification by legislatures on both sides of the Atlantic.

21. Geoffrey Edwards, "The European Community and Canada," *Behind the*

Headlines, Vol. 50, No. 2, (Toronto: Canadian Institute of International Affairs, 1993), p. 18.

22. Royal Bank of Canada, "Is Canada Ready for Europe 1992?" *Econoscope*, Volume l6, No. 1, February l992, p. 8, and for the figure on total world exports see Michael Smith and Stephen Woolcock, The United States and the European Community in a Transformed World (London: Royal Institute of International Affairs, 1993), p. 35.

23. Ibid., p. 9.

24. Smith and Woolcock, *The United States and the European Community*, p. 35. Or, put in another way, intra-EU exports have risen from 54 per cent of total EU exports in 1982 to more than 60 per cent in 1990; while on the import side the increase is from 50 per cent to 58 per cent during the same period.

25. Mark S. Mahaney, "The European Community as a Global Power: Implications for the United States," *SAIS Review*, Vol. 13, No. 1 (Winter-Spring 1993), p. 79; Smith and Woolcock (1993) discuss the relative weight of the EC and the United States in the world economy, pp. 34-40.; and Mark Nelson, "Transatlantic Travails," *Foreign Policy*, No. 92 (Fall 1993), on pp. 80-84 talks about the EC replacing the United States as an international power.

26. Austria , Sweden, Finland and Norway signed Treaties of Accession in 1994, membership being contingent upon ratification at the state and EU levels.

27. Smith and Woolcock, *The United States and the European Community*, p. 39.

28. From CANSIM statistical base, Statistics Canada.

29. European Commission, *1993 Report on US Barriers to Trade and Investment* (Brussels: Commission of the European Communities, April 1993), p. 7.

30. Canada, House of Commons, Standing Committee on External Affairs and International Trade, *Canada's Relations with the New Europe*, (June 1992), p. 2.

31. Fanny S. Demers and Michel Demers, "Europe 1992: Implications for North America," in Fenn Osler Hampson and Christopher J. Maule, eds. *Canada Among Nations 1992-93: A New World Order?* (Ottawa: Carleton University Press, 1993), p. 196.

32. The EU offers to Mexico, as to all developing countries, its generalized system of preferences. This system makes it possible for a complete range of manufactured and semi-manufactured industrial goods and a growing number of agricultural products from developing countries to enter the Community's market of 270 million consumers largely or entirely free of tariffs. The objective of the system is threefold, namely to stimulate trade flows, help the industrialization of the developing countries and thus diversify their economies.

33. A good example of the potential residual nature of Canadian exports to the EU is that since 1986 Scandinavian wood products and newsprint have been entering the Union at zero rates of duty; Canada remains outside these preferences.

34. The EU and Canada have always had different expectations, for their framework agreement. Measured against these differing expectations, it is not surprising that a 1992 Canadian Parliamentary report goes so far as to call the agreement a failure. It has neither prevented, nor helped to resolve many of the bilateral irritants over the last 10 years. Trade data covering the period since

1976 reveals that the composition of Canadian exports remains heavily dominated by resource exports; the EU continues to seek assured access to Canadian raw materials. See Canada, House of Commons Standing Committee on External Affairs and International Trade, *Canada's Relations with the New Europe*, p. 8.

35. Telephone interview with senior External Affairs and International Trade Canada official at Washington embassy, April 1992.

36. See Gary Hufbauer, "Beyond GATT," *Foreign Policy*, No. 77 (Winter 1989-90), pp. 64-76.

37. Canada, House of Commons, Standing Committee on External Affairs and International Trade, *Canada's Relations with the New Europe*, p. 9.

38. Royal Bank of Canada, "Is Canada Ready for Europe," *Econoscope*, p. 6.

39. See "Canada Risks Sideswipe in U.S., EC Telecom Spat," *The Globe and Mail* (Toronto), April 19, 1993.

40. Nelson, "Transatlantic Travails," p. 89.

41. For example, the flanking issue of the environment is very important in terms of Canadian exports, where the EC takes 17 per cent of all Canadian pulp and paper exports. The four major environmental issues today are: pine nemastode worm, forest management (UK), chlorin bleaching (Germany), and recycling. Consumers perceptions of how the Canada's forest industry is addressing these issues is beginning to influence their purchasing decisions and in some cases those perceptions are driving the imposition of regulations.

42. See "Canada and EC Mutual Recognition Agreements," *Europe 1992 Trade Winds* (Ottawa: Standards Council of Canada, January 1992). The regulated products are under EC technical harmonization directives and correspond to CEN/CENELEC/ETSI standards. The EU Commission is awaiting its mandate from the Council of Ministers to open discussions with third countries.

PART FIVE

Conclusion

14

Whither North America?

Charles F. Doran

Underlying the geostrategic logic of the North American Free Trade Agreement (NAFTA) from the perspectives of its three members, the United States, Canada and Mexico, is a set of questions that will shape its evolution profoundly over the next decade. Not only is there little agreement among the governments about the premises of involvement in NAFTA, there is also little conceptual clarification about the nature of the questions that will drive the future of integration a n d interdependence in North America. That is the purpose, in part, of this collection of essays and in particular of this chapter.

Shifts of Authority in International Political Economy

Where is the locus of decision and of political momentum regarding trade and commercial matters today? That is the first question confronting the scholar and policy-maker. It seems like a simple question whose answer is perhaps assumed to be self-evident. After all, governments negotiate international trade agreements. Firms implement those agreements. Nothing could be more clairvoyant. Yet behind this question lies more complexity and change than arises in most other matters of international political economy.

Traditionally the state has been regarded as sovereign in trade negotiations although interest groups and ideology mediated its decisions. For example, political parties in North America have had a role in shaping the policies adopted.

Indeed, one of the most interesting discoveries is that the major political parties in North America have not only changed their historical positions on free trade, but that they have flip-flopped in these positions. Moreover, the same thing has happened in both Canada and in the United States. Historically protectionist, the Republican party has become the champion of free trade in the late twentieth century. As the outcome of the NAFTA vote in the U.S. Congress shows, the Democratic party has changed its historical position of support for free trade to that of opposition, shaped in part by the pressure from organized labor to "save jobs" allegedly threatened by freer trade. In Canada, too, the Progressive Conservative party, historically cool to free trade, became, under former Prime Minister Brian Mulroney, the chief architect of NAFTA in Canada, while the governing Liberal Party, long the advocate of freer trade, has become the reluctant and belated supporter of the agreement.

Beneath the level of governmental decision, elite opinion, interest group pressure and the impulse of technological change are at work in the democratic polity forcing change in the decision of government as to whether trade liberalization is a good idea. Yet the final decision rests with the state, often with the head of government, and that decision has increasingly favored the choice of freer trade, as in Europe and now in North America, even when regional trade integration is the chosen instrument of trade liberalization.

Based on the economist's causal understanding of how trade and trade liberalization operate, NAFTA is a straight-forward imperative. For the economist, NAFTA trade liberalization is the logical result of pressures from the abundant factor of production, namely, capital in the capital-rich countries, and labor in the labor-rich countries, to seek the benefits of tariff reduction. According to the Stolper/Samuelson Theorem, there is a tendency for the returns to the factors in the various trade liberalizing countries to equalize after trade has been freed up. This means that wage rates in Mexico will eventually approach those in Canada and the United States. If some labor and a lot of capital in the form of investment move across those borders as well as a result of NAFTA, the efficiencies that follow will be even greater. Economic growth in all of the member countries should benefit from this regional trade liberalization. The justification for trade liberalization from the neo-classical economic point of view lies with the benefits that such liberalization can bring to the societies as a whole in terms of increased welfare. Government, in the view of the economist, ought to heed the conclusions of this analysis and support freer trade in the larger interest of society, though not from the perspective of all sub-groups such as U.S. and Canadian workers in labor-intensive industries, who might face accelerated job loss and therefore are likely to reject the analysis in their own self interest.

Yet, even beyond this qualification, the economic rationality of the free trade argument is not without some political ambiguity. What does the argument say about the merits of global trade liberalization versus regional trade liberalization? Perhaps which political party is in power, and who the president or prime minister is, does make a difference, at least regarding this more specific question, not of *whether* trade liberalization, but of *whither* trade liberalization, global or regional. Opting for a regional trade area is not so much a matter of believing in the benefits of trade liberalization as of selecting the mode or structural framework.

Admittedly, part of the explanation for the NAFTA option, at least from the U.S. perspective, was tactical. The United States needed NAFTA as a bluff to bring Europe and Japan to the bargaining table in the Uruguay Round of General Agreement on Tariffs and Trade (GATT) talks on grounds that were minimally acceptable to North Americans. NAFTA looked like enough of an alternative to global trade liberalization to up the ante in the GATT since neither the Europeans nor the Japanese wanted a trade world without additional GATT reforms but with an ascendant NAFTA. But if NAFTA was only a bluff, it was surely a costly initiative to undertake on these grounds alone, both with respect to political capital and to the risk of entrapment in an unwanted trade scheme.

Likewise, the Canadian motivation for NAFTA can be explained at least partially in tactical terms. Canada did not want a "hub and spoke" model with the United States at the center of a series of bilateral agreements with other trading partners but with no overarching agreement among these regional partners. These tactical explanations for NAFTA, the regional initiative, fit the Mexican motivation less well than the traditional economics explanation of access to a preferred market. Taken together these various motivations for NAFTA appear more compelling, but insufficient. Something is still missing.

The disappearance of hegemony by the United States means that it can no longer provide the disproportionate incentives to other states to make another round of global trade talks a success. This is true even if one discounts the exaggerated claims of some analysts concerning the extent of U.S. decline. System-wide explanations for how trade liberalization occurs have less appeal in the absence of an "unmoved mover" at the center of the system that can give trade liberalization its sense of direction and positive inertia. On the other hand, the individual nation-state provides a less compelling explanation for trade and commercial effort than ever before, regardless of the size of that polity, in a world of globalization and large regional economic enterprises elsewhere in the system. Perhaps the explanation for NAFTA lies with the insufficiency of the individual nation-state as a source of new economic impetus to growth.

Widening Versus Deepening

An issue that remains totally without resolution is whether only to "widen" NAFTA by adding new members, only to "deepen" it by adding new policies of harmonization, or gradually to try to do both at the same time. This same indecision is not unknown in other regional contexts. The European Union suffers from the same conundrum. Why does a decision about widening or deepening matter?

A scholarly interpretation is that there is no reason why both processes cannot occur simultaneously. The proverbial analogy is that one can "walk and chew gum at the same time." It is a catchy aphorism that bears the more intellectual appellation, complementarity. Complementarity works where the functions are independent, that is, where they use resources that are for the most part uncorrelated with each other. Walking uses feet; chewing occupies the jaws. That each is connected by the spinal column scarcely interferes with, indeed facilitates, simultaneous operation. But suppose that the functions were ballet dancing and kicking a soccer ball. The contradiction in function becomes obvious. Widening and deepening will only work in NAFTA if each is a truly complementary function.

Starting with six original members of the "Common Market" in 1958, Europe has proceeded to add members until it is estimated that by the end of this century the European Union may contain as many as 19 countries. Widening is comparatively easy to achieve in treaty terms. It is politically popular because greater size is popular. It is rewarding because it creates economies of scale and perhaps because it generates both trade creation (positive globally) and trade diversion (a beggar-thy-outside-neighbor policy). Widening is so attractive that, as a process, the founders of a trade area or of a common market, almost cannot resist its charm.

Is NAFTA likely to follow this same path, for both political and economic reasons? In addition to the possible economic benefits of a larger hemispheric trade area, the political pressures may be hard to resist. First, the concept of "doing something" for Latin America that reinforces political solidarity and enhances economic progress is irresistible in Washington and Ottawa. Second, trade diversion is likely to cause problems for governments outside NAFTA thus encouraging them to meet the conditions of admission.

Now the problem. As more states become members, more heterogeneity of interest and structure occurs within the common market or trade area. Insofar as the objective of a common market or trade area is to make progress in terms of deepening, that is, in terms of policy harmonization and possibly closer overall integration, creeping diversification is deadly to that objective. Greater heterogeneity means less consensus on the goals of the common enterprise. Less consensus involves more conflict that in turn generates an attempt to manage that conflict through the establishment of new supranational institutions. This trend is far advanced in the European Union with its Commission, Council, Parliament and Court, supported by a 10,000 member bureaucracy. NAFTA faced the same dilemma more narrowly in terms of labor practices and environmental policy, meeting the problem by creating two commissions, one located in Montreal (environment), the other located in Mexico City (labor). But all effects of heterogeneity are not met through the creation of institutions, especially where the institutions are expensive, inefficient and basically unwanted. Increased heterogeneity becomes a severe obstacle to effective deepening, that is, to meaningful policy harmonization.

Thus widening and deepening are not like walking and chewing gum. The functions are not strictly complementary. They are in many ways opposed. More than this, once widening is in place it makes deepening more difficult. It precludes some aspects of deepening because the increased structural diversity undermines the capacity to arrive at policy consensus. To a point, the establishment of overarching institutions helps to mute or manage the resulting inevitable conflict, but this strategy comes at high cost. More importantly perhaps, the creation of such institutions also involves the yielding of state sovereignty, something that peoples and their governments must want or at least tolerate.

There is, of course, an alternative route to progress within a common market or trade area. This route is to keep the regional effort small and inclusive so as to minimize the problems of interest and structural heterogeneity caused by the rampant addition of new members. But such a strategy presupposes two things. First, it assumes that the original members can keep the unit small by resisting the temptation to go for the easy benefits of enlargement first. Second, it presupposes that a strategy of deepening exists and that this strategy is minimally acceptable to the initial members.

In sum, two larger questions inform the future of economic interdependence and integration in North America. The first concerns where the locus of economic decision-making is today, with the individual nation-state, with the firm, or with some other combination of actors. An answer to this question is important because it will help determine whether the future of the trading system lies at the regional level, at the global level, or with some complex interrelationship between the two, and how this resulting nexus of trade ties will in turn affect the multinational firm and the modern nation-state, especially those involved in the NAFTA enterprise. The second question concerns how NAFTA itself is likely to evolve, via widening such that the very regional outline of the membership becomes so changed that the North American context is subsumed in a hemispheric or global state association, or via deepening such that a well-delineated regional entity emerges in North America. An answer to the first question will assist in an understanding of the second, and vice-versa. How the authors in this volume see these questions is thus of much interest.

What the Authors Say

Regarding the first question, the locus of decision-making on trade and investment today, Michael Hart is most direct. He claims that the old paradigm of trade between states has broken down. Firms no longer do business on the basis of territorially confined relationships. This comes as a blow to Canadians who might have preferred to stay out of larger trade areas. There is, for the most part, no such thing any longer as the "national firm." But he also notes that a new paradigm has yet to emerge to account for economic decision-making beyond the nation-state. The locus of authority has shifted. Hart calls upon the theorist and the academic to determine the new center of authority in trade and commerce and the new source of norm-creation for regularizing international political economy.

Alan Henrikson in essence agrees with Hart that the "nation is an insufficient unit of analysis" in trade terms. He considers use of the terms "continent," "hemisphere," "globe" and "region" but does not settle on any one category. He insists that to study the effects of trade and commerce on economic growth, the analyst must look at sub-regions inside the nation-state as a unit, and outside it within the international region. Thus Henrikson and Hart seem to be calling for the same thing, implicitly defending NAFTA because of the inadequacy of the territorial state as the spring board for global commerce.

On the other hand, movement toward decision-making on the basis of units larger than the nation-state is not easy or accepted readily. Denis Stairs observes that the weaker units like decision-making "by committee" where "power matters less, rules matter more, and supportive coalitions can sometimes be engineered." Similarly, Stephen Randall notes that Mexico is strongly committed to the multilateral resolution of conflicts, non-interventionism and national self-determination. Echoing some of these liberal preferences in favor of national independence, Gustavo del Castillo laments the "asymmetrical relationship" between the United States and its near neighbors, contending that this asymmetry has somehow kept Canada and Mexico apart.

Despite these North American anxieties about accepting the new paradigm that Hart and Henrikson, among others, claim is necessary, Neil Nevitte points to empirical evidence on public opinion in North America that surprisingly supports the shift toward the larger paradigm for trade and commerce, indeed toward political integration itself. He finds that one out of four Mexicans and Canadians is already prepared to accept political integration in some kind of new collectivity.

Lest either the proponents or the opponents of new paradigms for larger centers of economic decision-making become too emotional, Gretchen MacMillan has some realist warnings based on the experience of the European Union. Unlike NAFTA, she notes, the early forerunner of supranationalism in Europe, the European Coal and Steel Community, was "self-consciously supranational." Yet to date no sense of political community has emerged. National identity in Europe remains steadfastly with the nation-state. All the integration that has occurred has been "top-down," that is, managed by elites and reluctantly agreed to by the masses. Hence the experience of the European Union so far is neither a bellwether of procedure for integrative unions elsewhere in the system, nor an indication of a slippery slope toward inevitable full integration in North America.

Regarding the second large question, the strategy for future North American trade and commercial policy, the authors in this volume provide analytic if not skeptical commentary. Gilbert Winham and Heather Grant note that the motivations for joining NAFTA were remarkably divergent. Mexico wanted accelerated economic growth and access to the U.S. market. The United States sought long term stability along its southern border and perhaps closer coordination of policies throughout North America. Canada attempted to prevent the emergence of a "hub and spoke" model of integration by joining NAFTA.

So the objectives differed even if the resulting product, a regional trade area was the same.

Gustavo Vega Canovas makes a strong case for a widening approach beyond NAFTA. He notes that trade diversion is likely to force Venezuela and Colombia to consider meeting the terms necessary for admission to NAFTA. But Maxwell Cameron and Brian Tomlin assert that Canada itself is "unlikely" to take the initiative to extend membership within the hemisphere. If widening occurs, it will be because the United States takes the lead, they knowledgeably contend.

On the other side of this matter of widening versus deepening, Joseph Jockel recommends that Mexico, Canada and the United States consider three functional types of limited defense cooperation: sovereignty protection and the drug trade; environmental protection; and, rescue and disaster relief. If this kind of functional cooperation seems rudimentary, it is also quite feasible and perhaps essential. Evan Potter sounds a warning to those who reject deepening as either unnecessary or too difficult in his examination of Canadian trade access to the European Union. He reminds the critic that "sector and issue-specific agreements" are the new form of protectionism keeping North American goods out of European markets. It takes only a small step of logic to see that these same problems could emerge inside North America and that NAFTA will plausibly need to address these matters through some form of greater regional policy harmonization.

In short, the authors in this volume divide on the first question of whether the older paradigm of "national trade" is dead. Or perhaps more accurately, they divide over the matter of what a new paradigm should look like or politically entail. They also recommend various candidates for widening the present NAFTA membership while cautiously considering the implications of additional deepening. Throughout, prudence marks the judgments of the authors toward these strategies, as the three member polities attempt to digest the implications of NAFTA for their economies and societies. But the chapters individually and together raise sagacious commentary on the prospects for a regional trade area richer and more extensive than that provided by the hard-fought initial agreement. Are further insights possible concerning the two larger questions posed at the outset of this discussion?

New Paradigms, New Strategies

Without altering the tone or general conclusions of the previous chapters, a few amplifying observations regarding the future of trade regionalism in North America may be helpful. If the focus of decision authority in trade and commercial matters has shifted, where has it gone? If a number of the authors whose work is contained in this book are right that a new paradigm is needed, which paradigm? Why has the nation-state proven insufficient as a base for commerce and trade at exactly the time that the global system is facing fragmentation of its markets? I believe an answer to these questions is possible in theoretical and empirical terms.

Decision authority over matters of trade and commerce is always diffuse and shared across actors. But it is likely to reside *where the greatest confluence of trade and commercial activity resides.* When Britain accounted for a majority share of world trade at one point in the nineteenth century, it was dominant. In the 1950s and 1960s, when the United States held a predominant share of world trade and possessed more than 40 percent of the total world gross national product (GNP), the U.S. wielded greatly disproportionate power over the making of the norms of trade and finance. Hence, the theoretical key to the question where has decision authority over the direction, scale and momentum of trade liberalization shifted, is the further question where is trade and commercial activity now at its most intense?

Here empirical evidence is helpful, because the empirical answer is that clusters of intense trade interaction have emerged around regional dynamos of development and growth. These dynamos are the United States, Japan, and Germany respectively. But even more poignantly, the states in the vicinity have established most of their trade, commercial, and financial links with their own most proximate industrial dynamo.

That Canada has more than 70 percent of its external trade with the United States, and that the United States has more than 20 per cent of its trade with Canada, may seem high. But if one looks at the percent of foreign trade European states have with their immediate neighbors the figures are comparable. The same trend is gaining ground within Asia today. Trade and distance, for complex reasons that go beyond freight rates, are inversely correlated.

Thus trade dominance "by region" has replaced trade dominance "by individual state." Germany cannot act without the European Union. United States policy is shaped very much by the preferences of Canada and Mexico. Japan will not ignore the primary responsibilities it has in Asia.

Looked at from another perspective, the European Union did not create European regionalism, nor has NAFTA prepared the way for regionalism in North America. The intensity of trade and commercial activity within a region precedes and conditions the formal creation of treaties and institutions that highlight the regional outlook. The new paradigm has an unambiguous focus. An industrial dynamo surrounded by a regional network of trading partners is the new feature of the twenty-first century. NAFTA is its exemplification.

Regarding the second question, equally emphatic conclusions are possible. Which trend will take precedence, widening or deepening? Will the trend toward adding states to the trade area gain the lead, or will the movement toward policy harmonization among the existing members of NAFTA predominate? From the preceding discussion, it is clear that widening and deepening are not entirely separate functions. When widening is chosen first, it precludes deepening because of the increase of interest and structural heterogeneity that accompanies the addition of new members. This surely is the pattern in the European Union where the actual pace of movement toward an integrated political confederation has slowed, despite separate speeds for sets of members and complex institutions, even as the success of enlargement continues unabated. The two consequences, slower policy harmonization and continued accretion of new politically and culturally diverse members, are not at all unrelated.

Will NAFTA expand first, or concentrate its focus, or try, as the European Union has, to do both simultaneously with resulting mixed success? For reasons articulated well by scholars writing for this volume, NAFTA is likely to follow at least in these respects the European pattern, but for reasons that are distinctly North American. Since North Americans do not want to create a political union, they will choose to add new members to broaden the base of NAFTA, starting first with Chile, but following up with other hemispheric partners shortly thereafter.

The casualty of this strategy will be policy harmonization. As Evan Potter has noted regarding Europe, the problem this result creates is that new issue-specific and sectoral barriers will emerge that will tend to stymie trade flows and possibly investment openness inside the region and vis-à-vis third actors. NAFTA will become less North American, less regional in outlook, though still perhaps identifiable as a distinct trade-commercial grouping. Policy harmonization, never popular or politically easy, is likely to slow down.

There is one structural reality, however, that may tend to offset this negativism with respect to deepening. Of all the regions internationally, the North American region is the most hierarchic internally, not in terms of formal institutions, but in terms of size and power. Because of this hierarchic regionalism, North America, for example does not have to worry much about monetary union. It already exists under the rubric of the Federal Reserve Board. Given the very high proportion of Canadian trade and foreign investment associated with United States institutions, and the much bigger size of the American economy, the Canadian dollar responds very strongly to U.S. monetary policy. The economies in the European Union are relatively similar in size. Thus the task of creating a common monetary policy around the German deutschmark, everything else about the respective economies being equal, is far more different than would be the case in North America.

Similarly, the lack of progress in deepening will to some extent be offset by the greater concentration of decision authority that already exists within the region inside the United States. Whether other members of NAFTA will see the situation regarding the need for deepening as valid, and if valid whether in the same way as the United States, remains to be seen. In any case, NAFTA is likely to become more distinctive in comparison to other regional groupings even as its membership diffuses, and as it follows the same pattern of easy integration through accretion that other regional efforts have already pioneered.

Acronyms

ALADI	Latin American Integration Association
APEC	Asia Pacific Economic Cooperation
CACM	Central American Common Market
CAP	Common Agricultural Policy
CARICOM	Caribbean Common Market
CET	Common External Tariff
COECE	Coordinadora de Organismos Empresariales de Comercio Exterior
CSCE	Conference on Security and Cooperation in Europe
CUSFTA	Canada-U.S. Free Trade Agreement
DEW Line	Distant Early Warning Line
EAEG	East Asian Economic Grouping
EAI	Enterprise for the Americas Initiative
EAITC	External Affairs and International Trade Canada
EC	European Community
ECJ	European Court of Justice
ECLAC	United Nations Economic Commission for Latin America and the Caribbean
ECSC	European Coal and Steel Community
ECU	European Currency Unit
EEA	European Economic Area
EEC	European Economic Community
EFTA	European Free Trade Association
EMS	European Monetary System
EMU	Economic and Monetary Union
EOTC	European Organization for Testing and Certification
ERM	Exchange Rate Mechanism
ESCB	European System of Central Banks
EU	European Union
FDI	Foreign Direct Investment
FMLN	Faribundo Marti National Liberation Front
G3	Group of Three (Mexico, Colombia, Venezuela)

G7	Group of Seven (Canada, France, Germany, Italy, Japan, U.K., U.S.)
GATT	General Agreement on Tariffs and Trade
GDP	Gross Domestic Product
GNP	Gross National Product
GSP	Generalized System of Preferences
IGC	Intergovernmental Conference
ISI	Import Substitution Industrialization
ITAC	International Trade Advisory Committee
LAFTA	Latin American Free Trade Association
MERCOSUR	Southern Common Market (Argentina, Brazil, Paraguay, Uraguay)
MFN	Most Favored Nation
MOU	Memorandum of Understanding
MRA	Mutual Recognition Agreement
NAFTA	North American Free Trade Agreement
NATO	North Atlantic Treaty Organization
NEP	National Energy Program
NGO	Non-Governmental Organization
NORAD	North American Air Defense Command
NSC	National Security Council
OAS	Organization of American States
OECD	Organization for Economic Cooperation and Development
ONUSAL	United Nations Observer Mission in El Salvador
OPEC	Organization of Petroleum Exporting Countries
PEMD	Programme for Export Market Development
PJBD	Permanent Joint Board on Defense
PRI	Institutional Revolutionary Party
SAFTA	South American Free Trade Area
SAGIT	Sectoral Advisory Group on International Trade
SDI	Strategic Defense Initiative
SEA	Single European Act
SEM	Single European Market
TAD	Transatlantic Declaration (EC-Canada, EC-U.S.)
TAG	Trade Advisory Group
TEU	Treaty on European Union (Maastricht Treaty)
TPL	Tariff Preference Level
TRIP	Trade Related Aspects of Intellectual Property Rights
WHFTA	Western Hemispheric Free Trade Area

About the Editors and Contributors

Donald Barry is associate professor of political science at The University of Calgary. He is coauthor, with John Hilliker, of *Canada's Department of External Affairs: Coming of Age, 1946-1968* (1995) and editor of *Documents on Canadian External Relations*, Vol. 18, 1952 (1990) and Vol. 19, 1953 (1991).

Maxwell A. Cameron is assistant professor and associate director of the Centre for Negotiation and Dispute Resolution in the Norman Paterson School of International Affairs, Carleton University. He is coeditor, with Ricardo Grinspun, of *The Political Economy of North American Free Trade* (1993).

Mark O. Dickerson is professor of political science at The University of Calgary. He is the author of *Whose North? Political Change, Political Development and Self-Government in the Northwest Territories* (1992) and coeditor, with Stephen J. Randall, of *Canada and Latin America: Issues to the Year 2000 and Beyond* (1991).

Charles F. Doran is the Andrew W. Mellon Professor of International Relations and director of the Center of Canadian Studies at the Paul H. Nitze School of Advanced International Studies, The Johns Hopkins University. Among his publications are *Forgotten Partnership: U.S.-Canada Relations Today* (1984) *Canada and the United States: Enduring Friendship, Persistent Stress*, coedited with John H. Sigler (1986) and *Systems in Crisis: New Imperatives of High Politics at Century's End* (1991).

Gustavo del Castillo chairs the Department of North American Studies at El Colegio de la Frontera Norte. He is the author of *Ventajas y desventajas de Mexico en al GATT* (1985).

James D. Gaisford is associate professor of economics at The University of Calgary. He is the author of studies on the problem of domestic subsidies and countervailing duties, trade wars, and the liberalization of foreign investment.

Heather A. Grant received an LL.B from Dalhousie University in 1993 and was admitted to the bar of Ontario in 1994.

Michael Hart is senior advisor, trade policy studies in Canada's Department of Foreign Affairs and International Trade and adjunct professor in the Norman Paterson School of International Affairs at Carleton University. His publications include *A North American Free Trade Agreement: The Strategic Implications for Canada* (1990) *What's Next: Canada, the Global Economy an the New Trade Policy* (1994) and *Decision at Midnight: Inside the Canada-U.S. Free Trade Negotiations* (1994), with Bill Dymond and Colin Robertson.

Alan K. Henrikson teaches at the Fletcher School of Law and Diplomacy, Tufts University, where he is also director of the Fletcher Roundtable on a New World Order. He is the author of *Defining a New World Order: Toward a Practical Vision of Collective Action for International Peace and Security* (1991) and editor of *Negotiating World Order: The Artisanship and the Architecture of Global Diplomacy* (1986).

Joseph T. Jockel is senior fellow and director of the Canada Project at the Center for Strategic and International Studies, Washington, D.C. His publications include *No Boundaries Upstairs: Canada, the United States, and the Origins of North American Air Defence, 1945-1958* (1987) and *Security to the North: Canada and the Strategic Defense of North America* (1990).

Gretchen M. MacMillan is associate professor of political science at The University of Calgary. She has published *State Society and Authority in Ireland* (1993) and edited *The European Community, Canada and 1992* (1994).

Neil Nevitte is professor of political science at The University of Calgary. He is coauthor, with Roger Gibbins, of *New Elites in Old States* (1990) and coauthor, with Ronald Inglehart and Miguel Basañez, of *Convergence in North America* (forthcoming).

Evan H. Potter is editor of the journal *Canadian Foreign Policy* and coeditor, with Lorraine Eden, of *Multinational Corporations in the Global Political Economy* (1993).

Stephen J. Randall is Imperial Oil-Lincoln McKay Professor of American Studies and Dean of the Faculty of Social Sciences at The University of Calgary. He is coauthor, with John Herd Thompson, of *Canada and the United States: Ambivalent Allies* (1994) editor of *North American Without Borders? Integrating Canada, the United States and Mexico* (1992) and coeditor, with Mark O. Dickerson, of *Canada and Latin America: Issues to the Year 2000 and Beyond* (1991).

Denis Stairs is professor of political science at Dalhousie University. He has written *The Diplomacy of Constraint: Canada, the Korean War, and the United States* (1974) and coedited, with

Gilbert R. Winham, *Canada and the International Political/Economic Environment* (1985) *The Politics of Canada's Economic Relationship with the United States* (1985) and *Selected Problems in Formulating Foreign Economic Policy* (1985).

Brian W. Tomlin is professor and director of the Centre for Negotiation and Dispute Resolution in the Norman Paterson School of International Affairs, Carleton University. His book, *Faith and Fear: The Free Trade Story* (1991), coauthored with Bruce Doern, won the 1992 National Business Book Award in Canada.

Gustavo Vega Canovas is associate professor and academic coordinator of the United States-Canadian Studies Program, Center for International Studies, El Colegio de México. Among his publications are *Mexico and Free Trade With North America* (1991) *These and Those Integrations*, with Victor L. Urquidi, (1992) and *Economic Liberation and Free Trade in North America: Political, Social and Cultural Considerations* (1993).

Gilbert R. Winham is the Eric Dennis Memorial Professor of Government and Political Science at Dalhousie University. His publications include *International Trade and the Tokyo Round Negotiations* (1986) *Trading With Canada: the Canada-U.S. Free Trade Agreement* (1988) and *The Evolution of International Trade Agreements* (1992).

About the Book

The North American Free Trade Agreement (NAFTA) is a milestone in the affairs of the continent and in international trade. The first formal arrangement of any kind between Canada, the United States, and Mexico, it is also the first trade pact including countries of such disproportionate power and levels of development. For Canada and Mexico the agreement represents a reversal of long-standing efforts to resist the embrace of their superpower neighbor. For the United States it is the culmination of an equally enduring aim of achieving closer continental relations. In global economic terms, NAFTA furthers a trend toward regional economic arrangements and establishes a precedent for cooperation between developed and developing countries.

This comprehensive volume explores the management of Canadian-U.S.-Mexican relations in an era of emerging continental cooperation. Going beyond the economic considerations that have been the focus of much of the NAFTA-generated discussion, an international group of contributors examines a wide range of issues including the interrelationship between economic integration, national values and security, and the implications for national policies and community building in North America. Throughout the volume, contributors ask the question: Is NAFTA the first step in a wider integration process, or will its effects be more limited? They consider whether the agreement will become a point of departure for broader cooperation among the three countries and identify areas in which collaboration is likely.

Index